JOAN OF ARC

Major Literary Characters

**THE ANCIENT WORLD THROUGH
THE SEVENTEENTH CENTURY**

ACHILLES
Homer, *Iliad*

CALIBAN
William Shakespeare, *The Tempest*
Robert Browning, *Caliban upon Setebos*

CLEOPATRA
William Shakespeare, *Antony and
    Cleopatra*
John Dryden, *All for Love*
George Bernard Shaw, *Caesar and
    Cleopatra*

DON QUIXOTE
Miguel de Cervantes, *Don Quixote*
Franz Kafka, *Parables*

FALSTAFF
William Shakespeare, *Henry IV, Part I,
    Henry IV, Part II, The Merry Wives
    of Windsor*

FAUST
Christopher Marlowe, *Doctor Faustus*
Johann Wolfgang von Goethe, *Faust*
Thomas Mann, *Doctor Faustus*

HAMLET
William Shakespeare, *Hamlet*

IAGO
William Shakespeare, *Othello*

JULIUS CAESAR
William Shakespeare, *Julius Caesar*
George Bernard Shaw, *Caesar and
    Cleopatra*

KING LEAR
William Shakespeare, *King Lear*

MACBETH
William Shakespeare, *Macbeth*

ODYSSEUS/ULYSSES
Homer, *Odyssey*
James Joyce, *Ulysses*

OEDIPUS
Sophocles, *Oedipus Rex, Oedipus
    at Colonus*

OTHELLO
William Shakespeare, *Othello*

ROSALIND
William Shakespeare, *As You Like It*

SANCHO PANZA
Miguel de Cervantes, *Don Quixote*
Franz Kafka, *Parables*

SATAN
The Book of Job
John Milton, *Paradise Lost*

SHYLOCK
William Shakespeare, *The Merchant
    of Venice*

THE WIFE OF BATH
Geoffrey Chaucer, *The Canterbury
    Tales*

**THE EIGHTEENTH AND
NINETEENTH CENTURIES**

AHAB
Herman Melville, *Moby-Dick*

ISABEL ARCHER
Henry James, *Portrait of a Lady*

EMMA BOVARY
Gustave Flaubert, *Madame Bovary*

DOROTHEA BROOKE
George Eliot, *Middlemarch*

CHELSEA HOUSE PUBLISHERS

Major Literary Characters

DAVID COPPERFIELD
Charles Dickens, *David Copperfield*

ROBINSON CRUSOE
Daniel Defoe, *Robinson Crusoe*

DON JUAN
Molière, *Don Juan*
Lord Byron, *Don Juan*

HUCK FINN
Mark Twain, *The Adventures of
Tom Sawyer, Adventures of
Huckleberry Finn*

CLARISSA HARLOWE
Samuel Richardson, *Clarissa*

HEATHCLIFF
Emily Brontë, *Wuthering Heights*

ANNA KARENINA
Leo Tolstoy, *Anna Karenina*

MR. PICKWICK
Charles Dickens, *The Pickwick Papers*

HESTER PRYNNE
Nathaniel Hawthorne, *The Scarlet Letter*

BECKY SHARP
William Makepeace Thackeray, *Vanity Fair*

LAMBERT STRETHER
Henry James, *The Ambassadors*

EUSTACIA VYE
Thomas Hardy, *The Return of the Native*

TWENTIETH CENTURY

ÁNTONIA
Willa Cather, *My Ántonia*

BRETT ASHLEY
Ernest Hemingway, *The Sun Also Rises*

HANS CASTORP
Thomas Mann, *The Magic Mountain*

HOLDEN CAULFIELD
J. D. Salinger, *The Catcher in the Rye*

CADDY COMPSON
William Faulkner, *The Sound and the Fury*

JANIE CRAWFORD
Zora Neale Hurston, *Their Eyes Were
Watching God*

CLARISSA DALLOWAY
Virginia Woolf, *Mrs. Dalloway*

DILSEY
William Faulkner, *The Sound and the Fury*

GATSBY
F. Scott Fitzgerald, *The Great Gatsby*

HERZOG
Saul Bellow, *Herzog*

JOAN OF ARC
William Shakespeare, *Henry VI*
George Bernard Shaw, *Saint Joan*

LOLITA
Vladimir Nabokov, *Lolita*

WILLY LOMAN
Arthur Miller, *Death of a Salesman*

MARLOW
Joseph Conrad, *Lord Jim, Heart of
Darkness, Youth, Chance*

PORTNOY
Philip Roth, *Portnoy's Complaint*

BIGGER THOMAS
Richard Wright, *Native Son*

CHELSEA HOUSE PUBLISHERS

Major Literary Characters

JOAN OF ARC

Edited and with an introduction by
HAROLD BLOOM

CHELSEA HOUSE PUBLISHERS
New York ◊ Philadelphia

Jacket illustration: Constance Cummings as Joan of Arc in the 1939 production of George Bernard Shaw's *Saint Joan* with the Old Vic Company at the Golders Green Hippodrome (The Raymond Mander and Joe Mitchenson Theatre Collection).

Chelsea House Publishers

Editor-in-Chief   Remmel T. Nunn
Managing Editor   Karyn Gullen Browne
Picture Editor   Adrian G. Allen
Art Director   Maria Epes
Manufacturing Director   Gerald Levine

Major Literary Characters

Senior Editor   S. T. Joshi
Associate Editor   Richard Fumosa
Designer   Maria Epes

Staff for JOAN OF ARC

Picture Researcher   Ellen Barrett
Assistant Art Director   Howard Brotman
Production Manager   Joseph Romano
Production Coordinator   Marie Claire Cebrián

Printed and bound in the United States of America

First Printing

1   3   5   7   9   8   6   4   2

Library of Congress Cataloging-in-Publication Data

Joan of Arc / edited, and with an introduction, by Harold Bloom.
        p.   cm.—(Major literary characters)
        Includes bibliographical references and index.
        ISBN 0-7910-0960-2.—ISBN 0-7910-1015-5 (pbk.)
    1. Joan, of Arc, Saint, 1412–1431 in fiction, drama, poetry, etc.
                I. Bloom, Harold.   II. Series.
                        PN57.J4J63   1992
                        820'.9'351—dc20
                             91-25825
                                CIP

CONTENTS

viii   CONTENTS

THE ANALYSIS OF CHARACTER

Harold Bloom

"Character," according to our dictionaries, still has as a primary meaning a graphic symbol, such as a letter of the alphabet. This meaning reflects the word's apparent origin in the ancient Greek *charactēr*, a sharp stylus. *Charactēr* also meant the mark of the stylus' incisions. Recent fashions in literary criticism have reduced "character" in literature to a matter of marks upon a page. But our word "character" also has a very different meaning, matching that of the ancient Greek *ēthos*, "habitual way of life." Shall we say then that literary character is an imitation of human character, or is it just a grouping of marks? The issue is between a critic like Dr. Samuel Johnson, for whom words were as much like people as like things, and a critic like the late Roland Barthes, who told us that "the fact can only exist linguistically, as a term of discourse." Who is closer to our experience of reading literature, Johnson or Barthes? What difference does it make, if we side with one critic rather than the other?

Barthes is famous, like Foucault and other recent French theorists, for having added to Nietzsche's proclamation of the death of God a subsidiary demise, that of the literary author. If there are no authors, then there are no fictional personages, presumably because literature does not refer to a world outside language. Words indeed necessarily refer to other words in the first place, but the impact of words ultimately is drawn from a universe of fact. Stories, poems, and plays are recognizable as such because they are human utterances within traditions of utterances, and traditions, by achieving authority, become a kind of fact, or at least the sense of a fact. Our sense that literary characters, within the context of a fictive cosmos, indeed are fictional personages is also a kind of fact. The meaning and value of every character in a successful work of literary representation depend upon our ideas of persons in the factual reality of our lives.

Literary character is always an invention, and inventions generally are indebted to prior inventions. Shakespeare is the inventor of literary character as we know it; he reformed the universal human expectations for the verbal imitation of personality, and the reformation appears now to be permanent and uncannily inevitable. Remarkable as the Bible and Homer are at representing personages, their characters are relatively unchanging. They age within their stories, but their habitual modes of being do not develop. Jacob and Achilles unfold before us, but without metamorphoses. Lear and Macbeth, Hamlet and Othello severely modify themselves not only by their actions, but by their utterances, and most of all through *overhearing themselves,* whether they speak to themselves or to others. Pondering what they themselves have said, they will to change, and actually do change, sometimes extravagantly yet always persuasively. Or else they suffer change, without willing it, but in reaction not so much to their language as to their relation to that language.

I do not think it useful to say that Shakespeare successfully imitated elements in our characters. Rather, it could be argued that he compelled aspects of character to appear that previously were concealed, or not available to representation. This is not to say that Shakespeare is God, but to remind us that language is not God either. The mimesis of character in Shakespeare's dramas now seems to us normative, and indeed became the accepted mode almost immediately, as Ben Jonson shrewdly and somewhat grudgingly implied. And yet, Shakespearean representation has surprisingly little in common with the imitation of reality in Jonson or in Christopher Marlowe. The origins of Shakespeare's originality in the portrayal of men and women are to be found in the *Canterbury Tales* of Geoffrey Chaucer, insofar as they can be located anywhere before Shakespeare himself. Chaucer's savage and superb Pardoner overhears his own tale-telling, as well as his mocking rehearsal of his own spiel, and through this overhearing he is emboldened to forget himself, and enthusiastically urges all his fellow-pilgrims to come forward to be fleeced by him. His self-awareness, and apocalyptically rancid sense of spiritual fall, are preludes to the even grander abysses of the perverted will in Iago and in Edmund. What might be called the character trait of a negative charisma may be Chaucer's invention, but came to its perfection in Shakespearean mimesis.

The analysis of character is as much Shakespeare's invention as the representation of character is, since Iago and Edmund are adepts at analyzing both themselves and their victims. Hamlet, whose overwhelming charisma has many negative components, is certainly the most comprehensive of all literary characters, and so necessarily prophesies the labyrinthine complexities of the will in Iago and Edmund. Charisma, according to Max Weber, its first codifier, is primarily a natural endowment, and implies a primordial and idiosyncratic power over nature, and so finally over death. Hamlet's uncanniness is at its most suggestive in the scene of his long dying, where the audience, through the mediation of Horatio, itself is compelled to meditate upon suicide, if only because outliving the prince of Denmark scarcely seems an option.

Shakespearean representation has usurped not only our sense of literary character, but our sense of ourselves as characters, with Hamlet playing the part of the largest of these usurpations. Insofar as we have an idea of human disinterestedness, we tend to derive it from the Hamlet of Act V, whose quietism has about it a ghostly authority. Oscar Wilde, in his profound and profoundly witty dialogue, "The Decay of Lying," expressed a permanent insight when he insisted that art shaped every era, far more than any age formed art. Life imitates art, we imitate Shakespeare, because without Shakespeare we would perish for lack of images. Wilde's grandest audacity demystifies Shakespearean mimesis with a Shakespearean vivaciousness: "This unfortunate aphorism about art holding the mirror up to Nature is deliberately said by Hamlet in order to convince the bystanders of his absolute insanity in all art-matters." Of *Hamlet*'s influence upon the ages Wilde remarked that: "The world has grown sad because a puppet was once melancholy." "Puppet" is Wilde's own deconstruction, a brilliant reminder that Shakespeare's artistry of illusion has so mastered reality as to have changed reality, evidently forever.

The analysis of character, as a critical pursuit, seems to me as much a Shakespearean invention as literary character was, since much of what we know about how to analyze character necessarily follows Shakespearean procedures. His hero-villains, from Richard III through Iago, Edmund, and Macbeth, are shrewd and endless questers into their own self-motivations. If we could bear to see Hamlet, in his unwearied negations, as another hero-villain, then we would judge him the supreme analyst of the darker recalcitrances in the selfhood. Freud followed the pre-Socratic Empedocles, in arguing that character is fate, a frightening doctrine that maintains the fear that there are no accidents, that overdetermination rules us all of our lives. Hamlet assumes the same, yet adds to this argument the terrible passivity he manifests in Act V. Throughout Shakespeare's tragedies, the most interesting personages seem doom-eager, reminding us again that a Shakespearean reading of Freud would be more illuminating than a Freudian exegesis of Shakespeare. We learn more when we discover Hamlet in the Freudian Death Drive, than when we read *Beyond the Pleasure Principle* into *Hamlet.*

In Shakespearean comedy, character achieves its true literary apotheosis, which is the representation of the inner freedom that can be created by great wit alone. Rosalind and Falstaff, perhaps alone among Shakespeare's personages, match Hamlet in wit, though hardly in the metaphysics of consciousness. Whether in the comic or the modern mode, Shakespeare has set the standard of measurement in the balance between character and passion.

In Shakespeare the self is more dramatized than theatricalized, which is why a Shakespearean reading of Freud works out so well. Character-formation after the passing of the Oedipal stage takes the place of fetishistic fragmentings of the self. Critics who now call literary character into question, and who proclaim also the death of the author, invariably also regard all notions, literary and human, of a stable character as being mere reductions of deeper pre-Oedipal desires. It becomes clear that the fortunes of literary character rise and fall with the prestige of normative conceptions of the ego. Shakespeare's Iago, who wars against being, may be the first deconstructionist of the self, with his proclamation of "I am not what I am." This constitutes the necessary prologue to any view that would regard a fixed ego as a virtual abnormality. But deconstructions of the self are no more modern than Modernism is. Like literary modernism, the decentered ego came out of the Hellenistic culture of ancient Alexandria. The Gnostic heretics believed that the psyche, like the body, was a fallen entity, mechanically fashioned by the Demiurge or false creator. They held however that each of us possessed also a spark or pneuma, which was a fragment of the original Abyss or true, alien God. The soul or psyche within every one of us was thus at war with the self or pneuma, and only that sparklike self could be saved.

Shakespeare, following after Chaucer in this respect, was the first and remains still the greatest master of representing character both as a stable soul and a wavering self. There is a substance that endures in Shakespeare's figures, and there is also a quicksilver rendition of the unsettling sparks. Racine and Tolstoy, Balzac and Dickens, follow in Shakespeare's wake by giving us some sense of pre-Oedipal sparks or drives, and considerably more sense of post-Oedipal character and personality, stabilizations or sublimations of the fetish-seeking drives. Critics like Leo Bersani and René Girard argue eloquently against our taking this mimesis as the only proper work of literature. I would suggest that strong fictions of the self, from the Bible through Samuel Beckett, necessarily participate in both modes, the sublimation of desire, and the persistence of a primordial desire. The mystery of Hamlet or of Lear is intimately invested in the tangled mixture of the two modes of representation.

Psychic mobility is proposed by Bersani as the ideal to which deconstructions of the literary self may yet guide us. The ideal has its pathos, but the realities of literary representation seem to me very different, perhaps destructively so. When a novelist like D. H. Lawrence sought to reduce his characters to Eros and the Death Drive, he still had to persuade us of his authority at mimesis by lavishing upon the figures of *The Rainbow* and *Women in Love* all of the vivid stigmata of normative personality. Birkin and Ursula may represent antithetical and uncanny drives, but they develop and change as characters pondering their own pronouncements and reactions to self and others. The cost of a non-Shakespearean representation is enormous. Pynchon, in *The Crying of Lot 49* and *Gravity's Rainbow*, evades the burden of the normative by resorting to something like Christopher Marlowe's art of caricature in *The Jew of Malta*. Marlowe's Barabas is a marvelous rhetorician, yet he is a cartoon alongside the troublingly equivocal Shylock. Pynchon's personages are deliberate cartoons also, as flat as comic strips. Marlowe's achievement, and Pynchon's, are beyond dispute, yet they are like the prelude and the postlude to Shakespearean reality. They do not wish to engage with our hunger for the empirical world and so they enter the problematic cosmos of literary fantasy.

No writer, not even Shakespeare or Proust, alters the available stock that we agree to call reality, but Shakespeare, more than any other, does show us how much of reality we could encounter if only we retained adequate desire. The strong literary representation of character is already an analysis of character, and is part of the healing work of a literary culture, which implicitly seeks to cure violence through a normative mimesis of ego, *as if it were stable,* whether in actuality it is or is not. I do not believe that this is a social quest taken on by literary culture, but rather that we confront here the aesthetic essence of what makes a culture *literary,* rather than metaphysical or ethical or religious. A culture becomes literary when its conceptual modes have failed it, which means when religion, philosophy, and science have begun to lose their authority. If they cannot heal violence, then literature attempts to do so, which may be only a turning inside out of the critical arguments of Girard and Bersani.

I conclude by offering a particular instance or special case as a paradigm for the healing enterprise that is at once the representation and the analysis of literary character. Let us call it the aesthetics of being outraged, or rather of successfully representing the state of being outraged. W. C. Fields was one modern master of such representation, and Nathanael West was another, as was Faulkner before him. Here also the greatest master remains Shakespeare, whose Macbeth, himself a bloody outrage, yet retains our imaginative sympathy precisely because he grows increasingly outraged as he experiences the equivocation of the fiend that lies like truth. The double-natured promises and the prophecies of the weird sisters finally induce in Macbeth an apocalyptic version of the stage actor's anxiety at missing cues, the horror of a phantasmagoric stage fright of missing one's time, of always reacting too late. Macbeth, a veritable monster of solipsistic inwardness but no intellectual, counters his dilemma by fresh murders, that prolong him in time yet provoke him only to a perpetually freshened sense of being outraged, as all his expectations become still worse confounded. We are moved by Macbeth, however estrangedly, because his terrible inwardness is a paradigm for our own solipsism, but also because none of us can resist a strong and successful representation of the human in a state of being outraged.

The ultimate outrage is the necessity of dying, an outrage concealed in a multitude of masks, including the tyrannical ambitions of Macbeth. I suspect that our outrage at being outraged is the most difficult of all our affects for us to represent to ourselves, which is why we are so inclined to imaginative sympathy for a character who strongly conveys that affect to us. The Shrike of West's *Miss Lonely-hearts* or Faulkner's Joe Christmas of *Light in August* are crucial modern instances, but such figures can be located in many other works, since the ability to represent this extreme emotion is one of the tests that strong writers are driven to set for themselves.

However a reader seeks to reduce literary character to a question of marks on a page, she will come at last to the impasse constituted by the thought of death, her death, and before that to all the stations of being outraged that memorialize her own drive towards death. In reading, she quests for evidences that are strong representations, whether of her desire or her despair. Such questings constitute the necessary basis for the analysis of literary character, an enterprise that always will survive every vagary of critical fashion.

EDITOR'S NOTE

The book brings together a selection of the best criticism that has been devoted to Joan of Arc, in her varied representations as a major literary character, particularly as a dramatic character. Four essays and thirteen critical extracts are given to her part in G. B. Shaw's *Saint Joan* (1923), while other essays and extracts consider her appearances in plays, poems, and novels by the very diverse company of Shakespeare, Voltaire, Robert Southey, Schiller, Mark Twain, Anatole France, Georg Kaiser, Brecht, Maxwell Anderson, Jean Anouilh, and Thomas Keneally. I am most grateful to S. T. Joshi for his erudition and acumen in helping me to edit this volume.

My introduction centers upon Shaw's Saint Joan, emphasizing both the strengths and the limitations of Shaw's treatment of her. The very rich grouping of critical extracts covers the full range of Joan of Arc's manifestations in Western literature. Among the most interesting are Coleridge on Southey, Carlyle on Schiller, Howells on Twain, Shaw and Pirandello on Shaw, Eric Bentley on Shaw and Brecht, and Leslie A. Fiedler on Shakespeare.

Fuller scale critical essays begin with the great historian Johan Huizinga on the relation of Shaw's Saint Joan to the historical Joan of Arc. Roger B. Salomon follows with the contrary emphasis, arguing for Mark Twain's *Joan of Arc* as an escape from the squalors of history.

Schiller's Joan of Arc, so dimmed for us by changes in sensibility, is defended by Frank M. Fowler, after which Hans Mayer shrewdly compares some of Joan's more startling aspects in Schiller, Shaw, and Brecht.

Anouilh is employed as foil to Shaw by Paul Hernadi, meditating upon different modes of historical revisionism. Shakespeare's Joan receives a masterly analysis by Gabriele Bernhard Jackson, who shows how much more there is to the figure than the surface might indicate.

In this book's final essay, John A. Bertolini reads Shaw's Saint Joan as the playwright's unified defense both of the self and of the imagination.

INTRODUCTION

As a literary character, Joan of Arc has provoked an extraordinary range of representations, none of which has been adequate to her mythological force in Western (let alone exclusively French) tradition. The strongest of all writers, Shakespeare, unfortunately portrayed Joan at the very beginning of his career as dramatist, with most unhappy results. The Joan of *Henry VI, Part One* is a strident strumpet and witch, though at times shrewd in her military-political stratagems. At that, she is less rancid than Voltaire's heroine, who is the whorish daughter of a priest. Schiller's idealized Joan is rather too virtuous and holy to be interesting (at least to us, now) while Mark Twain's version is scarcely worthy of so grand a comic writer. In our time, Brecht rather unconvincingly recruited Joan for Marxist purposes in the wake of Shaw's *Saint Joan,* where the Marxism is more subtly blended into the Protestantism of the play. Since Brecht cheerfully pillaged Shaw (as T. S. Eliot more gloomily managed *his* pilfering from *Saint Joan* in *Murder in the Cathedral*), the honors at representing Joan of Arc to date clearly remain with Shaw. If our current feminist criticism inspires a new wave of revisionist women novelists and dramatists, here and on the Continent, perhaps we will have a vision of Joan of Arc that will challenge or surpass Shaw's. But as of now I have never encountered a single work of literature portraying Joan from the hand of a woman.

Shaw's Joan is set forth in his preface as a kind of paradigm for feminist emulation (in his notion of feminism):

> She was the pioneer of rational dressing for women, and, like Queen Christina of Sweden two centuries later, to say nothing of Catalina de Erauso and innumerable obscure heroines who have disguised themselves as men to serve as soldiers and sailors, she refused to accept the specific woman's lot, and dressed and fought and lived as men did.
>
> . . . it is hardly surprising that she was judicially burnt, ostensibly for a number of capital crimes which we no longer punish as such, but essentially for what we call unwomanly and insufferable presumption.

This is wonderful fun, though we might remember that "rational dressing for women" amounts to arms and armor, in the case of Joan. Shaw's Joan, like Shaw himself, is invariably presumptuous, but neither in history nor in *Saint Joan* was she burned for that. Shaw remarks in the same preface: "She was in fact one of the first Protestant martyrs." In fact she was not; in *Saint Joan* she most certainly is. But then she very nearly is Shaw himself, and she manifests his remarkable amalgam of ideas: from Schopenhauer, Nietzsche, Ruskin, Samuel Butler, Shelley, Marx, William Morris, Lamarck, Bergson, among others. Her religion is Shavian Life-Force worship, or self-worship (if you would have it so). Shaw evades her Catholicism, but has no way of avoiding her French nationalism, her Gaullism, as it were. He tropes it simply as another category of her will, and it is her will that interests him most. Her motto might be Shelley's: "I always go on until I am stopped and I never am stopped." She is another in the great progression of literary characters who are heroines of the Protestant will, and her closest analogues in modern literature are the sisters, Ursula and Gudrun, in D. H. Lawrence's *Women in Love*.

As a literary and dramatic character, Shaw's Joan is a mixed success. She is overwhelmingly vivid, and doubtless Shaw's healthy self-love is transferred to what essentially is a representative of the playwright-polemicist's own soul. As an incarnation of the Life Force, as a Protestant saint and martyr, Joan manifests individuality, but did Shaw manage to create a coherent personality for her? The question is a difficult one because Shaw does nothing in the course of the play to portray a development in Joan that could relate the girl of the opening scenes to the heroine of the trial and the epilogue. Joan does not change as the play proceeds, and yet she is altogether changed at the end. Shaw was a superb comic polemicist but a very uncertain dramatist when it came to tragedy. Critics have tried to maintain that Joan is the most Shakespearean of Shaw's heroines, but she is only an ideological cartoon compared to Rosalind, Desdemona, or Cleopatra. Shaw, always dreadful in his remarks upon Shakespeare, was absurd when he asserted that one could read Shakespeare "from one end to the other without learning that the world is finally governed by forces expressing themselves in religions and laws which make epochs rather than by vulgarly ambitious individuals who make rows." Individuals, as Shakespeare should have taught Shaw, are the aesthetic center of tragedy or tragicomedy. Saint Joan is in no way vulgar, but she is superbly ambitious, and she made an epoch, at least for France.

Shaw's heroine lacks tragic intensity, but is so likeable that her considerable pathos engrosses us, despite Shaw's laziness in working through her personal development. Nothing will ever convince any playgoer or reader that there is the slightest resemblance between Shaw's Joan and the historical-mythological Joan of Arc, but Shaw was too sly to suggest much of a similarity. It is a curious irony that the most impressive literary version to date of the French Catholic warrior-saint should be Shaw's Anglo-Irish Protestant Life Force, but the irony is deeply worked into the play, and Shaw takes every advantage of it. The strongest element in his creation of Joan is the pathos of her loneliness. For me, her most moving speech comes at the end of Scene V, when she realizes that king, archbishop, and comrades-in-arms all will abandon her. The solitary communion of the Protestant temperament, alone with her God, is splendidly conveyed:

I see now that the loneliness of God is His strength: what would He be if He listened to your jealous little counsels? Well, my loneliness shall be my strength too; it is better to be alone with God; His friendship will not fail me, nor His counsel, nor His love. In His strength I will dare, and dare, and dare, until I die.

Poor Joan is in effect Shaw's Jesus, but the Life Force cannot save her from martyrdom. As a playwright, Shaw wrote little that was effective after *Saint Joan*. At the least, he had outdone every competitor at representing Joan of Arc. Perhaps he was content to have crowned his career with so sublimely unlikely a Protestant saint.

—H. B.

CRITICAL EXTRACTS

JOHN AIKIN

We are sorry to observe, in the preface to this work (*Joan of Arc* by Robert Southey), certain facts stated in order to display the extreme rapidity with which it was written. An epic poem in 12 books finished in six weeks, and, on its improved plan in 10 books, almost entirely recomposed during the time of printing! Is it possible that a person of classical education can have so slight an opinion of (perhaps) the most arduous effort of human invention, as to suffer the fervour and confidence of youth to hurry him in such a manner through a design which may fix the reputation of a whole life? Though it may be that a work seldom gains much by remaining long in the bureau, yet is it respectful to the public to present to it a performance of bulk and pretension, bearing on its head all the unavoidable imperfections of haste? Does an author do justice to himself, by putting it out of his power to correct that which he will certainly in a few years consider as wanting much correction? To *run a race with the press, in an epic poem,* is an idea so extravagant, that Mr. S. must excuse us if it has extorted from us these animadversions. We now proceed to the work itself.

How far the story of the *Maid of Orleans* is happily chosen for an epic poem is a question which will, doubtless, be differently decided by different persons. The bad success of the present poet's *serious* predecessor, Chapelain, may fairly be ascribed to his want of poetical talents. The good success of his *comic* predecessor, Voltaire, is a much more formidable obstacle; for it is certain that the association made in the minds of those who have read that supremely witty, splendid, and licentious poem, has almost as much unfitted *la Pucelle* for becoming a heroine, as Butler has done his Hudibras for becoming a hero. Nor can any one, well acquainted with the history and manners of that period, really bring himself to acquiesce in a picture of immaculate purity, humanity, and philosophical enlargement of sentiment, personified under the name of a country girl who was either a wild fanatic, an artful impostor, or more probably a mixture of both. With respect to the objection which Mr. S. anticipates, that the subject of the poem is so far from

5

national to an Englishman that it records the defeat of his country, we should be sorry not to feel with him that the approbation of those who cannot wish well to the cause of justice, by whomsoever supported, is not worth endeavouring to obtain: yet human nature being what it is, the author must not be surprised if this circumstance diminishes the popularity of his work. Indeed, if, as we think is very evident, he has chosen the subject with a view to modern application, nothing can be more natural than that it will displease those of opposite sentiments, for the very same reasons which have rendered it pleasing to him.

—JOHN AIKIN, Review of *Joan of Arc* by Robert Southey,
Monthly Review N.S. 19, No. 4 (April 1796): 301–2

SAMUEL TAYLOR COLERIDGE

I looked over the 5 first Books of the 1st. (Quarto) Edition of *Joan of Arc* yesterday, at Hood's request, in order to mark the lines written by me.—I was really astonished, 1. at the school-boy wretched Allegoric Machinery—2. at the transmogrification of the fanatic Virago into a modern novel-pawing Proselyte of the age of Reason, a Tom Paine in Petticoats, but *so* lovely!—& in love, moreover!—'*on her rubied Cheek Hung Pity's crystal gem'!* 3. at the utter want of all rhythm in the verse, the monotony & dead *plumb down* of the Pauses—& the absence of all Bone, Muscle, & Sinew in the single Lines.—His Carmen Triumphale!—Is he grown silly?

—SAMUEL TAYLOR COLERIDGE, Letter to J. J. Morgan (16 June 1814),
Collected Letters of Samuel Taylor Coleridge, ed. Earl Leslie Griggs
(Oxford: Clarendon Press, 1959), Vol. 3, p. 510

THOMAS CARLYLE

Considered as an object of poetry or history, Jeanne d'Arc, the most singular personage of modern times, presents a character capable of being viewed under a great variety of aspects, and with a corresponding variety of emotions. To the English of her own age, bigoted in their creed, and baffled by her prowess, she appeared inspired by the Devil, and was naturally burnt as a sorceress. In this light, too, she is painted in the poems of Shakspeare. To Voltaire, again, whose trade it was to war with every kind of superstition, this child of fanatic ardour seemed no better than a moonstruck zealot; and the people who followed her, and believed in her, something worse than lunatics. The glory of what she had achieved was forgotten, when the means of achieving it were recollected; and the Maid of Orleans was deemed the fit subject of a poem, the wittiest and most profligate for which literature has to blush. Our illustrious *Don Juan* hides his head when contrasted with Voltaire's *Pucelle:* Juan's biographer, with all his zeal, is but an innocent, and a novice, by the side of this arch-scorner.

Such a manner of considering the Maid of Orleans is evidently not the right one. Feelings so deep and earnest as hers can never be an object of ridicule: whoever pursues a purpose of any sort with such fervid devotedness, is entitled to awaken emotions, at least of a serious kind, in the hearts of others. Enthusiasm puts on a different shape in every different age: always in some degree sublime, often it is dangerous; its very essence is a tendency to error and exaggeration; yet it is the fundamental quality of strong souls; the true nobility of blood, in which all greatness of thought or action has its rise. *Quicquid vult valdè vult* is ever the first and surest test of mental capability. This peasant girl, who felt within her such fiery vehemence of resolution, that she could subdue the minds of kings and captains to her will, and lead armies on to battle, conquering, till her country was cleared of its invaders, must evidently have possessed the elements of a majestic character. Benevolent feelings, sublime ideas, and above all an overpowering will, are here indubitably marked. Nor does the form, which her activity assumed, seem less adapted for displaying these qualities, than many other forms in which we praise them. The gorgeous inspirations of the Catholic religion are as real as the phantom of post-humous renown; the love of our native soil is as laudable as ambition, or the principle of military honour. Jeanne d'Arc must have been a creature of shadowy yet far-glancing dreams, of unutterable feelings, of 'thoughts that wandered through Eternity.' Who can tell the trials and the triumphs, the splendours and the terrors, of which her simple spirit was the scene! 'Heartless, sneering, god-forgetting French!' as old Suwarrow called them,—they are not worthy of this noble maiden. Hers were errors, but errors which a generous soul alone could have committed, and which generous souls would have done more than pardon. Her darkness and delusions were of the understanding only; they but make the radiance of her heart more touching and apparent; as clouds are gilded by the orient light into something more beautiful than azure itself.

It is under this aspect that Schiller has contemplated the Maid of Orleans, and endeavoured to make us contemplate her. For the latter purpose, it appears that more than one plan had occurred to him. His first idea was, to represent Joanna, and the times she lived in, as they actually were: to exhibit the superstition, ferocity, and wretchedness of the period, in all their aggravation; and to show us this patriotic and religious enthusiast beautifying the tempestuous scene by her pres-ence; swaying the fierce passions of her countrymen; directing their fury against the invaders of France; till at length, forsaken and condemned to die, she perished at the stake, retaining the same steadfast and lofty faith, which had ennobled and redeemed the errors of her life, and was now to glorify the ignominy of her death. This project, after much deliberation, he relinquished, as too difficult. By a new mode of management, much of the homeliness and rude horror, that defaced and encumbered the reality, is thrown away. The Dauphin is not here a voluptuous weakling, nor is his court the centre of vice and cruelty and imbecility: the misery of the time it touched but lightly, and the Maid of Arc herself is invested with a certain faint degree of mysterious dignity, ultimately represented as being in truth a preternatural gift; though whether preternatural, and if so, whether sent from above or from below, neither we nor she, except by faith, are absolutely sure, till the conclusion.

The propriety of this arrangement is liable to question; indeed, it has been more than questioned. But external blemishes are lost in the intrinsic grandeur of the piece: the spirit of Joanna is presented to us with an exalting and pathetic force sufficient to make us blind to far greater improprieties. Joanna is a pure creation, of half-celestial origin, combining the mild charms of female loveliness with the awful majesty of a prophetess, and a sacrifice doomed to perish for her country. She resembled, in Schiller's view, the Iphigenia of the Greeks; and as such, in some respects, he has treated her.

The woes and desolation of the land have kindled in Joanna's keen and fervent heart a fire, which the loneliness of her life, and her deep feelings of religion, have nourished and fanned into a holy flame. She sits in solitude with her flocks, beside the mountain chapel of the Virgin, under the ancient Druid oak, a wizard spot, the haunt of evil spirits as well as of good; and visions are revealed to her such as human eyes behold not. It seems the force of her own spirit, expressing its feelings in forms which react upon itself. The strength of her impulses persuades her that she is called from on high to deliver her native France; the intensity of her own faith persuades others; she goes forth on her mission; all bends to the fiery vehemence of her will; she is inspired because she thinks herself so. There is something beautiful and moving in the aspect of a noble enthusiasm, fostered in the secret soul, amid obstructions and depressions, and at length bursting forth with an overwhelming force to accomplish its appointed end: the impediments which long hid it are now become testimonies of its power; the very ignorance, and meanness, and error, which still in part adhere to it, increase our sympathy without diminishing our admiration; it seems the triumph, hardly contested, and not wholly carried, but still the triumph, of Mind over Fate, of human volition over material necessity.

All this Schiller felt, and has presented with even more than his usual skill. The secret mechanism of Joanna's mind is concealed from us in a dim religious obscurity; but its active movements are distinct; we behold the lofty heroism of her feelings; she affects us to the very heart. The quiet, devout innocence of her early years, when she lived silent, shrouded in herself, meek and kindly though not communing with others, makes us love her: the celestial splendour which illuminates her after-life adds reverence to our love. Her words and actions combine an overpowering force with a calm unpretending dignity; we seem to understand how they must have carried in their favour the universal conviction. Joanna is the most noble being in tragedy. We figure her with her slender lovely form, her mild but spirit-speaking countenance; 'beautiful and terrible'; bearing the banner of the Virgin before the hosts of her country; travelling in the strength of a rapt soul; irresistible by faith; 'the lowly herdsmaid,' greater in the grandeur of her simple spirit than the kings and queens of this world. Yet her breast is not entirely insensible to human feeling, nor her faith never liable to waver. When that inexorable vengeance, which had shut her ear against the voice of mercy to the enemies of France, is suspended at the sight of Lionel, and her heart experiences the first touch of mortal affection, a baleful cloud overspreads the serene of her mind; it seems as if Heaven had forsaken her, or from the beginning permitted demons or earthly dreams to deceive her. The agony of her spirit, involved in endless and horrid labyrinths of doubt, is powerfully portrayed. She has crowned the king at Rheims; and all is joy, and pomp, and jubilee, and almost adoration of Joanna: but Joanna's thoughts are not of joy. The sight of her poor but kind and true-hearted sisters in the crowd, moves her to the soul. Amid the tumult and magnificence of this royal pageant, she sinks into a reverie; her small native dale of Arc, between its quiet hills, rises on her mind's eye, with its straw-roofed huts, and its clear greensward; where the sun is even then shining so brightly, and the sky is so blue, and all is so calm and motherly and safe. She sighs for the peace of that sequestered home; then shudders to think that she shall never see it more. Accused of witchcraft, by her own ascetic melancholic father, she utters no word of denial to the charge; for her heart is dark, it is tarnished by earthly love, she dare not raise her thoughts to Heaven. Parted from her sisters; cast out with horror by the people she had lately saved from despair, she wanders forth, desolate, forlorn, not knowing whither. Yet she does not sink under this sore trial: as she suffers from without, and is forsaken of men, her mind grows clear and strong, her confidence returns. She is now more firmly fixed in our admiration than before; tenderness is united to our other feelings; and her faith has been proved by sharp vicissitudes. Her countrymen recognise their error; Joanna closes her career by a glorious death; we take farewell of her in a solemn mood of heroic pity.

Joanna is the animating principle of this tragedy; the scenes employed in developing her character and feelings constitute its great charm. Yet there are other personages in it, that leave a distinct and pleasing impression of themselves in our memory. Agnes Sorel, the soft, languishing, generous mistress of the Dauphin, relieves and heightens by comparison the sterner beauty of the Maid. Dunois, the Bastard of Orleans, the lover of Joanna, is a blunt, frank, sagacious soldier, and well described. And Talbot, the grey veteran, delineates his dark, unbelieving, indomitable soul, by a few slight but expressive touches: he sternly passes down to the land, as he thinks, of utter nothingness, contemptuous even of the fate that destroys him, and

> On the soil of France he sleeps, as does
> A hero on the shield he would not quit.

—THOMAS CARLYLE, *The Life of Friedrich Schiller* [1825], *The Works of Thomas Carlyle*, ed. H. D. Traill (London: Chapman & Hall, 1899), Vol. 25, pp. 154–59

HENRY, LORD BROUGHAM

In the year 1730 Voltaire wrote part of another poem, which he finished at intervals during the seven or eight years following—his too famous mock-heroic, the *Pucelle d'Orléans*. It is painful and humiliating to human genius to confess, what yet is without any doubt true, that this is, of all his poetical works, the most perfect, showing most wit, most spirit, most of the resources of a great poet, though of course the nature of the subject forbids all attempts at either the pathetic or the sublime; but in brilliant imagery—in picturesque description—in point and epigram—in boundless fertility of fancy—in variety of striking and vigorous satire— all clothed in verse as natural as Swift's, and far more varied as well as harmonious—no prejudice, however naturally raised by the moral faults of the work, can prevent us from regarding it as the great masterpiece of his poetical genius. Here of course the panegyric must close, and it must give way to indignation at such a perversion of such divine talents. The indecency, often amounting to absolute obscenity, which pervades nearly the whole composition, cannot be ex- cused on the plea that it is only a witty licentiousness, instead of one which excites the passions; still less can it be palliated by citing bad precedents, least of all by referring to such writers as Ariosto, who more rarely violates the laws of decorum; whereas Voltaire is ready to commit this offence at every moment, and seems ever to take the view of each subject that most easily lends itself to licentious allusions. But this is not all. The *Pucelle* is one continued sneer at all that men do hold, and all that they ought to hold, sacred, from the highest to the least important subjects, in a moral view—from the greatest to the most indifferent, even in a critical view. Religion and its ministers and its professors—virtue, especially the virtues of a prudential cast—the feelings of humanity—the sense of beauty—the rules of po- etical composition—the very walks of literature in which Voltaire had most striven to excel—are all made the constant subjects of sneering contempt, or of ribald laughter; sometimes by wit, sometimes by humour, not rarely by the broad grins of mere gross buffoonery. It is a sad thing to reflect that the three masterpieces of three such men as Voltaire, Rousseau, Byron, should all be the most immoral of their compositions. It seems as if their prurient nature had been affected by a bad but criminal excitement to make them exceed themselves.—Assuredly if such was not Voltaire's case, he well merits the blame; for he scrupled not to read his *Pucelle* to his niece, then a young woman.

—HENRY, LORD BROUGHAM, "Voltaire," *Lives of Men of Letters and Science
Who Flourished in the Time of George III* (London: Charles Knight, 1845),
pp. 42–44

DENTON J. SNIDER

Shakespeare, or the author of the First Part of *Henry the Sixth,* has not taken much advantage of the imposing figure of Joan of Arc; he has rather left her character and her mission in a state of perplexing doubt. When the French speak, full justice is done to her wonderful power; she is divinely sent; she has beheld in a vision the one thing needful in the present emergency; she is inspired of Heaven to be the deliverer of her country. But the English ridicule her claims; they even assail her womanly honor, which she, among the French, is represented as having kept unstained; and, finally, they burn her for a witch. English feeling, perhaps, dictated such a portraiture. Between these two opinions the character fluctuates; it has no unity in its development, but sways from one side to the other, finally resting under an English cloud of suspicion. Still the main fact cannot be obscured—a woman of humble station rises to be a national heroine, heroic above all men of that age; the champion of the Family has become the champion of the State.

—DENTON J. SNIDER, *"Henry the Sixth," The Shakespearean Drama: A Commentary: The Histories* (St. Louis: Sigma Publishing Co., 1889), pp. 434–35

W. D. HOWELLS

I wish his ⟨Mark Twain's⟩ personal recollections of Joan could have been written by some Southwestern American, translated to Domremy by some such mighty magic of imagination as launched the Connecticut Yankee into the streets of many-towered Camelot; but I make the most of the moments when the Sieur Louis de Conte forgets himself into much the sort of witness I could wish him to be. I am not at all troubled when he comes out with a bit of good, strong, downright modern American feeling; my suffering begins when he does the supposed mediæval thing. Then I suspect that his armor is of tin, that the castles and rocks are pasteboard, that the mob of citizens and soldiers who fill the air with the clash of their two-up-and-two-down combats, and the well-known muffled roar of their voices have been hired in at so much a night, and that Joan is sometimes in an awful temper behind the scenes; and I am thankful when the brave Sieur Louis forgets himself again. I have my little theory that human nature is elementally much the same always and everywhere, and that if the man of intelligence will study this in his own heart he will know pretty well what all other men have been in essentials. As to manners, I think that a man who knew the Southwest in the days of slavery, when the primitive distinctions between high and low, bond and free, lord and villein, were enforced with the violence of passions stronger than the laws, could make a shrewd guess at mediæval life; and I am inclined to accept Mark Twain's feudal ruffians, gentle and simple, as like enough, or as much like as one can get them at this late day. At least, they are like something, and the trouble with the more romantic reproductions is that they are like nothing.

A jolly thing about it, and a true thing, is the fun that his people get out of the affair. It is a vast frolic, in certain aspects, that mystical mission of the inspired Maid, and Joan herself is not above having her laugh at times. Her men-at-arms, who drive the English before them under her miraculous lead, are "the boys" who like to drink deep and to talk tall; to get the joke on one another, and the dead wood. Without this sort of relief I own that I should find their campaigns rather trying, and, without the hope of overhearing some of their lusty drollery, I should not care to follow them in all their hard fighting. I fancy it is the chance of this that gives the author himself so much stomach for battle; it seems worth while to lay a lot of fellows in plate-armor low if you can have them clatter down to the music of a burly jest and a roaring laugh. He is not at the trouble to maintain the solemnity of the dominant strain throughout; and he has made his Sieur de Conte not only a devout believer in the divine authority of Joan, but a delicately tender sympathizer with her when she suffers as a poor, simple shepherd-girl for the deeds of the prophetess. De Conte is a very human and lovable character, and is rather apt to speak with the generous feeling and the righteous love and hate of Mark Twain, whose humor has never been sullied with anything mean or cruel. The minor note is heard mostly through De Conte's story of the trial and martyrdom of Joan, which is studied faithfully from the histories, and which I think is the best part of the book. It is extremely pathetic at moments, and as one reads the heart swells with pity for the victim of one of the cruelest wrongs ever done, as if the suffering from it were not over four hundred years ago.

It would not be easy to convey a sense of the reverent tenderness with which the character of Joan is developed in this fiction, and she is made a "sensible, warm motion" from the myth that she seems in history. The wonder of her career is something that grows upon the reader to the end, and remains with him while he is left tingling with compassion for the hapless child who lived so gloriously and died so piteously.

What can we say, in this age of science, that will explain away the miracle of that age of faith? For these things really happened. There was actually this peasant maid who believed she heard voices from Heaven bidding her take command of the French armies and drive the English out of her country; who took command of them without other authority than such as the belief of her prince and his people gave her; who prophesied of the victories she should win, and won them; who broke the power of the invaders; and who then, as if God thought she had given proofs enough of her divine commission, fell into their power and was burned for a heretic and an idolater. It reads like a wild and foolish invention, but it is every word most serious truth. It is preposterous, it is impossible, but it is all undeniable.

What can we say to it in the last year of this incredulous old century, nodding to its close? We cannot deny it. What was it all? Was Joan's power the force dormant in the people which her claim of inspiration awoke to mighty deeds? If it was merely that, how came this poor, ignorant girl by the skill to lead armies, to take towns, to advise councils, and to change the fate of a whole nation? It was she who recreated France, and changed her from a province of England to the great monarchy she became. Could a dream, an illusion, a superstition, do this? What, then, are dreams and illusions and superstitions, that our wisdom should be so eager to get rid of them?

We know that for the present the force which could remove mountains is pretty much gone out of the world. Faith has ceased to be, but we have some lively hopes of electricity. We now employ it to exanimate people; perhaps we shall yet find it valuable to reanimate them. Or will faith come back again, and will the future ages be some of them religious?

I shall not attempt to answer these questions, which have, with a good number of others, been suggested by this curious book of the arch-humorist of the century. I fancy they will occur to most other readers, who will share my interest in the devout, the mystical, the knightly treatment of the story of Joan of Arc by Mark Twain. Voltaire tried to make her a laughingstock and a by-word. He was a very great wit, but he failed to defame her, for the facts were against him. It is our humorist's fortune to have the facts with him, and whatever we think Joan of Arc, inspired or deluded, we shall feel the wonder of them the more for the light his imagination has thrown upon them. I dare say there are a good many faults in the book. It is unequal; its archaism is often superficially a failure; if you look at it merely on the technical side, the outbursts of the nineteenth-century American in the armor of the fifteenth-century Frenchman are solecisms. But, in spite of all this, the book has a vitalizing force. Joan lives in it again, and dies, and then lives on in the love and pity and wonder of the reader.

—W. D. HOWELLS, *"Joan of Arc"* [1896], *My Mark Twain* (New York: Harper & Brothers, 1910), pp. 152–56

WILLIAM HALLER

Southey's interest in his heroine was, of course, as a political rather than as a human figure. As De Quincey pointed out, he shows her merely doing, never suffering. He invents an infancy and childhood for her, makes her share the terrible effects upon the poor country people of the English invasion, and gives her a romantic education with a hermit in the forest. Roused to action by visions, an angel, and reports of the horrors of war perpetrated by her country's enemies, she resolves to save France. She meets Dunois wounded, cures him, convinces him of her mission, and is led by him to the king at Chinon. There she convinces also the court and clergy in the traditional manner, leads an army to the relief of Orleans, repulses the English, defeats them at Patay, and crowns the king in triumph at Rheims. There Southey's interest in Joan stopped, for from that point on her story is personal rather than political. The French people had conquered in the fight for liberty against the English, and that was sufficient for his purposes at the time. It is necessary to add, however, that even if he had not been so preoccupied with this aspect of the story, the other was little likely to have occurred to him or to anyone, even to Shakespeare. The reason for this was that the marvelous detailed documents relating to Joan's sufferings and displaying her most intimate nature became generally accessible only in 1790 in the work of L'Averdy, who made the first scholarly effort to study the sources of Joan's history, and superseded all other works on the subject until the monumental publications of Quicherat (1841–1849) made Joan a world-wide heroine. Of the existence of L'Averdy's work, Southey was informed, as he tells us in the preface to his first edition (1796), but he appears never to have seen the book itself, certainly never, in later editions, to have made use of it.

The general outline of the story, as given in the poem, was thus easily applicable to the situation obtaining in 1793. It also offered many opportunities for pertinent and, at the time, startling allusions to the ideas and affairs of the same momentous year. The exigencies of the narrative compelled the author to represent the triumph of a king, but the facts of history also permitted him to depict the awakening of a people to national consciousness and the resolution to throw off a tyrant Englishman; as for Charles VI, he was a fit object against whom to vent republican spleen, and he consequently makes a sorry figure in Southey's hands. He is a king always eager to order a fast for the people and a feast for the courtiers, who are said to be "insects," "summer-flies," "blood-suckers" sprung from the "court dunghill," and loath to do battle against the invaders. Joan, on the contrary, assisted by her follower Conrade, a figure supplied by Southey, is the voice of the people urging the king to burst his fetters and lead the nation against the common foe. Charles trembles at her words, but the implication is that he is incapable of becoming the hero she intends herself to be. Thereupon her satellite Conrade calls down destruction upon the heads of those mighty ones, those "prime ministers of death" (no uncertain reference to the prime ministry of England at the time), who send thousands to massacre merely in order to rear pyramids of glory out of the bodies of the innocent.

> Oh groves and woodland shades
> How blest indeed were you, if the iron rod
> Should one day from Oppression's hand be wrenched
> By everlasting Justice! come that hour
> When in the Sun the Angel of the Lord
> Shall stand and cry to all the fowls of Heaven,
> "Gather ye to the supper of your God,
> That ye may eat the flesh of mighty men,
> Of Captains and of Kings!" Then shall be peace
> When ... author of all ills that flesh endures,
> OPPRESSION, in the bottomless abyss
> Shall fall to rise no more!

In the ninth book Southey sends Joan in a dream on a journey to a kind of purgatorial inferno, where she beholds, chief among other marvels, the monarchs of the earth, "the MURDERERS OF MANKIND," enthroned under a black dome, and "each bearing on his brow a crown of fire," In this gallery sit Nimrod, Alexander, Cæsar "accurst liberticide," Octavius, Titus "the Conqueror of the Jews," and lastly Henry V, who addresses her on the pertinent subject of invading France. He confesses that he might have reigned in happiness, peace, and prosperity if his appetite for glory had not been tempted by the spectacle of France, torn by faction and apparently an easy prey. Therefore, though himself a man of temperate life, he sent forth murder and rape to work for him, and persecuted those who taught new doctrines which, albeit true, opposed his wishes. He can now have no hope of escape from punishment until the whole human race is as happy as the French were by him rendered wretched, until it forms "one brotherhood, one universal family of love."

Such principles could not be made the sole basis of the action of the poem, but they could be enforced by many such prophetic strains looking forward to the poet's own day. Thus he refers to Brissot and Madame Roland as martyred patriots who have sowed by toil and manured by blood a mighty tree beneath which the sons of men hereafter will pitch their tents in amity. Or he alludes to the Bastille as a hell-house of France before the sublime, almighty people dashed the iron rod from their tyrant's hand. In the bolder tones of a funeral speech by Joan over the dead on the field of Patay, Southey brings home the application of all this to England by making his heroine pray to the God of peace and love to forgive the blood-guilty men who came to desolate France and compel its people to bow the knee before a tyrant, and by making her prophesy that England's chiefs will drain their people's blood and wealth in vain if they attempt to force by arms the yoke of slavery upon France, who will repel the mercenary thousands sent upon her and blast the despots with the thunderbolt of vengeance. Finally, the concluding scene of the poem consists of a warning and a prophecy to the king of France. Let him remember to be a friend to the weak and lowly; let him not shroud himself in his robes of royalty when hunger is abroad in the land; let him protect his people; he will then be heaven's true representative, and never need hireling guards fleshed in slaughter to fight in vain defense of a tottering, blood-cemented throne. If he should fail to follow her advice, may God be merciful to him when the spirits of the murdered innocent cry out for justice! The poet concludes the whole work with a last fling at England; the maid has redeemed her country, and the hope is uttered that the arms of "FREEDOM" may always meet with such success.

For his conception of Joan as an heroic figure in a struggle for popular liberty, Southey was not indebted to any previous treatment of the story. Chapelain's La Pucelle (1656) did, indeed, attempt to treat Joan seriously, but could hardly be so read. Southey knew of the existence of this poem from Boileau at the time of the composition of his own work, but was unable to obtain a copy of it until the publication of his second edition (1798). At that time, with his passion for giving information, he printed an analysis of Chapelain's work which, he there says, "comprises all the beauties, and most of the absurdities of twelve thousand lines. I believe no person less interested than myself in the story could persevere through it." As for the ribald burlesque that Voltaire produced after Chapelain, Southey had now long since passed out of the mood in which he could take the cynic sympathetically, and he wrote, "I have never been guilty of reading the Pucelle of Voltaire." These words were not printed, however, until the second edition, for the benevolent Cottle could not speak harshly even of a dead Voltaire, and altered the statement in the preface of the first edition to "The Pucelle of Voltaire I have not read." Southey's inspiration and model were really to be found in Leonidas, and, we should add, Lucan's Pharsalia, a great favorite with all the young romantic revolutionists.

To these influences and to these sentiments must be added others more far-reaching. Joan is the champion of popular liberty only because she has grown up in the freedom of nature. For this notion, of course, Southey was indebted not only to revolutionary theories sweeping in upon him from all sides, but also to that "head-full" of Rousseau which he got at school. Yet references to Rousseau in his extant letters are few and, except in one or two cases, never specific. It was rather the poet Akenside to whom he acknowledged a direct obligation for the principles that had imbued his youthful mind. This almost forgotten writer bears a striking relation to all the romantic nature-poets which betrays much concerning the origin of their ideas. Akenside attempted the impossible task, in which Pope had already failed, of building poetry out of the thin notions of Deism before Deism was more than the a priori theology and shallow optimism of Bolingbroke and Shaftesbury. The poetic problem was to provide their doctrine of a vague, all-powerful, benefi- cent deity with images as concrete as the dramatic mythology of the Christian trinity, saviour, devil, and judgment day. Akenside, always theoretical and never apprehending religion by faith, flounders badly, but strikes out the main lines that later poets of natural religion were to follow. Through nature the deistic god makes men good, and through nature he manifests himself. Akenside conveys all this by an adaptation to his needs of the classical mythology, as in the "Hymn to the Naiads," or by the new mythology of personifications in Pleasures of Imagination. The theme of the latter poem is in crude form that theory of the poetic function later elabo- rated by Coleridge and Wordsworth minus the notions about using the language of the middle and lower classes of society. The imagination, according to Akenside, is the faculty by which man perceives and reveals the divine,—or the good, the true, and the beautiful,—as it exists only in nature. Consistently with his theories, he has much to say in addition about liberty and the rights of man, but his theories were never sufficiently fused within him by passion to make him a poet. Deism ran off by other channels to France, and there became the religion of popular revolution. When it returned flaming to England, ardent spirits like Southey and Coleridge, welcoming it, rejoiced to find their hopes already expressed in Akenside, to whom they frequently refer, and plunged at once to the enterprise so coldly attempted by the older writer of representing the religion of nature poetically. The artistic prob- lem was still the same,—to find an imagery that would make their religion concrete,—and the same solutions were tried. For Akenside's warmed-over clas- sical mythology Southey merely substituted history in Joan and nonclassical mythol- ogy in later poems, and like Wordsworth, fused most, but, like Wordsworth again, not all of Akenside's demi-deities of personification into the grand personification of Nature. If Southey failed to become a great poet, it was in part due to the fact that revolutionary Deism lacked roots and body for great epic, and found its final expression only in the lyric of Wordsworth.

With Akenside as an authority, therefore, the poet makes Joan owe all her power to the fact that she has been educated by nature to be natural, or in other words, good, and that good is naturally omnipotent; consequently she has but to confront the wicked, unnatural English in order to drive them pell-mell into anni- hilation. The weakness of this faith was, of course, the weakness of the poem; there can be no struggle, because one party is invincible, the other unhuman, and neither is interesting. In describing the education of Joan, then, Southey accepts wholeheartedly the theory that in the blest era of the infant world, "ere man had learnt to bow the knee to man," love and happiness had gone hand in hand. Honesty then reigned; vice had not yet appeared; gold, and hence avarice, had not yet been discovered; the worship of justice had not yet given way to the worship of wealth and power; only when that occurred did oppression and poverty, parents of misery, appear. Nevertheless this decay was ordained by the "All-Wise" for the best, for man would thereby learn to regain and keep by means of wisdom that state of bliss which he had lost through ignorance. For Joan, the lucky circumstances of her education insured this happy state so far as it could be attained in her own experience. Her parents had been driven by the English from Harfleur, her mother was dead, she was left alone as a child beside her father's body in a forest, and there a holy hermit with the educational principles of Rousseau had found her and brought her up. Her infancy was spent in the forest. The hermit taught her to pray to an all-gracious God as her creator and preserver, taught her also in seraphic rapture to behold God in the works of nature about them.

The faith which Joan thus learned she also learned to preach, for when she is examined by the priests endeavoring to determine her divine inspiration, and is asked whether she has duly attended divine confessional, her reply is unhesitating. To be sure she admits that she knows not the abstruse points of nice religion, the subtle and narrow bounds of orthodoxy, but condemns all forms of devotion, chaunted mass, altar and robe, wafer and cup, priest-created Gods, storied panes, trophied pillars, the imaged cross. These things have waked in her no artificial awe. But she has beheld the eternal energy pervading the boundless range of nature; morning and evening her soul has been called forth to devotion by the sun and flowers. The priests reply that nature is sinful, but she flouts the suggestion. Nature cannot teach sin; nature is all benevolence, all love, all beauty. Only if it be sin to bind the wounds of the lamb and bathe them in tears, has nature taught sin, for this is what nature has taught her to do. Suggestions to the contrary are blasphemous. There is no vice in the greenwood, no misery, no hunger, such as will one day plead with damning eloquence against the rulers of society.

In the second edition of the poem (1798) Southey made still further use of the teachings of the romantic thinkers. He there attempted to eliminate from his narrative all the miraculous elements included in the earlier form. Where an angel comes, therefore, in the first edition, to inspire Joan with her lofty mission, in the later version her inspiration more consistently rises from nature through a romantic reverie or trance. There is a lonely spring called the fountain of the fairies. It is deep in the forest, with no sound except of the passing wind or murmuring stream. Here Joan's soul may enjoy solitude, freedom, holy quiet, and escape from human kind. While sitting in this place one night she is enveloped in a storm and filled with the glory of tempest, thunder and lightning, so that all thought is annihilated in her, her powers suspended, and she herself "diffused into the scene." In this state it occurs to her to save France. Such was the romantic machinery of the natural supernatural.

Before leaving the discussion of *Joan of Arc,* it must be noted that the choice of a female hero by the young poet was no accident, though of feminine characteristics she displays none. But among Southey's sympathies for the oppressed was the sympathy for the lot of woman. The "Inscription for a Tablet at Godstow Nunnery" in memory of Rosamund gave some indication of this, and it is signallized still more by the composition, during this very visit at Brixton Causeway, of "The Triumph of Woman" with a dedication to Mary Wollstonecraft which coupled her name with that of Joan, Madame Roland, and Charlotte Corday. The poem itself was simply a variant upon the same theme and situation as the epic just composed.

The poetical qualities of *Joan of Arc* are easy to distinguish. They are a faithful reflection of the qualities of Southey himself. The poem has vigor, but coupled with a certain stridency, an unstoical lack of restraint. At best, it has the qualities of good rhetorical declamation and clear narrative, but it is too hurried, in spite of being also too long, to achieve beauty of phrase or rhythm. The blank verse, indeed, is scarcely distinguishable as such; it never sings, yet it shows promise of developing into swift and lucid prose. Contrary to expectation, the poem as a whole is not dull so much as thin, and sharp with the sharpness of unripe fruit. All these are qualities rising naturally from the character of the young author. He was a lean, greyhound creature with hawk-like head, and the quick intensity of an animal highly bred for speed. His passion for headlong expression and for committing himself conspicuously, his constitutional incapacity for patience,—which is a different thing from persistence or fortitude,—are all here displayed. The character of Joan herself is a projection of Southey. Her self-confidence, her self-assertiveness, her lack of humility, her vehemence, her voluble preachiness, her unrestrained impulse to be doing,—these are the traits of an eager, overstimulated, unreflecting boy, and such a boy Southey was when he wrote himself into his poem; unreflecting, for the whirl of romantic and revolutionary ideas came to him, not as things to be apprehended and weighed by the intelligence, but as impulses to be caught by the emotion. What Southey had as boy and man were not so much opinions and judgments, as sympathies and antipathies. Hence he contributed nothing to the revolutionary notions he had received except immediate, vigorous, copious expression in words and also in actions. We are interested in *Joan of Arc,* therefore, as the first full manifestation of Southey's personality, and as a sharp delineation of the rising current of the age in which he lived. The latter consideration gave the poem a contemporary reputation of an obvious nature which inevitably and rapidly faded.

—WILLIAM HALLER, *The Early Life of Robert Southey 1774–1803*
(New York: Columbia University Press, 1917), pp. 102–12

GEORGE BERNARD SHAW

English readers would probably like to know how these idolizations and reactions have affected the books they are most familiar with about Joan. There is the first part of the Shakespearean, or pseudo-Shakespearean trilogy of *Henry VI*, in which Joan is one of the leading characters. This portrait of Joan is not more authentic than the descriptions in the London papers of George Washington in 1780, of Napoleon in 1803, of the German Crown Prince in 1915, or of Lenin in 1917. It ends in mere scurrility. The impression left by it is that the playwright, having begun by an attempt to make Joan a beautiful and romantic figure, was told by his scandalized company that English patriotism would never stand a sympathetic representation of a French conqueror of English troops, and that unless he at once introduced all the old charges against Joan of being a sorceress and a harlot, and assumed her to be guilty of all of them, his play could not be produced. As likely as not, this was what actually happened: indeed there is only one other apparent way of accounting for the sympathetic representation of Joan as a heroine culminating in her eloquent appeal to the Duke of Burgundy, followed by the blackguardly scurrility of the concluding scenes. That other way is to assume that the original play was wholly scurrilous, and that Shakespear touched up the earlier scenes. As the work belongs to a period at which he was only beginning his practice as a tinker of old works, before his own style was fully formed and hardened, it is impossible to verify this guess. His finger is not unmistakeably evident in the play, which is poor and base in its moral tone; but he may have tried to redeem it from downright infamy by shedding a momentary glamor on the figure of The Maid.

When we jump over two centuries to Schiller, we find *Die Jungfrau von Orleans* drowned in a witch's caldron of raging romance. Schiller's Joan has not a single point of contact with the real Joan, nor indeed with any mortal woman that ever walked this earth. There is really nothing to be said of his play but that it is not about Joan at all, and can hardly be said to pretend to be; for he makes her die on the battlefield, finding her burning unbearable. Before Schiller came Voltaire, who burlesqued Homer in a mock epic called *La Pucelle*. It is the fashion to dismiss this with virtuous indignation as an obscene libel; and I certainly cannot defend it against the charge of extravagant indecorum. But its purpose was not to depict Joan, but to kill with ridicule everything that Voltaire righteously hated in the institutions and fashions of his own day. He made Joan ridiculous, but not contemptible nor (comparatively) unchaste; and as he also made Homer and St Peter and St Denis and the brave Dunois ridiculous, and the other heroines of the poem very unchaste indeed, he may be said to have let Joan off very easily. But indeed the personal adventures of the characters are so outrageous, and so Homerically free from any pretence at or even possibility of historical veracity, that those who affect to take them seriously only make themselves Pecksniffian. Samuel Butler believed *The Iliad* to be a burlesque of Greek Jingoism and Greek religion, written by a hostage or a slave; and *La Pucelle* makes Butler's theory almost convincing. Voltaire represents Agnes Sorel, the Dauphin's mistress, whom Joan never met, as a woman with a consuming passion for the chastest concubinal fidelity, whose fate it was to be continually falling into the hands of licentious foes and suffering the worst extremities of rapine. The combats in which Joan rides a flying donkey, or in which, taken unaware with no clothes on, she defends Agnes with her sword, and inflicts appropriate mutilations on her assailants, can be laughed at as they are intended to be without scruple; for no sane person could mistake them for sober history; and it may be that their ribald irreverence is more wholesome than the beglamored sentimentality of Schiller. Certainly Voltaire should not have asserted that Joan's father was a priest; but when he was out to *écraser l'infâme* (the French Church) he stuck at nothing.

So far, the literary representations of The Maid were legendary. But the publication by Quicherat in 1841 of the reports of her trial and rehabilitation placed the subject on a new footing. These entirely realistic documents created a living interest in Joan which Voltaire's mock Homerics and Schiller's romantic nonsense missed. Typical products of that interest in America and England are the histories of Joan by Mark Twain and Andrew Lang. Mark Twain was converted to downright worship of Joan directly by Quicherat. Later on, another man of genius, Anatole France, reacted against the Quicheratic wave of enthusiasm, and wrote a *Life of Joan* in which he attributed Joan's ideas to clerical prompting and her military success to an adroit use of her by Dunois as a *mascotte:* in short, he denied that she had any serious military or political ability. At this Andrew saw red, and went for Anatole's scalp in a rival *Life* of her which should be read as a corrective to the other. Lang had no difficulty in shewing that Joan's ability was not unnatural fiction to be explained away as an illusion manufactured by priests and soldiers, but a straightforward fact.

It has been lightly pleaded in explanation that Anatole France is a Parisian of the art world, into whose scheme of things the able, hardheaded, hardhanded female, though she dominates provincial France and business Paris, does not enter; whereas Lang was a Scot, and every Scot knows that the grey mare is as likely as not to be the better horse. But this explanation does not convince me. I cannot believe that Anatole France does not know what everybody knows. I wish everybody knew all that he knows. One feels antipathies at work in his book. He is not anti-Joan; but he is anti-clerical, anti-mystic, and fundamentally unable to believe that there ever was any such person as the real Joan.

Mark Twain's Joan, skirted to the ground, and with as many petticoats as Noah's wife in a toy ark, is an attempt to combine Bayard with Esther Summerson from *Bleak House* into an unimpeachable American school teacher in armor. Like Esther Summerson she makes her creator ridiculous, and yet, being the work of a man of genius, remains a credible human goodygoody in spite of her creator's infatuation. It is the description rather than the valuation that is wrong. Andrew Lang and Mark Twain are equally determined to make Joan a beautiful and most ladylike Victorian; but both of them recognize and insist on her capacity for leadership, though the Scots scholar is less romantic about it than the Mississippi pilot. But then Lang was, by lifelong professional habit, a critic of biographies rather than a biographer, whereas Mark Twain writes his biography frankly in the form of a romance.

—GEORGE BERNARD SHAW, "Preface" [1924] to *Saint Joan, Collected Plays with Their Prefaces* (London: Max Reinhardt/The Bodley Head, 1973), Vol. 6, pp. 39–43

LUIGI PIRANDELLO

In none of Shaw's work that I can think of have considerations of art been so thoroughly respected as in *Saint Joan.* The four acts of this drama begin, as they must begin, with Joan's request for soldiers of Robert de Beaudricourt to use in driving the English from "the sweet land of France." And they end, as they must end, with the trial and execution of Joan. Shaw calls this play a chronicle. In fact, the drama is built up episode by episode, moment by moment, some of them rigorously particular and free from generality—truly in the style of the chroniclers—though usually they tend to be what I call deliberate "constructiveness." The hens have not been laying, when suddenly they begin to lay. The wind has long been blowing from the east, and suddenly it begins blowing from the west. Two miracles! Then there are other simple, naïve things, such as the recognition of the "blood royal" in the third act, which likewise seems to be a miracle.

But these moments are interspersed with other moments of irony and satire, of which either the Church or the English are the victims. However, this attempt to present the chronicle inside what is really history does not seem to me quite as happy as it was in *Caesar and Cleopatra.* In *Saint Joan,* history, or rather character historically conceived, weighs a bit too heavily on the living fluid objectivity of the chronicle, and the events in the play somehow lose that sense of the unexpected which is the breath of true life. We know in advance where we are going to come out. The characters, whether historical or typical, do not quite free themselves from the fixity that history has forced upon them and from the significant rôle they are to play in history.

Joan herself, who is presented to us as a fresh creature of the open fields, full of burning faith and self-confidence, remains that way from the beginning to the end of the play: and she makes a little too obvious her intention not to be reciting a historical rôle and to remain that dear, frank, innocent, inspired child that she is. Yes, Joan, as she really was in her own little individual history, must have been much as Shaw imagined her. But he seems to look on her once and for all, so to speak, quite without regard for the various situations in which she will meet life in the course of the story.

And she is kept thus simple and unilinear by the author just to bring her airy, refreshing ingenuousness into contrast with the artificial, sophisticated—or, as I say, "deliberate" or "constructed"—complexity of her accusers. There is, in other words, something mechanical, foreordained, fixed, about her character. Much more free and unobstructed in his natural impulses, much more independent of any deliberate restraints, and accordingly much more "living" (from my point of view) is the Chaplain, de Stogumber, the truly admirable creation in this drama, and a personage on which Shaw has surely expended a great deal of affectionate effort.

At a certain moment Joan's faith in her "voices" is shaken. And this charming little creature, hitherto steadfastly confident in the divine inspiration which has many times saved her from death in battle, is suddenly filled with terror at the torment awaiting her. She says she is ready to sign the recantation of all that she has said and done. And she does sign it. But then, on learning from her judges that the sentence of death is only to be changed into a sentence of life imprisonment, she seizes the document in a sudden burst of emotion and tears it to pieces. "Death is far better than this!" she cries. She could never live without the free air of the fields, the beauty of the green meadows, the warm light of the sun. And she falls fainting into the arms of the executioners, who drag her off to the stake.

At this moment Shaw carries his protagonists to a summit of noble poetry with which any other author would be content; and we may be sure that any other author would have lowered the curtain on this scene. But Shaw cannot resist the pressure and the inspiration of the life he well knows must be surging in such circumstances in his other character—the Chaplain. He rushes on toward a second climax of not less noble poetry, depicting with magnificent elan the mad remorse, the hopeless penitence of Stogumber, thus adding to our first crisis of exquisite anguish another not less potent and overwhelming.

Rarely has George Bernard Shaw attained higher altitudes of poetic emotion than here. There is a truly great poet in Shaw; but this combative Anglo-Irishman is often willing to forget that he is a poet, so interested is he in being a citizen of his country, or a man of the twentieth century society, with a number of respectable ideas to defend, a number of sermons to preach, a number of antagonists to rout from the intellectual battlefield. But here, in *Saint Joan,* the poet comes into his own again, with only a subordinate rôle left, as a demanded compensation, to irony and satire. To be sure *Saint Joan* has all the savor and all the attractiveness of Shaw's witty polemical dialogue. But for all of these keen and cutting thrusts to left and right in Shaw's usual style of propaganda, *Saint Joan* is a work of poetry from beginning to end.

This play represents in marvelous fashion what, among so many elements of negation, is the positive element, indeed the fundamental underpinning, in the character, thought and art of this great writer—an outspoken Puritanism, which brooks no go-betweens and no mediations between man and God; a vigorous and independent vital energy, that frees itself restlessly and with joyous scorn from all the stupid and burdensome shackles of habit, routine and tradition, to conquer for itself a natural law more consonant with the poet's own being, and therefore more rational and more sound. Joan, in fact, cries to her judges: "If the Church orders me to declare that all that I have done and said, that all the visions and revelations I have had were not from God, then that is impossible. I will not declare it for anything in the world. What God made me do, I will never go back on; and what He has commanded, or shall command, I will not fail to do, in spite of any man alive. That is what I mean by impossible. And in case the Church should bid me do anything contrary to the command I have from God, I will not consent to it, no matter what it may be."

Joan, at bottom, quite without knowing it, and still declaring herself a faithful daughter of the Church, is a Puritan, like Shaw himself—affirming her own life impulse, her unshakable, her even tyrannical will to live, by accepting death itself. Joan, like Shaw, cannot exist without a life that is free and fruitful. When she tears up her recantation in the face of her deaf and blind accusers, she exemplifies the basic germ of Shaw's art, which is the germ also of his spiritual life.

—LUIGI PIRANDELLO, "Pirandello Distills Shaw," New York Times Magazine,
January 13, 1924, pp. 1, 14

GEORGE JEAN NATHAN

This *Saint Joan* seems to me to be for the major portion as affectation on Shaw's part to prove late in his career to a doubting world that he has, after all, a heart. Why Shaw should want to convince the world that he has a sympathetic heart baffles me quite as much as if Darwin or Huxley or Einstein had wished or would wish similarly to convince the world of the fact in their own cases. But age ever grows sentimental, and Shaw, whose genius lay in tonic cynicism and disillusion, has grown comfortably sweet. Relatively so, true enough, but the genius of incredulity and dissent cannot compromise with the angels and survive. Yet one cannot convince one's self that this late compromise on Shaw's part is not very largely another instance of his sagacious showmanship, or in other words, conscious hokum. Shaw is undoubtedly just selling his soulfulness to the box-office devil. The sentiment of his rare Cleopatra was wise, and not without its leaven of irony, and very truly beautiful. The sentiment of his Joan of Arc is the bald sentiment of a wartime soapbox plea for money to buy milk for French babies. It is effective in an open and shut way, but its artistic integrity is suspect. Now and again in the course of his play, Shaw, with the ghost of the Shaw of fifteen years ago mocking him, becomes for a moment himself again, and we get a flash of the old-time quick mind playing its smiling skepticism in counterpoint to the Rubinstein "Melody in F" dramatic motif. But splendid though these isolated moments are—the speeches of the Archbishop of Rheims in the second episode and of the bench of the Inquisition in the episode before the last are Shaw at his best—they yet paradoxically, because of the confusion of the sentimental and rational keys, weaken considerably the texture of the drama as a whole. The greatest love scene in all the drama of all the world, a scene of tenderness and passion and glory all compact, would fall promptly to pieces were the heroine to hiccough or the hero, embarrassingly finding an alien particle in his mouth, to spit. Shaw's hiccoughing is amusing and his expectorations are corrective and prophylactic, but they do not jibe with the story of Joan as he has set out to tell it and as actually he has told it. The story of Joan is perhaps not a story for the theatre of Shaw, after all. It is a fairy tale pure and simple, or it is nothing—an inspiring and lovely fairy tale for the drunken old philosophers who are the children of the world. It vanishes before the clear and searching light of the mind as a fairy vanishes before the clear and searching light of dawn and day. It is a tale for the night of the imagination, and such a tale is not for the pen of a Shaw. It is a tale for a Rostand, or a Barrie at his best, or maybe for some Molnar. If irony creeps into it, that irony should be an irony that springs not from the mind but from the heart.

—GEORGE JEAN NATHAN, "The Theatre," *American Mercury* 1, No. 2
(February 1924): 241–42

IVOR BROWN

The stricter Shavians must be sorely troubled by the gush of praise that has welled up from a score of geysers from which their hero has nothing to expect as a rule but the hottest of hot water. Those who spat upon *Methuselah* do more than bow the knee to Joan; they grovel on their bellies before her. Some of this praise from the haters of the Metabiological Pentateuch may come by way of mere reaction. After an ill-graced actor leaves the stage, their eyes are kind to those that follow him. But that explanation is not enough and the true disciples must be expecting to visit a very bad play of which so much good has been said and dreading lest their author has denied his own Methuselist doctrine, collapsed in old age, repented of genius, and descended to a Drinkwaterish level of common-place chronicle. Let me assure all such that Mr. Shaw has done nothing of the kind and that *Saint Joan* is a perfectly fitting piece of work for the author of *The Quintessence of Ibsenism*.

Because Mr. Shaw has not guyed a pillar of the Church as he recently guyed some pillars of the State, it is suggested that his play is all handsome reverence and as easy a diet for school-girls as *Oliver Cromwell* and *Robert E. Lee*. This view is only tenable for those who refuse to look beneath the surface of the chronicle or even to glance at the author's note upon the programme. In *Back to Methuselah!* it was prophesied that a prudent posterity would canonize Ibsen, and Mr. Shaw has now the satisfaction of demonstrating that one good Ibsenite has already been admitted to the canon. Saint Joan appeals to him precisely because she would have appealed to Saint Henrik. She is the alone-standing woman, the realist at war with romantic shams, the critic and victim of "the damned compact majority." The fact that she fears no foe in shining armour has tricked the injudicious romantics into believing that Mr. Shaw has capitulated to the British theatre at last and given us the usual twaddling, romantic heroine. Hence the almost hysterical enthusiasm. Do not be deceived by the coats of mail. These but the trappings and the suits of twaddle. Under the coat is a modern skin. Scratch Saint Joan and you find Saint Henrik.

Always in this play the Maid stands for the One against the Many, for Experience against System, and for the real against the romantic. She does not say as much, because she did not know as much. Mr. Shaw does not make the mistake of intellectualizing Joan; her revolt is more instinctive than rational, but it is none the less a revolt on reason's side. She does not argue her case; she acts it. The argument is left to others, as in that central and crucial scene when the Earl of Warwick and the Bishop of Beauvais discuss ways and means of laying the troublesome maid by the heels. This is the one scene in which Joan does not appear and it gives Mr. Shaw his chance to do the talking for Joan. It is shown that the Church has canonized a good Protestant, nay even a good Quaker. It is shown too that Joan was a champion of nationalist democracy against the medievalism of privileged groups. She was fighting the Syndicalism of the priests, the Syndicalism of the feudal barons, and the Syndicalism of the incompetent soldiers.

The Maid claimed direct communication with God; that was her offence. She short-circuited priest-craft. The Bishop of Beauvais defended the authority of which he was a part. If any country wench can walk and talk with God, what is the use of Bishops save as ornaments? Joan's doctrine was equalitarian. Her claim to be led by "voices" which are above all earthly sovereigns was precisely similar to the Quaker's claim to be guided by a Light which is above all earthly luminaries. The Quakers, being logical equalitarians, have no clergy. For them the Light shines as fully and truly on one man as on another. The Bishop, being also logical, saw that Joan's "voices" proclaimed the doom of his own kind. Therefore, as Mr. Shaw informs us on the programme, did the Church of England have Quaker women flogged; therefore was Joan sent to the fire. The first-fruits of independence are stripes and stakes.

Joan's Quakerly doctrine did not, of course, lead her to any conscientious objection against war; it led her to a conscientious protest for war. Here she speaks for herself in the play. Her grievance against the knights was their unknightly conduct; they were not soldiers, but play-boys, and the war against the English invader was not war at all but a glorified game of Prisoner's Base, in which the object was to tumble a bundle of armour containing a knight off his horse and then chaffer for a thumping ransom. Joan's instinctive Ibsenism revolted against this sham chivalry and romantic hocus-pocus. She made her army fight realistically and so made it win, not because she was blood-thirsty, but because she saw that if swords were to be drawn they had better be drawn thoroughly. Her only object was to get the English out of France; God meant them to stay where He put them.

The third aspect of Joan's realism is in her distrust of the feudal oligarchy of the time. She stood for the nation, united under a king, against the confusion of government by robber barons. The Earl of Warwick speaks for his class and speaks shrewdly. If Joan were to persuade the people that God gave the land to the king, how long would it take them to amend His doctrine into "God gave the land to the people"? Monarchy and democracy have always stood closer together than oligarchy stands to either. Nationalism tends to be despotic or democratic and Joan's life was an essay in nationalist prophecy; therefore dangerous to feudal Syndicalism. Another reason for the infamy of Rouen. Yet people find this play romantic!

Mr. Shaw, it is said, has whitewashed Joan's judges. He clears them, certainly, of the stain of corruption and makes them honest authoritarians in pursuit of heresy. But the crime of the burning cannot be washed away; if the judges were bought, the Church is less culpable, since basely served. If they were true, faithful Churchmen, then the whiter their hands the blacker the Church. Not much comfort is there in fact for those who see rosy tints in the Shavian colour-scheme. The epilogue (a vision of the King's at the time of the Rehabilitation) is equally bitter. We see Joan's enemies in the most damnable state of all, the state of penitence without reform. They will speak fair of Joan, canonize Joan, and literally idolize Joan; but they will not learn her lesson. They will crowd the streets with her statues but they will join the crowd that hounds a new Joan to destruction. Those who trust to themselves and God, should have no trust in the people. The mob is not yet fit for them. "Now that Ibsen is no longer frantically abused and is safe in the Pantheon, his message is in worse danger of being forgotten or ignored than when he was in the pillory." Thus wrote Mr. Shaw in 1923. For Ibsen read Joan and thus writes Mr. Shaw to-day.

I have left myself very little space to deal with the presentment of the play, because I have been so astonished at the way in which its ideas have been overlooked. On the surface it is exciting, colourful, and informed with a brave thinker's pride in a brave performer. The action swings along in the richest of robes through the stateliest of Gothic arches. Mr. Ricketts has done the decoration so handsomely that, by feasting the eye, he is in danger of putting the mind to sleep. And Miss Thorndike's Joan is dashing, debonair, and sufficiently ecstatic; it is not her best part (what's Joan to Hecuba?) but it gives her masculinity of style full range and she makes no mistakes. Mr. O. B. Clarence is all silvery excellence as the Inquisitor, Mr. Ernest Thesiger uncannily cunning as the Dauphin, Mr. Lyall Swete too exquisitely intellectual as Warwick, and Mr. Eugene Leahy profoundly sinister as the Bishop. It should be added that Miss Thorndike spoke in a dialect of uncertain origin (it struck me as a mixture of Lancashire and Wessex), that Mr. Shaw has filled his text with modern slang, and that there is still the old Shavian ragging of all things English. This ceased to be funny about 1905. In conclusion it is a good play for the Ibsenites, and as the anti-Ibsenites are too dense to see the point through the coats of steel and cloth of gold, it will probably be a Shavian best-seller.

—IVOR BROWN, "Saint Joan and Saint Henrik," *Saturday Review* (London),
April 5, 1924, pp. 349–50

GEORGE BERNARD SHAW &
ARCHIBALD HENDERSON

HENDERSON. It is a rather singular fact that men who make a business of exciting other people's laughter—whether by humor, wit, satire, or irony—should show such a predisposition toward Joan of Arc as a subject for novel and drama—heroic, tragic, saintly figure that she unquestionably is. I think of Mark Twain, the American humorist, who regarded *Joan of Arc* as his best work, and it was certainly his own favorite; Anatole France, the ineffably sophisticated and silken ironist; Andrew Lang, a wit if there ever was one; and yourself—whom we claim as our leading satirist of to-day. Why do you mirth-provoking, laughter-loving, people write about Joan of Arc?

SHAW. Because Joan in her rough shrewd way, was a little in that line herself. All souls of that sort are in conflict with the official gravity in which so much mental and moral inferiority disguises itself as superiority. Joan knocked over the clerical,

legal, and military panjandrums of her time like ninepins with her trenchant commonsense and mother wit; and though they had the satisfaction of burning her for
making them ridiculous, they could not help raising up indignant champions for her
by that same stroke. Besides, pious as Joan was, she was an anti-clerical, devoted
to the Church Triumphant in heaven, but with a deep mistrust of *"les gens d'Eglise"*
who constitute the Church Militant on earth. Well, the three writers you mention
are all anti-clericals. Andrew Lang, the least of the three, made the fewest mistakes
about her. If he had not made her a border-ballad beauty (Joan was neither pretty
nor ugly: she was completely neutral in that respect) he would be less open to
criticism than the other two, who were men of genius. Mark Twain made her a
compound of a Victorian schoolmarm in armor and six petticoats with the Duke of
Wellington. Both he and Lang made her the heroine of a melodrama with the
Catholic Church as the villain, which is utter nonsense: her trial and sentence were
quite as legal as, and much fairer than most modern political trials. Anatole France
was disabled by his Anti-Feminism: he could not credit Joan with mental superiority
to the Statesmen and Churchmen and Captains of her time; and as her superiority
is the simple explanation of the whole affair, he makes very good shooting at the
Church, but misses the bull's eye.

HENDERSON. My dear G. B. S., you are commonly charged by those who do not
know you personally with being inordinately vain. Yet I observe that you modestly
omitted your name from the catalogue. Would you mind telling me why *you* chose
Joan of Arc as a dramatic subject?

SHAW. Why not? Joan is a first-class dramatic subject ready made. You have a
heroic character, caught between "the fell incenséd points" of the Catholic Church
and the Holy Roman Empire, between Feudalism and Nationalism, between Protestantism and Ecclesiasticism, and driven by her virtues and her innocence of the
world to a tragic death which has secured her immortality. What more do you
want for a tragedy as great as that of Prometheus? All the forces that bring about
the catastrophe are on the grandest scale; and the individual soul on which they
press is of the most indomitable force and temper. The amazing thing is that the
chance has never been jumped at by any dramatic poet of the requisite caliber. The
pseudo-Shakespearean Joan ends in mere jingo scurrility. Voltaire's mock-Homeric
epic is an uproarious joke. Schiller's play is romantic flapdoodle. All the modern
attempts known to me are second-rate opera books. I felt personally called on by
Joan to do her dramatic justice; and I don't think I have botched the job.

—GEORGE BERNARD SHAW AND ARCHIBALD HENDERSON, "A Dialogue on Things
  in General," *Harper's Monthly Magazine* 148, No. 6 (May 1924): 716–17

T. S. ELIOT

The Kibbo Kift may be what Professor Gamble calls "the renewal of life at a lower
level of complexity." The true "dominant" of our time (with "the inevitable price of
diminished progress") is Mr. Bernard Shaw. Mr. Shaw stands in fact for "the great

middle-class liberalism" (I am not now quoting from Professor Gamble) "as Dr. Newman saw it, and as it really broke the Oxford movement." *St. Joan* has been called his masterpiece. I should be inclined to contest this judgment in favour of *Man and Superman,* but certainly (unless we owe our clairvoyance solely to the lapse of time) *St. Joan* seems to illustrate Mr. Shaw's mind more clearly than anything he has written before. No one can grasp more firmly an idea which he does not maintain, or expound it with more cogency, than Mr. Shaw. He manipulates every idea so brilliantly that he blinds us when we attempt to look for the ideas *with which he works.* And the ideas with which he works, are they more than the residue of the great Victorian labours of Darwin, and Huxley, and Cobden? We must not be deceived by the fact that he scandalised many people of the type to which we say he belongs: he scandalised them, not because his first principles were fundamentally different, but because he was much cleverer, because his thought was more rapid, because he looked farther in the same direction. The animosity which he aroused was the animosity of the dull toward the intelligent. And we cannot forget on the other hand that Mr. Shaw was the intellectual stimulant and the dramatic delight of twenty years which had little enough of either: London owes him a twenty years' debt. Yet his Joan of Arc is perhaps the greatest sacrilege of all Joans: for instead of the saint or the strumpet of the legends to which he objects, he has turned her into a great middle-class reformer, and her place is a little higher than Mrs. Pankhurst. If Mr. Shaw is an artist, he may contemplate his work with ecstasy.

—T. S. ELIOT, "A Commentary," *Criterion* No. 9 (October 1924): 4–5

CARL VAN DOREN

At one point the paths of Mark Twain and Bernard Shaw run so close together that their two attitudes can be studied side by side. The *Personal Recollections of Joan of Arc* raises the white banner of romantic goodness against the evil and malicious world. The flawless heroism of Joan, for Mark Twain, lies in her utter innocence. She comes from her distant province to the center of the French cause, able to save it with her virtues if only its vices will allow her to. For a time its vices tremble before her virtues, but not longer than might be expected in a universe bound to protect itself from the dissolving power of simple goodness. Envy raises its head, and crude superstition, and deliberate hate. The qualities neither of Joan nor of her enemies are analyzed in detail. She is a heroine, and they are villains. With that simple conception of character to start with, Mark Twain unfolds his panorama. He is interested in the picturesque items of battle and siege, in the humorous episodes which vary the tragic march of events, in the eloquence of Joan, in the melodramatic plots of those who undo her, in the clash of good and evil which occurs at her trial, in the pathetic outcome of another chapter in the endless warfare between inno-cence and villainy. Having hit upon a great theme, long the subject of controversy, he tries to extract the story from a tangle of arguments and to turn it into the language of ordinary human experience. But he does not modernize it by discarding the romantic idiom in which such stories were customarily told in his generation as he does not modernize it by exhibiting in it any conflict of doctrines such as he had observed. He leaves it still in history, merely freshening an ancient chronicle by touching it with charm and tenderness and humor.

In *Saint Joan* Mr. Shaw, though possibly more learned in the matter than Mark Twain, takes the Maid out of history and sets her in effect among his contemporaries. Like all his favored characters, she is the incarnation of an idea. Having fixed her will upon one purpose, which is the expulsion of the English from her native land, she refuses to be deflected by any of the excuses which the French make for not having accomplished it already. Ridiculing their formalities, dissipating their cowardice, she carves her way to her goal. But in so doing she comes up against the mighty obstacle of institutions, just as the rebels of Mr. Shaw's age have done. As he sees it, the opposition is not between good and evil; it is between initiative and inertia. The bishop and the inquisitor desire genuinely to be just. They give Joan every opportunity to recant her dangerous heresies. They plead with her in order that they may save her soul. Their idea is pitted against hers, and they are no less convinced than she. Between these warring ideas there can be no peace, because they are both, in the judgment of their holders, right. These learned men hold that mankind must be preserved by its establishments, by the perpetuation of an order which subordinates the individual to the general. This village girl holds that the individual must, when there is a difference of opinion, trust to his own certainty. Mr. Shaw knows that only the decision of posterity can say which party to such a conflict was justified. More magnanimous than in any other of his plays, he does not, as a member of posterity, too severely assess the blame. He is content to make a drama out of the conflict, the kind of drama which can hardly be matched when emotions only are at stake, and the irresistible has less chance than here to meet the immovable.

—CARL VAN DOREN, "Mark Twain and Bernard Shaw," *Century Magazine* 109, No. 5 (March 1925): 707–8

JOSEPH WOOD KRUTCH

Maxwell Anderson's *Joan of Lorraine* (Alvin Theater) is, though for very different reasons, likely to achieve almost as much success as Miss Hellman's piece (*Another Part of the Forest*). Its elaborate scheme, by means of which various characters are permitted to comment on the significance of Joan of Arc during the course of the rehearsal of a play about her, is ingeniously managed and well sustained. Perhaps because Mr. Anderson has been taken to task so often of recent years by critics who complained of turgidity and pretentiousness, the prose of the present work is straightforward enough and sensible enough. But the whole seemed to me something which could, with uncomfortable accuracy, be described as Shaw and water. A good many things in *St. Joan* have been left out, including, for example, the hard-boiled conclusion that heretics cannot be distinguished from saints until after they have been burned. Nevertheless, most of what *Joan of Lorraine* says about faith, Shaw seems to me to have said first. Ingrid Bergman plays the leading role with a certain wholesome, well-scrubbed charm and is, indeed, almost too far removed from the usual Hollywood glamour girl not to suggest sensible shoes and pigtails, but I can hardly follow most of my colleagues in hailing her as a great actress. The presence of hordes of movie fans who Oh'd and Ah'd like fond parents at a school play whenever they thought their favorite was being cute made both the play and the performance somewhat hard to judge.

—JOSEPH WOOD KRUTCH, "Drama," *Nation,* December 7, 1946, pp. 671–72

ROSAMOND GILDER

Mr. Anderson has shown a certain boldness in depriving himself of the usual paraphernalia of theatrical glamour—the full stage set, the lights and color, the illusion of reality. He could not count on a nightly repetition of the 'miracle' of which the director in his play speaks—the miracle which occurs sometimes in rehearsal when an actor in ordinary street clothes, on an empty stage, under a harsh work-light, suddenly taps the wellspring of creative inspiration—and the play is born. Theatre people know this 'miracle' and have seen rehearsals which have had a beauty and intensity that no finished performance has obtained—but, like all miracles, such moments cannot be summoned at will. Mr. Anderson has tried to recreate some elements of the atmosphere in which it flowers by showing the form, if not the substance, of a play in rehearsal. This is of course as great an artifice as any other but it serves admirably Mr. Anderson's purpose of relating the symbol which is Joan to the immediate preoccupations of today.

To obtain his effect, he brings his curtain up on a company in the last days of rehearsal. The bare stage is adorned with kitchen chairs only, the director's table is on one side, the backs of flats lean against the wall, a last exhortation is being addressed to the company. As the scenes progress, there is manifest a disagreement between director and star—on no less a subject than the meaning of the play. The author—offstage—is rewriting with the director's approval. The star feels that he is betraying the very core of Joan's nature. The actress sees Joan as pure, single, incapable of compromise. The director argues that compromise is necessary in a realistic world, that even Joan found it necessary. Before long the whole cast is involved in a heated discussion not only of this point but of the whole subject of what men live by. The rehearsals are resumed. The scenes of Joan's life point the argument with growing intensity. Finally, when Joan denies the abjuration torn from her by her dread of the fire, the actress suddenly sees the solution of her own dilemma. Joan never for a moment compromised with the things that matter—her faith, her conviction of her vocation, her belief in her voices. In Joan's own words (from the Procès) 'If I should say that God had not sent me, I should damn myself. It is true that God sent me.' By this Joan lived—and died.

Ingrid Bergman has many natural gifts that fit her for the role. She is built along peasant lines, feet well planted on the ground, shoulders broad, legs stocky. Her face, square and strong, can shine with the tenderest radiance lit by a smile that is at once childlike and mysteriously candescent. Miss Bergman does not bring to her interpretation any startling revelation; she is throughout a winning, forthright Joan, the Joan of sheepcote and countryside, able, courageous and devoted, rather than the oriflamme of battle, the inspired visionary who transformed and freed a people. Sam Wanamaker gives a vivid, intelligent performance as the director while Romney Brent supplies what light relief there is in the role of a frivolous Dauphin, the unwilling recipient of a troublesome royal crown. The play, directed by Margo Jones, flows easily in and out of its two phases, the transitions being marked by Lee Simonson's ingenious and atmospheric light. Just enough costumes are introduced to please the eye and vary the monotony of modern clothes. Mr. Anderson's Joan may add nothing new to the gallery of portraits of The Maid (one might, in fact, take exception to the validity of certain elements in his delineation)—but her story serves Mr. Anderson well as a sounding board for argument and the focal centre of an absorbing play.

> —ROSAMOND GILDER, "New Year, New Plays: Broadway in Review,"
> *Theatre Arts* 31, No. 1 (January 1947): 12, 15–16

JOHN GASSNER

Shaw's Joan is sent to the stake as a heretic to the feudal state and the medieval church. The former looks upon her as a proto-Nationalist, the latter as a proto-Protestant and, according to Shaw, she is actually *both* while trying only to be loyal to the State and the Church. In each case, her simplicity is both her glory and her suffering. She has the simplicity to believe that a king should be a king when all the more sophisticated people of her time know that a king is, properly speaking, only a puppet of the feudal nobility, and are content that this should be so. Her simplicity tells her that this should not be the case especially when a divided France is being conquered by England. In her simplicity, she also believes in private revelation. When she hears voices, she knows they must come from a divine source because she has unquestioning faith in a providence that gives direct guidance. Her simplicity gets her in trouble with the Inquisition. Her faith earns her the crown of martyrdom—and canonization. But what the voices whisper is the common sense that her own intelligence approves. Peasant and saint, medieval woman and proto-feminist, pragmatist and believer—the portraits mingle, dissolve, and recombine to produce the human being. No one after the death of Chekhov ever gave the modern theatre a greater example of dramatic characterization. Originality can be accurately attributed to both that characterization and the play that contains it. And originality is precisely the quality that could be expected of a man in whom one could usually find "the right mind cooperating with the finest sensibility, and then freely expressing it," which Herbert Read considers the final condition of literary genius.

The tent scene in which her fate is sealed in a long discussion that is a masterpiece of dialectical analysis does not, indeed, exhaust the power and meaning of the play. The great trial scene, in which Joan prefers death to imprisonment and recovers total integrity, is yet to come. The dream scene of the Epilogue, too, has yet to make its contribution with its mordant and anguished view that dead saints are much preferred to live ones. The tent scene, however, is our best reminder that Shaw's reverence and sympathy were compounded of more durable stuff than sentiment. He remained loyal to the "drama of ideas" which, in his view, was the distinctive quality of dramatic modernism. A unique combination of realism with idealism, or of rationalism with the poetry of faith, makes *Saint Joan* a modern affirmation, as analytical as it is fervent, rather than a genuflection to traditional piety and heroics. Shaw was no less strenuous when he discovered values he could accept as when he found values he had to reject.

—JOHN GASSNER, "Saint George and the Dragon," *The Theatre in Our Times* (New York: Crown, 1954), pp. 145–46

LOUIS L. MARTZ

There is nothing complex about the character of Shaw's Joan; it is the whole fabric of the play that creates something like a tragic tension. For whatever he may say in his preface, Shaw the dramatist, through his huge cast of varied human types, probes the whole range of belief and disbelief in Joan's voices. "They come from your imagination," says the feeble de Baudricourt in the opening scene. "Of course," says Joan, "That is how the messages of God come to us." Cauchon believes the girl to be "inspired, but diabolically inspired." "Many saints have said as much as Joan," Ladvenu suggests. Dunois, her only friend, senses some aura of divinity about her, but becomes extremely uneasy when she talks about her voices. "I should think," he says, "you were a bit cracked if I hadnt noticed that you give me very sensible reasons for what you do, though I hear you telling others you are only obeying Madame Saint Catherine." "Well," she replies, "I have to find reasons for you, because you do not believe in my voices. But the voices come first; and I find the reasons after: whatever you may choose to believe." *Whatever you may choose to believe:* there is the point, and as the figure of Joan flashes onward through the play, with only one lapse in confidence—her brief recantation—Shaw keeps his play hovering among choices in a highly modern state of uncertainty: we know and do not know: until at the close Shaw seems to send us over on the side of affirmation. We agree, at least, with the words of the French captain in the opening scene: "There is something about her.... Something.... I think the girl herself is a bit of a miracle."

She is, as Eliot would say, "a white light still and moving," the simple *cause* of every other word and action in the play; and her absolute simplicity of vision cuts raspingly through all the malign or well-intentioned errors of the world, until in its wrath the world rises up in the form of all its assembled institutions and declares by the voice of all its assembled doctors that this girl is—as Shaw says—*insufferable.*

Thus Joan's apparent resemblance to the Aristotelian hero: her extreme self-confidence, her brashness, her appearance of rash impetuosity—all this becomes in the end a piece of Shavian irony, for her only real error in the play is the one point where her superb self-confidence breaks down in the panic of recantation. And so the hubris is not Joan's but Everyman's. The characters who accuse Joan of pride and error are in those accusations convicting themselves of the pride of self-righteousness and the errors of human certitude. It is true that the suffering that results from this pride and error remains in Shaw's play rather theoretical and remote: and yet we feel it in some degree: in the pallor and anguish of Joan as she resists the temptation to doubt her voices, in the rather unconvincing screams of de Stogumber at the close, and, much more effectively, in the quiet, controlled sympathy of Ladvenu. It would seem, then, that some degree of tragedy resides in this failure of Everyman to recognize absolute Reality, the secret cause, when it appears in the flesh. Must then, cries Cauchon in the Epilogue, "Must then a Christ perish in torment in every age to save those that have no imagination?" It is the same symbolism that Eliot has evoked in the beginning of his play, where the Chorus asks: "Shall the Son of Man be born again in the litter of scorn?"

We need not be too greatly concerned with Shaw's bland assertions that he is letting us in on the truth about the Middle Ages, telling us in the play all we need to know about Joan. Books and articles have appeared—a whole cloudburst of them—devoted to proving that Shaw's methods of historical research in his play and in his preface are open to serious question. But Shaw gave that game away long ago when he announced: "I deal with all periods; but I never study any period but the present, which I have not yet mastered and never shall"; or when he said, with regard to Cleopatra's cure for Caesar's baldness, that his methods of scholarship, as compared with Gilbert Murray's, consisted in "pure divination." The preface to *Saint Joan* lays down a long barrage of historicity, which in the end is revealed as a remarkable piece of Shavio-Swiftian hoaxing: for in the last few pages of that long preface he adds, incidentally, that his use of the "available documentation" has been accompanied by "such powers of divination as I possess"; he concedes that for some figures in his play he has invented "appropriate characters" "in Shakespear's manner"; and that, fundamentally, his play is built upon what he calls "the inevitable flatteries of tragedy." That is, there is no historical basis for his highly favorable characterizations of Cauchon and the Inquisitor, upon which the power and point of the trial scene are founded.

I do not mean to say, however, that our sense of history is irrelevant to an appreciation of Shaw's play. There is a point to be made by considering such a book as J. M. Robertson's *Mr. Shaw and "The Maid,"* which complains bitterly, upon historical grounds, against Shaw's "instinct to put things both ways." This is a book, incidentally, which Eliot has praised very highly because it points out that in this kind of subject "Facts matter," and that "to Mr. Shaw, truth and falsehood . . . do not seem to have the same meaning as to ordinary people." But the point lies rather in the tribute that such remarks pay to the effectiveness of Shaw's realistic dramaturgy.

Shaw is writing, as he and Ibsen had to write, within the conventions of the modern realistic theater—conventions which Eliot escaped in *Murder in the Cathedral* because he was writing this play for performance at the Canterbury Festival. But in his later plays, composed for the theater proper, Eliot has also been forced to, at least he has chosen to, write within these stern conventions.

Now in the realistic theater, as Francis Fergusson has suggested, the artist seems to be under the obligation to pretend that he is not an artist at all, but is simply interested in pursuing the truth "in some pseudo-scientific sense." Thus we find the relation of art to life so often driven home on the modern stage by such deep symbolic actions as removing the cubes from ice trays or cooking an omelette for dinner. Shaw knows that on this stage facts matter—or at least the appearance of facts—and in this need for a dramatic realism lies the basic justification for Shaw's elaborately argued presentation of Joan as a Protestant and Nationalist martyr killed by the combined institutional forces of feudalism and the Church. Through these historical theories, developed within the body of the play, Joan is presented as the agent of a transformation in the actual world; the theories have enough plausibility for dramatic purposes, and perhaps a bit more; this, together with Shaw's adaptation of the records of Joan's trial, gives him all the "facts" that he needs to make his point in the modern theater.

Some of Joan's most Shavian remarks are in fact her own words as set down in the long records of her trial: as, for example, where her questioner asks whether Michael does not appear to her as a naked man. "Do you think God cannot afford clothes for him?" answers Joan, in the play and in the records. Shaw has made a skillful selection of these answers, using, apparently, the English translation of the documents edited by Douglas Murray; and he has set these answers together with speeches of his own modeled upon their tone and manner. In this way he has been able to bring within the limits of the realistic theater the very voice that rings throughout these trial records, the voice of the lone girl fencing with, stabbing at, baffling, and defeating the crowd of some sixty learned men: a voice that is not speaking within the range of the other voices that assail her. Thus we hear her in the following speech adapted from half-a-dozen places in the records: "I have said again and again that I will tell you all that concerns this trial. But I cannot tell you the whole truth: God does not allow the whole truth to be told. . . . It is an old saying that he who tells too much truth is sure to be hanged. . . . I have sworn as much as I will swear; and I will swear no more." Or, following the documents much more closely, her answers thus resound when the questioners attempt to force her to submit her case to the Church on earth: "I will obey the Church," says Joan, "provided it does not command anything impossible."

If you command me to declare that all that I have done and said, and all the visions and revelations I have had, were not from God, then that is impossible: I will not declare it for anything in the world. What God made me do I will never go back on; and what He has commanded or shall command I will not fail to do in spite of any man alive. That is what I mean by impossible.

And in case the Church should bid me do anything contrary to the command I have from God, I will not consent to it, no matter what it may be.

In thus maintaining the tone of that—extraordinary—voice, Shaw has, I think, achieved an effect that is in some ways very close to the effect of the "intersection of the timeless with time" which Eliot has achieved in his play, and which he has described in "The Dry Salvages":

Men's curiosity searches past and future
And clings to that dimension. But to apprehend
The point of intersection of the timeless
With time, is an occupation for the saint—
No occupation either, but something given
And taken, in a lifetime's death in love,
Ardour and selflessness and self-surrender.

—LOUIS L. MARTZ, "The Saint as Tragic Hero: *Saint Joan* and *Murder in the Cathedral*," *Tragic Themes in Western Literature*, ed. Cleanth Brooks (New Haven: Yale University Press, 1955), pp. 159–64

S. JOHN

Like Giraudoux, Anouilh is occasionally over-fascinated by the theatrical machine. Thus, *L'Alouette* (1952), Anouilh's ambitious attempt to recreate the legend of Joan of Arc, is fatally damaged at its centre because of an irresistible urge to exploit mere technical effect. The central dramatic device of the play is a form of cutting and 'flash-back' common in films. Joan relives her past life in a series of dramatic episodes which are inserted into the progress of her trial. This device is brilliantly successful in making vivid and actual the incidents and words which are now embedded in the charges brought against the Maid. So long as these episodes—a sort of play within a play—follow the proper chronology of Joan's life, they seem naturally integrated with the course of the trial. Difficulty arises when the past inset-scenes culminate in the trial's present and in Joan's conviction. Joan confesses her guilt, recants, is condemned to the stake. The audience at the trial raises a pyre on the stage. The faggots are lit. At this critical moment Baudricourt charges on and complains that, in enacting Joan's past, the crowd have overlooked the Coronation at Rheims, the summit of her exertions. The pyre is hastily dismantled, an altar raised, and the coronation re-enacted with all pomp and colour, so that the curtain falls on a graphically satisfying tableau in which Joan is petrified for ever in the conventional posture of story books ('cette belle image de livre de prix'). The agony at the stake, the long ordeal of the individual conscience pitted against authority are both obliterated in the posthumous reputation. Whatever the merits of this interpretation—and it seems to me to lessen greatly the tragic force of Joan's career—Anouilh's methods border on the frivolous. Technique triumphs over feeling. By reversing the normal order of events at the very moment of the burning,

Anouilh powerfully reinforces in the minds of his audience the notion that they have witnessed, not some tragic and exemplary passion in which they were sympathetically involved, but the adroit manipulation of a theatrical illusion. Attention has been diverted from the creature so as to fall on the creator.

—S. JOHN, "Obsession and Technique in the Plays of Jean Anouilh," *French Studies* 11, No. 2 (April 1957): 115–16

N .   J U S S E M - W I L S O N

Péguy has left us in his poetry a monument to his rediscovery of belief, but very little precise explanation as to how and when it came about. In 1908 he confided to Lotte: 'I have found faith again,' and two years later he proclaimed it publicly in the *Mystery of the Charity of Joan of Arc.*

But these dates are convenient rather than decisive or definitive milestones, for the journey back to faith had evidently started long before 1908—he himself insisted that there had been no conversion, no sudden illuminating mystical experience, but a 'deepening'—and Joan was not the end of the journey.

If one were to look for a common denominator to the many and very diverse problems which Péguy deepened, and at the end of which he found Christianity, one would not go very far wrong with the denominator of time. He had felt the shiver of time in many ways. Through history; through the mystery of birth and presences: to be born and not to be born at a certain moment of time, to come too soon or too late, at the right moment or the wrong moment. Most frequently he approached it from its tragic end because in one form or another he had come up against the inevitable descent down the slope of time in all fields of human activity from politics to man's psychic and moral life. In time, the child loses its purity and innocence; in time, the youthful spirit of adventure degenerates into balancing risks against security; the young man's sense of freedom becomes imprisoned in the old man's sense of systems; in time, everything becomes a habit; in time, absolute ideals turn into relative interests, mystique ends in politique. The greatest civilisations have had their peaks and their decadence, and the greatest civilisations have died, in time. This ageing and dying was Péguy's despair. 1905 is an important milestone on his Christian journey not because he discovered Christ among the monuments of Paris, but because he could not resign himself to their mortality and began to look towards Christianity which speaks of eternal life and salvation. Christianity, however, also speaks of Hell and damnation. It is significant that this is the subject of his first Christian work, almost as if he had to exorcise an old nightmare before he could concentrate on the now much more important question of time. After the first *Mystery of Joan of Arc* Hell and damnation will not appear again. But time, transferred to a Christian plane and discussed in a Christian context, will remain a constant problem, a problem which Christianity, even if it relieved Péguy by removing the absurdity of mortality, could not altogether solve for him. In various forms, the problem of time already appears

in the *Joan Mystery* and already there we see Péguy oscillating between two opposing poles: the Bergsonian and the Pascalian.

In his wish to show that the rediscovery of belief had introduced no division
into his adult life, Péguy first had the original idea of writing an extended commentary on the *Joan* trilogy of 1897, the latter to be reproduced word for word
without any suppressions.

One can only regret that he had to abandon the project; understandably
enough, since the additions appended to the first two acts of the first play alone
filled a volume of 230 pages and the original trilogy had a total of 24 acts! The
Mystery as published by Péguy himself in 1910 consists of commentaries incorporated into two of the dialogues of the original first play: the opening conversation
between Joan and Hauviette and the confrontation of Joan and Madame Gervaise
which followed. These dialogues are each preceded by Joan's monologues, which
do not figure in the play of 1897 and which are a measure of the depth of despair
of the Christian Joan.

The Joan of 1910 still wishes to save better than Christ and this is still the crux
of the debate; but now she also questions some fundamentals. To begin with, the
whole purpose of the crucifixion. Fourteen centuries of Christianity, she exclaims,
and evil still exists. God has sent his Son who suffered and died, and he has sent
Saints who suffered and died, and evil still exists. And now, more than ever. Was
it all in vain? Where in God's justice does the vanity of such a sacrifice fit in? This
is the formidable subject of her first monologue which begins with a recital of Our
Father. The words 'Thy Kingdom come' stick in Joan's throat. She can see no signs
of this in fourteen centuries. A consolation suggests itself to her. Perhaps God has
miscalculated something. 'If there have not been enough saints send us more, send
us as many as it needs—. We shall follow them.' And finally she makes a suggestion:
'what we need, Lord, what you should send us is a Saint, a woman, who will
succeed'.

Hauviette is the same earthy commonsense peasant, but she is considerably
more articulate than in 1897. It is she in fact who dominates the conversation and
she tells Joan a few truths about herself. In Hauviette's depiction of Joan we have
Péguy's Bergsonian portrait of his Pascalian alter ego: an insatiable soul, consumed
by 'a fever of sadness' and feeling the sufferings of others more than the sufferer
himself, seeing only suffering and almost looking for evil, perpetually praying, perpetually anguished at the thought of the future and of eternal damnation. Why, asks
Hauviette in her common sense, why does Joan go on working if everything is
vanity and evil? Hauviette is an earthy sort of Bergsonian. She actually quotes the
words discussed at great length in the Bergson *cahier:* 'sufficient unto the day is the
evil thereof', and she proceeds to give an endearing peasant explanation of what
this means: one prays at certain times of the day just as one eats at certain times
of the day. Six days of the week are reserved for work and Sunday for God. There
is a time for everything. The present is the present and the future must not be
forced into it.

The down to earth wisdom of Hauviette has no effect on Joan. Left alone, she resumes the subject of her monologue: has the crucifixion been in vain? Then, after two stage directions of 'silence' and 'en vision' she becomes preoccupied with 'the frightening mystery of time'. Joan trembles at this thought: 'happy is he who has seen him in time'. She would like to fathom this mystery of presences, the election of certain witnesses in preference to others, the mysterious promotion of normally insignificant places to an everlasting inscription in history. 'To be present,' all is there. How she envies the Jews of those days who knew Christ as a man, could touch his body and see the colour of his eyes. Since then Christianity is a Christianity of the eleventh hour which can see Christ only in eternity, a spatial time which man can fill with abstractions to his heart's content. Joan's shiver at the thought that it is all a question of being born at the right or the wrong moment, is intimately linked with her need—Péguy's need—for incarnation, for everything to take on form and shape in the physical and tangible world. She comes close to suggesting that Christianity since the 'first hour' is something entirely abstract because Christ has been absent. 'If you were here, God, things wouldn't happen the way they do. They would never have happened that way.' And this is the link between the two monologues. Evil exists because for fourteen centuries Christ has been absent. Now he can only be contemplated in his eternity. Thus, Joan has answered, to her own satisfaction and to Madame Gervaise's horror, the initial question. The crucifixion has not been in vain for the time in which it happened. But since then there has been a very long absence.

Madame Gervaise, supposedly unseen by Joan and also 'en vision', appears and exclaims by way of reply:

He is here.
He is here as on the first day.
He is here among us as on the day of his death . . .

The longest and the most remarkable additions have been made to the dialogue between Joan and the nun. And here we move away from Christ's long absence from the earth and Joan's loneliness as an individual, as a Saint in the making who is conscious of this absence and despairing because she can see no solution; from this we move to the loneliness of the damned and Christ's eternal absence from Hell. The debate is still the same as in 1897, but it has a new width and depth because the protagonists have developed. The young nun has grown immensely in stature. In 1897 she hardly understood Joan and was not a little intimidated by her. Now she could be a perceptive and sympathetic 'directeur de conscience' with an understanding of some of the psychological factors involved in Joan's loneliness and despair. She guesses that Joan's failure at her first Communion—this scandalised some Catholic critics—was a decisive moment in her spiritual loneliness. The child had expected that the experience would make Christ's presence palpable. All her hopes had been centred on this event in her life. And she found, to her despair, that Communion made no difference to the vacuum.

The young nun also understands that Joan's increasing contempt for those nearest to her makes her an increasingly lonely figure among men and heightens her moral despair. In Joan's scale of justice her family and friends weigh most heavily on the guilty side, the side of those who, by watching evil, become accomplices of it. One is most exacting with those one loves best. Péguy knew this well.

Gervaise now understands how an obsession with the triumph of evil, if deeply felt, can become a desire to save from evil, and how Joan through this ardent desire and in her immense pity for man, blasphemes against the divine, isolates herself from ordinary humanity, and finally exposes herself to all the varieties of pride. She warns Joan against pride and despair. They can lead towards God and man but also away from them.

Joan too has developed. Her sense of vocation has given her some bold certainties against which the humble nun with her unsanctimonious but slightly mechanical theology battles in vain. One of these certainties concerns another question of time. It forms a strange sequel to the meditation of the second monologue. After having listened to Madame Gervaise's realistic *recitative* of the Crucifixion, Joan cannot bear the thought that the people she knows would ever have consented to such suffering. Hence the bold postulate that God's Son was born at the wrong moment. Had he lived in France at a later date, in Domrémy of the fifteenth century for instance, the Crucifixion would not have taken place, for no Frenchman would have permitted that. A little later she adds that not even the English would have endured such a sacrifice. In other words, in Joan's own times, in the Middle Ages, Christ the man would not have died. Unimpressed by Madame Gervaise's arguments about the fulfilment of the Scriptures, and unmoved by the nun's painful admission that she too might have witnessed the Crucifixion without revolting, Joan follows her train of thought and now harshly condemns those 'happy contemporaries' of the previous monologue. At the mention of the Apostles, she repeats almost hypnotised: Peter! 'Three times. Three times he betrayed him.' The Christians of the first hour were privileged witnesses who allowed themselves to become criminal spectators. In spite of, or perhaps because of, such bold certainties this passage has an intimately tragic note. The reader remembers that Joan's contemporaries will prove to be similar criminal spectators though Péguy, by a curiously 'optimistic' ending, encourages us to remember Joan's *success*. 'Orléans, in the country of the Loire.' With these words Joan abruptly concludes the discussion on damnation. And on this cryptic note of temporal success ends a drama of intense spiritual despair.

Incorporated into this battle between resignation and revolt, between a serene Saint accepting what is and basing her certainties on texts, and an angry Saint concerned with what might be and posing certainties of the heart, we have something altogether new: a recitative of the Passion and a *Pietà*. It is *sung*, so to speak, by an inspired young nun who here envisages things quite as physically and concretely as Joan, and who will gradually retreat and let the suffering Christ and Mary tell their own stories in *free indirect speech*. There will not even be the *eyewitness* between the listener, Joan, and the victims. Joan's need for physical presence, her need to be made to feel suffering, is amply satisfied.

Again and again in this complete but unchronological history of Christ's life evoked by Gervaise, Mary and Christ, we come back to the blood and sweat, the hands and feet pierced by nails, the burning throat, even the terrible 'cramps' caused by the unusual position of the body on the cross.

Here is the beginning of one of many passages depicting Christ's bodily pain. The emphasis is on the burning throat.

Sa gorge qui lui faisait mal.
Qui lui cuisait.
Qui lui brûlait.
Qui lui déchirait.
Sa gorge sèche qui avait soif.
Son gosier sec.
Son gosier qui avait soif.

In the moving *Pietà* we see Mary, her eyes swollen, eyelids bruised, eyelashes stuck together, swallowing back tears with her saliva, grow old and ugly. A stupefied, hideous and very touching Mater Dolorosa who tries to understand how it all happened as she walks and weeps, and who only succeeds in remembering without comprehending. She is the eternal mother, with touches here and there of an earthy peasant mother with a sense of reality, and no less moving for that, in her immense grief. Similarly, Pilate is the harmless and indifferent senior civil servant concerned with order, and the crowds are the crowds of always: watching an execution and taking pity on the relatives of the condemned. 'Péguy re-presents the past,' André Gide aptly remarked in one of the most perceptive studies to appear on the *Mystery*. This is how Péguy intended to develop this ancient genre, a genre comparable with the tragedy of the ancients, he thought, or with French Classical tragedy.

Structurally speaking, the Passion and the *Pietà*, linked to the main debate by the slenderest of links, form a long digression which unbalances the work as a whole. It is, however, the most original part of the *Mystery* and stylistically certainly the most interesting.

For thirteen years, ever since the few regular Alexandrines contained in the first Joan drama, Péguy had not written any poetry and now he suddenly revealed himself a poet, and a very modern poet. 'All the attempts at *vers libres* for the past twenty years have put into my hands a marvellous instrument,' he told a friend. And with an immodesty in which enthusiasm and excitement play a large part, he continues to sing the praise of the 'resonances and harmonies' contained in the *Mystery*. 'There is nothing comparable in musical prose.'

He was to perfect the irregular *vers libre* in the following two *Mysteries* (1911–12) but then, as in his first effort, he combined with what was then a new and sophisticated verse technique his own very distinctive manner of communication.

The invasion of *vers libre* by blank spaces, the fullstop and repetitions was unique. No other poet at the time was so passionately concerned with obliging the reader to reduce the speed of his thoughts. Blank spaces, breaking the flow of the verse, were provided for meditation. The fullstop, breaking up logical sentence units into the smallest, i.e. one word, units, fulfils the same purpose; and so of course does the repetition with the added effect of stress.

In the repetition which does not quite repeat, an accumulation of synonyms for instance, the reader was invited to join the poet on a special journey of discovery, sometimes as exasperating as the *digressions* and for similar reasons: one word was shown to be capable of infinite growth, capable of calling to mind new images and releasing new emotions. Within the flowing *vers libre* the arrangement of one synonym per line and each line made into an independent thought-unit by the fullstop, was even more unusual and striking than the unbroken accumulation of synonyms found in his prose. That with all these immobilising elements Péguy managed to create movement and flow, his own rhythm of obstinate thoughts spoken aloud and caught on the move, so to speak, that was his special art.

—N. JUSSEM-WILSON, "The Christian Joan," *Charles Péguy*
(New York: Hillary House, 1965), pp. 76–85

DAVID M. BEVINGTON

In the meeting of the Dauphin and Joan of Arc (I.ii), Shakespeare clearly lampoons the right relation of men and women in a dazzling array of epic and Biblical allusions. One myth familiar for his purposes was that of Mars and Venus, who in their right relationship display the qualities of rationality, honor, and action in hierarchical supremacy to subservient fleshly pleasure. When reason is pandered to sense, however, the masculine principle becomes debased and emasculated. Bestial man wallows in Circean excess. The woman domineers, becoming progressively masculine. Accordingly, when Joan overcomes the Dauphin in a test of physical strength, he apostrophizes her as

> Bright star of Venus, fall'n down on the earth,
> How may I reverently worship thee enough?   (I.ii.144–145)

Yet earlier, in his first speech, the Dauphin had identified his fortunes with those of Mars: "Now we are victors; upon us he smiles" (I.ii.4). Even in their first conjunction, the soldier and the lady have assumed unnatural roles of enervated warrior and seductress, signifying disorder in the cosmos and in the state as well.

Other allusions reinforce the theme of sexual inversion and blasphemous parody. The allusions are complexly ironic, sometimes contrasting Joan with positive ideals of divine harmony and sometimes likening her to infamously wanton women. Her diabolical powers of prophecy, for instance, bear only a perverted resemblance to the prophetic spirit of "the nine sibyls of old Rome" (I.ii.56), or of St. Philip the Evangelist's daughters who were prophesying virgins, or of Constantine's mother Helen who reputedly discovered the true cross. Serving as object of the Dauphin's veneration, Joan displaces true respect for the divine wisdom of Homer's *Iliad*, encased in Darius' rich-jewelled casket. She is the Dauphin's Saint, and will intercede for him in place of the traditional Saint of Paris, St. Denis. Beneath the anti-Catholic jesting on saint-worship are darker suggestions of pagan idolatry and conversation with evil spirits.

As a blasphemous type of incarnation, Joan competes even more impudently with otherworldly visitors of divine inspiration, both Christian and classical. Her chief identification is with the Virgin Mary, yet Joan is herself a strumpet. Her claim of pregnancy to avoid execution (V.ii) is an outrageous travesty of the Virgin birth. As her English captors, York and Warwick, wrily comment, "Now, heaven forfend, the holy maid with child!" "The greatest miracle that e'er ye wrought" (V.iv.65–66). Like Mohammed, who claimed to partake directly of the secrets of God by means of a dove, Joan boasts of visitations from the Holy Ghost. After her first and greatest victory at Orleans (I.vi), she is likened to Astraea's daughter, embodiment of justice in a mythic golden age, and now descended to earth once more in a type of incarnation. Comparison with the genius of the garden of Adonis calls up, to Joan's manifest discredit, an image of pervasive harmony transcending worldly mutability.

When Joan is compared with the Hebrew prophetess Deborah, Judge of Israel, the similitude is complex. Deborah, with the help of another woman, overthrew the mighty Sisera: "for the Lord shall sell Sisera into the hand of a woman" (Judges, iv.9). Joan is domineering like her, but is no heroine of ancient testament. More directly, with obviously reprehensible pride she likens herself to mighty Caesar (I.ii.138–139), who boasted himself to be above the reach of fortune, even natural catastrophe. The Dauphin proclaims Joan an "Amazon." He also sees her as another Rhodope, a profligate woman who captivated a king and usurped his role as performer of masculine deeds of glory, such as the building of the third Egyptian pyramid. By praising Rhodope and identifying himself with the Memphian king, the Dauphin denies once again any intention of challenging Joan's mastery.

Even the allusion to Venus is laden with significant diabolical meaning in a pun familiar to the Renaissance: "Bright star of Venus, fall'n down on the earth." In this Joan is both the goddess of love and the morning (or evening) star, bright Lucifer, whose description in Isaiah, xiv.12 was taken to mean the fall of Satan after his disobedience: "How are thou fallen from heaven, O Lucifer, son of the morning!" The Dauphin's apostrophe of Venus is thus a complex and ironic conceit, playing on the identification of Venus with Lucifer-Satan, and envisaging another descent or incarnation blasphemously analogous to that of Astraea, the Holy Ghost, and the angel of the annunciation. Joan therefore not only practises with devils but is a devil herself, and the Dauphin's deification of her is devil-worship even if he is unconscious of the irony of his allusions. The Dauphin's fall is ethically more allencompassing than the surrender to mere physical pleasure: it is the chaos of natural order in himself, his followers, and his country. He is bewitched. When he asks, in courtly parlance, "Let me thy servant and not sovereign be" (I.ii.111), he surrenders the crown itself to a Frenchwoman as Henry VI will also do in the play's ending.

Joan's method of seduction, in an ageless antifeminist tradition, is a hypocritical combination of modesty and availability. She is not interested in sex for its own sake; she yields her body for power. This discrepancy between appearance and intention is treated by Shakespeare as a comic discrepancy, and produces an emphasis on salacious double entendres throughout her conversations. The pun is not simply an undignified form of wit intended to provoke coarse laughter, but a thematic device. In virtually every instance, the point is that sexual war is replacing military war. When Joan proposes to the Dauphin that she become his "warlike mate" (I.ii.92), she suggests not only sexual companionship but that sex become their battlefield, usurping the English war. The Dauphin responds in kind, proposing that "in single combat thou shalt buckle with me" (l. 95). And so the metaphor continues through the Dauphin's surrender and request for mercy, to Joan's hinting at a ransom.

Of course their union at first produces success against the English as well as in bed, but the inversion of masculinity can ultimately lead only to the Dauphin's enervation as a soldier. Dallying results in a neglecting of the guard and English recapture of Orleans. The Dauphin's watchfulness has been shamefully nonmilitary:

And for myself, most part of all this night
Within her quarter and mine own precinct
I was employed in passing to and fro (II.i.67–69)

As a witch desiring mastery over men, Joan is not content with the Dauphin alone. Effortlessly she adds the Duke of Burgundy to her menagerie, wooing him to the French side with rhetoric and with witchcraft: "enchant him with thy words" (III.iii.40), "she hath bewitched me with her words" (l. 58). "I am vanquished" (l. 78). Having overcome, she contemptuously dismisses her victim with "Done like a Frenchman—turn and turn again" (l. 85). The line is in character for a "foul fiend" and "hag of all despite" (III.ii.52) who uses rousing jingoistic speech only as a veneer to deceive her victims. Similarly she employs her military authority over the French to seduce Reignier, Alençon, and other of the Dauphin's courtiers. Finally she turns to sexual practices with spirits as well as men.

Three men whom Joan cannot seduce, however, are Lord Talbot, his son John, and his successor as conqueror of the French, the Duke of York. Her attempts to win these champions to her lust are explicit, as York observes in capturing her:

Unchain your spirits now with spelling charms
And try if they can gain your liberty.
A goodly prize, fit for the devil's grace!
See how the ugly witch doth bend her brows
As if, with Circe, she would change my shape. (V.iii.31–35)

The allusion to Circe, one of two actual citations of her name in Shakespeare, emphasizes the ugliness of temptation when viewed by the temperate man. York, despite his less attractive qualities of political ambition, is at least indifferent to feminine allure. It is Talbot, however, who most valiantly withstands Joan's power in repeated encounters. In so rejecting temptation he accomplishes what the effete

French Dauphin failed to do. The structural comparison between the two as Joan's "wooers" is emphasized once again by the language of double entendre. Just as the Dauphin offers to "buckle" with Joan, Talbot vows to "have a bout with thee" (I.v.4; III.ii.56). She taunts him in the same metaphor with "Are ye so hot, sir?" (III.ii.58). She challenges young Talbot, "Thou maiden youth, be vanquished by a maid" (IV.vii.38).

Joan is able for a time to practice upon Talbot's physical capacities with her magic spells (I.v.9). Heaven can of course permit the temporary ascendancy of a scourge, afflicting the innocent soldier as well as the corrupted English politicians whom he serves. Yet the devil's power is limited in tormenting the virtuous, as it is with the Old Man in *Doctor Faustus.* Joan may dazzle Talbot momentarily but she cannot transform him to her will.

—DAVID M. BEVINGTON, "The Domineering Female in *I Henry VI,"*
Shakespeare Studies 2 (1966): 51–54

ERIC BENTLEY

Half a dozen years after the première of *Saint Joan,* Bertolt Brecht wrote *Happy End,* which a couple of years later had grown into *Saint Joan of the Stockyards.* It can serve here as a cue for continued analysis of *Saint Joan* itself and for an exploration of the difference between Shaw and Brecht. The relation between the two dramatists was never closer than here, since *Saint Joan of the Stockyards* owes much not only to *Saint Joan* but to *Major Barbara.*

As usual with Brecht, one can begin with surprise at how much he saw fit to borrow. "A Salvation Army officer forsaken by God" could be considered the central image of *Major Barbara,* and Brecht appropriated it. That the officer is a girl, with all that femininity connotes of delicacy in feeling and ardor in aspiration, is not lost on Brecht, either, and the general reason for the loss of God is the same in both authors: the dependence of the otherworldly institution upon a capitalistic world. However, though both authors rely upon a Marxist analysis of the Salvation Army, they approach the subject from opposite ends. Shaw shows that the teetotalism of the Army, being promoted by brewers' money, is compromised at the start: the "idealism" of an Army officer has to be either ignorant or corrupt. Realizing this, Major Barbara feels emptied out, devastated, abandoned by her God. She will remain in this state of mind and heart until a niche is found for her within the existing social order. The finding of such a niche is the psychospiritual solution to what has already been shown as a psychospiritual problem. Brecht, on the other hand, is little concerned with the usefulness of capitalism to the Salvation Army. He is concerned with the usefulness of the Salvation Army to capitalism. If his Joan, too, suffers a psychospiritual crisis—and she does, though the phrase itself begins to let us down in a Brechtian context—it is from the sensation not of being deserted but of being cheated. God has not gone: he was never there. Joan discovers not a void of unbelief but an active atheism which offers an alternative to deity in the idea of Man On His Own—man's fate is man himself. It is at this point that one can imagine the playwright Brecht asking whether, if one Shaw play wouldn't do his job for him, another might serve the purpose. Though *Saint Joan of the Stockyards* is mostly a *Major Barbara,* ultimately it is indeed a *Saint Joan:* for Barbara turns into Joan when Brecht's protagonist moves from false to true consciousness and from passivity disguised as action to action which is positive and revolutionary.

Brecht probably noted what most of Shaw's critics have missed: that Shaw himself goes part of the way toward making Joan a revolutionary leader whose final support comes from the people. She is his only nonbourgeois superman, for even his Caesar is bourgeois in spirit, as is his superking Magnus, and this fact yields much more broadly conceived political drama than Shaw was wont to attempt. In the great scene (Five) which is the turning point of the story, Joan stands forth as the patron saint of all future National Liberation Fronts:

> Common folks understand . . . they follow me half naked into the moat and up the ladder and over the wall. . . . You locked the gates to keep me in; and it was the townsfolk and the common people that followed me, and forced the gate. . . . I will go out now to the common people, and let the love in their eyes comfort me for the hate in yours. You will all be glad to see me burnt; but if I go through the fire, I shall go through it to their hearts for ever and ever.

Though, unlike Shaw's Major Barbara, Brecht's Joan Dark has, in the Communist Party, an alternative to both the Salvation Army and big business, unlike Shaw's Joan she is not permitted a true martyrdom but only a fake one. Her death is a "setup," and so she remains in death what she had been in life: a victim. The politics of *Saint Joan* and *Saint Joan of the Stockyards* are thus revealed, in their respective endings, to be diametrically opposite. Shaw calls for a democracy of supermen that shall be worthy of his democratic superwoman. Brecht appeals for solidarity among those people (the working class, the victims) by whom the myths of sainthood will be shattered along with the social order which the myths serve to flatter and conceal.

—ERIC BENTLEY, "Ibsen, Shaw, Brecht" [1969], *Theatre of War: Comments on 32 Occasions* (New York: Viking Press, 1972), pp. 201–2

MAXWELL GEISMAR

God, King, Patriotism, Nationalism, Purity, Self-sacrifice, Religious Devotion, the Supernatural, Sentimentality, Chastity—Saint Joan embodied every trait that Sam Clemens, in his right mind, could not bear. What was there in this sexless and non-nubile Maid of Orléans which so attracted Clemens, definitely beyond all need for even a best seller which was completely "edifying" for respectable young Americans? One remembers his fervid and frank descriptions of the pagan ladies of the Sandwich Isles; probably his admiration and affection for the women of the darker races (though he equally admired the physical grace of the men) had certain sexual undertones. How could the Twainian narrator of the tale, the Sieur Louis de Conte, remembering in his old age "the dear little figure, with breast bent to the flying horse's neck"—the marvelous child's meteoric flight across the firmament of France—describe her as "the most noble life that was ever born into this world save only One"? One also remembers Sam Clemens' notions about Jesus, God, and the Church—which last still however remains as the official villain in *Joan of Arc,* obstructing the Maid's natural converse with her heavenly Voices. ⟨. . .⟩

There is not the slightest hint here of those intuitive and penetrating social-historical insights which mark the most irregular of Clemens' other writings. This is all romance melodrama in a vein of "historical" fantasy worthy of Henry James— and here indeed these two polar opposites of the late nineteenth-century American literary scene meet in a common cultural hypocrisy and sentimentality. But what still remains curious in *Joan of Arc* is the force of Clemens' narrative power—or the force of his illusionary sense—in that, realizing all these fatal flaws in the story, we still can't quite drop the book; we still continue to read it, and even in a sense to enjoy it. Is this some curious vestige of infantile fantasy which the mature, satiric, radical Mark Twain still shared with the feudal romantic royalist Henry James—and which a supposedly mature reader still feels in such literary works? There *is* a pleasure left in reading *Joan of Arc,* not unlike that when we enjoy a bad movie. The narrative still manages to keep our interest; it is only the quality, tone, content of the narrative which is so appalling. This is the most unlikely Mark Twain to be still Mark Twain.

—MAXWELL GEISMAR, "Failure and Triumph," *Mark Twain: An American Prophet*
(Boston: Houghton Mifflin, 1970), pp. 152–53, 155

ERNST SCHÜRER

One of Kaiser's latest but decidedly Expressionistic plays is his *Gilles und Jeanne* (1923), a drama about Jeanne d'Arc, who had been canonized in 1920. However, Kaiser's main figure is not Joan of Arc, but Gilles de Rais (1404–40). Kaiser had learned of him when reading Joris-Karl Huysmans's novel *Là-Bas,* a work about mysticism and satanism which gives a detailed account of Gilles, a rich French nobleman who became marshal of France at the age of twenty-five. He raised an army against the English at his own expense and was entrusted with the guard and defense of the maid before Orléans in 1429. Huysmans does not mention Gilles's erotic attraction to Joan, but he thinks that her religiosity influenced him. He makes her responsible for his development; for in his opinion it is but one step from lofty mysticism to basest satanism. Huysmans further states that there had been rumors that Gilles had committed treachery after the English capture of the maid in 1430. After his return to his castle, Gilles turned to alchemy and the occult sciences, then to debauchery, murder, and the most beastly crimes, abducting children from the neighboring villages and torturing them in order to enjoy their pain. He was finally captured and burned at the stake. Although he is often considered the original

Bluebeard, the assumption is false since he did not kill women, as did the hero of Charles Perrault's French fairy tale. Kaiser, however, used this motif, probably also influenced by the show trial against the French woman murderer, Landru, in 1922.

Considering Kaiser's treatment of history, it is not to be expected that he would present a drama about la Pucelle d'Orléans! Although he uses certain details of her story, these only serve as a convenient outline for his plot. The differences become evident at once: the play is not concerned with the struggle against the English, the raising of the siege of Orléans, and the liberation of France, but with the regeneration of an individual, Gilles de Rais. With his mercenary army, he fights alongside Jeanne and wins the victories for her—not for patriotic reasons but only to win Jeanne. And she was not inspired to leave Domremy for nationalistic purposes but to save a single human individual:

> I was looking for you—Gilles. I was sent for you—Gilles. I was pushed into armor and battle to find you, Gilles. Obediently I went my way through terror and horror—to arrive at the lowest depravity:—into the dark hell of the most damnable man!!!! . . . Greater is the victory over an individual who conquers all. For you I am fighting—Gilles. What is the worth of weapons which kill?!! Unarmed I shall conquer. You I want to conquer—Gilles!!!!

Blinded by passion, Gilles desires her during the battle, but when she refuses to yield to him, he holds back his troops, thereby enabling the English to carry the day and capture the maid. Accused of being a sorceress, her life depends on evidence only Gilles can give. Again he appeals to her to give herself to him in return for her freedom, and again she declines. His ensuing testimony that she had been the devil's paramour leads to her conviction and burning at the stake.

But Gilles cannot forget the dead Jeanne, and his mad desire turns into a raging frenzy. His alchemist first promises him reincarnation of the dead maid, then abducts peasant girls whom he dresses in Jeanne's armor. At first Gilles believes the man, but when he discovers the deception he strangles his victims. He considers himself the devil: "Countless sacrifices fall!!!! Mine is the murder!!!! I am Lucifer!!!!" When he tries to kidnap a seventh victim, the alchemist is apprehended just as he is attempting to sneak into the castle. But before he can open his mouth, Gilles stabs him to death. Gilles is nevertheless arraigned before the same court that had convicted Jeanne. Since his alchemist has burned the corpses, no evidence exists against him, and he is acquitted. Suddenly, he sees an apparition of Jeanne in her silvery armor, bathed in light. The apparition grows stronger as she takes off the armor and puts down her sword. The regeneration is not caused by force, but by love and purity of heart in the service of one's fellow man. Gilles recognizes his guilt and confesses. After his self-accusation, he feels cleansed, for he considers his crimes a necessary station on the road to salvation: "The road to man is far—and until *one* individual has not sunk to his neck into a swamp of blood and has risen again—: nobody is won!!—The murder is mine—mine the confession!!—What redeems the fault more deeply??!!!!" The papal nuncio considers Gilles a sacrifice for all men, a second Christ: "More has happened than our conviction atones for!! A man pleaded guilty!! Who is not like him?!—We shall gather the logs and erect the wood-pile:—everybody burns with Gilles, who burns for all!!!!" The blood of Jeanne and the six victims has purified Gilles, and his blood washes away the sins of the world.

One can hardly imagine a greater contrast than that between Jeanne and Gilles. It is already evident in their outer appearance: the black knight of darkness is arraigned against the shining crusader of the light, the forces of evil against those of good, depravity against innocence, sensualism against purity. At the end, they are nevertheless equated: they both voluntarily sacrifice their lives for the good of humanity. Gilles's sudden elevation is a shock for the audience, since the combination of idealistic messianism and superhuman criminality is repulsive. But it is also found in other Expressionist plays. The hero of Hans Kaltnecker's *Die Opferung* (The Sacrifice, 1918) commits murder, incurring guilt in order to be able to sacrifice himself for humanity. In Franz Werfel's *Schweiger* (1922), evil is seen as "an instrument of divine mercy: 'The blacker the evil, the greater man's readiness for grace!' " Lämmert writes about this tendency: "Self-sacrifice for its own sake is the best security for future salvation"; and he rightly criticizes the excesses of an ethical attitude which sees evil as a necessary station on the way to a new world, an attitude which could serve as an excuse for the elimination of the enemies of the Nazi regime in 1933.

The strange notion that a confession of guilt will result in instant innocence and redemption and even elevate the sinner above the rest of humanity, found in a large number of plays by Kaiser, is influenced by the ethics of the Catholic Church. *Gilles und Jeanne* is Kaiser's contribution to the mystical trend in Expressionism; it possesses characteristics of the medieval mystery play, especially in the final act in the cathedral. Gilles's conversion is essentially a religious experience caused by the miracle of the apparition of the maid, who bears similarities to the Madonna. The play also shows the characteristic merger of erotic and religious experience, a feature which, according to Thomas, links Expressionism with the Baroque mystics. In this play, the Expressionist vision is actually seen on the stage: it suggests the presence of a metaphysical world and a higher existence. But God is never mentioned, and man is saved by man. This basic antireligious attitude also prevented Kaiser from joining the church, a step many other Expressionists actually took. The play's action may be looked upon as a parable of the aims of Expressionism, as seen by many of its disciples. On its way through disorder and chaos, humanity arrives at a new spirituality.

—ERNST SCHÜRER, "The Visions of a New Man: The Expressionist Plays,"
Georg Kaiser (New York: Twayne, 1971), pp. 120–23

LESLIE A. FIEDLER

For those who, in the interest of art and mental health, demand the angelification of the eternal alien, woman, her mythicizing *upward,* Joan remains an object of

adoration, however heterodox. The honorable list of her admirers comes immediately to mind: Friedrich Schiller, Bernard Shaw, Jean Anouilh, Eugène Sue, and
Mark Twain, dissenters in a Protestant or post-Protestant culture grown too aus-
terely patriarchal to honor the Great Goddess. There have been pious Roman
Catholic glorifiers of Joan, too, ever since her second, posthumous trial revoked her
condemnation as a witch and prepared the way for her to become a saint; but they
seem less interesting somehow, since orthodoxy tends to neutralize myth by
turning it into dogma. But the vilifiers of Joan, those driven to mythicize her
downward, are of at least equal importance and interest, particularly in France,
where her official cult, that redeification of woman inside the myth of nationalism,
has seemed to some more malign than beneficial to art and sanity alike.

James Joyce, himself an heir of precisely those writers, has provided a clue to
the significance of their attack on Joan in an extraordinary little critical essay, which
begins as a study of Daniel Defoe but includes before it is through an illuminating
series of observations on the development of realism-naturalism (*verismo* is the
term Joyce uses, for he wrote it originally in Italian) in modern European literature.
"Modern realism," he argues, "is perhaps a reaction. The great French Nation, which
venerates the legend of the Maid of Orleans, nevertheless disfigures her through
the mouth of Voltaire, lasciviously defiles her in the hands of the engravers of the
nineteenth century, riddles and shreds her in the twentieth century with the cutting
style of Anatole France. . . ."

But is this not just what Shakespeare, achieving in verse the victory which
eluded "English John Talbot" on the field of battle, is doing in *Henry VI, Part I*
—disfiguring, lasciviously defiling, riddling and shredding the Maid—though surely
not with the same intention as the realists with whom Joyce is concerned. Their
attack, no matter how little they may have been conscious of its final implications,
was ultimately as an act of aesthetic blasphemy, a denial of the Muse herself, since
they were, all of them, in theory as in practice, bent on reinterpreting their art not
as a gift of the creative spirit, traditionally felt to be female, but as the pursuit of
cold, hard (mythologically speaking, *male*) facts by cold, hard (in fact, male once
more) authors. *Le style, c'est l'homme,* they liked to say, or, *Madame Bovary, c'est
moi,* which rendered in plain English becomes: "every man his own muse," or, "my
heroine is me."

Primarily, Shakespeare is interested, like the Tudor chroniclers on whom he
drew and those who sat in the ecclesiastical court which originally condemned the
Pucelle to be burned, on making a case for England, or rather against France. But
there is in him, too, despite what allegiance he may have felt he owed the old
Roman faith of his mother, a Protestant, Puritan, Hebraic, finally patriarchal distrust
of Mariolatry in all its forms, any attempt to smuggle into Christianity or patriotic
piety homage to the Goddess. For him, in general as well as particular, the virgin is
a whore; which is why he, through his mouthpiece Talbot, begins by calling the
Pucelle "puzzel," and why he lingers so obscenely over Joan's desperate attempts
to escape the fire by claiming pregnancy—though by which of her many lovers she
finds it hard to be sure.

In any case, the plea which, in French ignorance, she hoped would save her, in the eyes of English morality doubly condemns her. She begins her confession, "I am with child, ye bloody homicides. / Murder not then the fruit within my womb. . . ." York answers scornfully, "Now Heaven forfend! The holy maid with child!" And when she concludes by crying, "Oh, give me leave, I have deluded you. / 'Twas neither Charles nor yet the Duke I named, / But Reignier, King of Naples, that prevailed," that same interlocutor responds, "And yet, forsooth, she is a virgin pure! / Strumpet, thy words condemn thy brat and thee." From "puzzel" to "strumpet," the English charge remains the same, though the spokesmen shift with the tides of war.

It is not merely the fact of Joan's having been a whore that stirs the fury of English Shakespeare and his English heroes against her ("Break thou in pieces and consume to ashes, / Thou foul accursèd minister of Hell!"). Even more it is the fact of her having claimed to be the total opposite, of having been a liar as well. Like Chaucer, Shakespeare seems to have felt that the three natural gifts of God to women are "Deceite, wepyng, spynnyng" (lies, tears, and skill with the distaff). Unlike Chaucer, however, he could not contain that belief in ironical acceptance, not even in the *Sonnets,* where he makes a show of such containment ("I do believe her, though I know she lies"), and certainly not in the first part of *Henry VI.* Everything about Joan enrages Shakespeare, because everything about her is a lie, an illusion. She enters, for instance, in the guise of a golden girl; but she is revealed, before all the play is played, a swarthy hag in disguise, as Shakespeare has all along suspected every woman is in essence. Joan herself confesses the fact with a kind of pride on first meeting the Dauphin.

> And, whereas I was black and swart before,
> With those clear rays which she infused on me
> That beauty am I blessed with which you see.

It is the Blessed Virgin herself, "God's Mother . . . in cómplete glory," supreme symbol in the Christian world of divine womanhood, whom she claims as the source of her magical transformation. And, indeed, before that initial encounter is over, a whole gamut of mythological or semimythological females has been evoked, from classical antiquity and medieval hagiography as well as the Testaments, Old and New: Saint Katherine, Deborah, the Amazons, the "mother of Great Constantine," "Saint Philip's daughter," and at last the goddess of love herself. "Bright star of Venus, fall'n down on the earth," the Dauphin says toward the scene's end, "How may I reverently worship thee enough?"

Interestingly, of the three saints whom Joan claimed to have seen in visions— Michael, Margaret, and Katherine—only the last is alluded to in Shakespeare's play. Margaret is omitted, perhaps, in order to save the name for Joan's successor as "the English scourge"; and Michael is suppressed, surely, because, along with that other slayer of dragons, Saint George (as already noticed in the florid eulogy by York), he belongs to the other side, which is to say, the male side, Talbot's side. Moreover, Shakespeare may have found Katherine, who was the patron saint of childbirth, ironically appropriate to the final revelation of the Maid's pregnancy, real or imaginary.

In any case, Shakespeare, for all his hostility to Joan, apparently sensed what more sympathetic churchmen have ever since felt obliged to deny, that the Pucelle was, throughout her short life, an adherent of the underground cult of the Great Goddess. This she seems to have believed finally compatible with orthodox Christianity, and at the moment of her sacrificial death, she apparently felt herself to be the avatar of the female force she had worshipped in all innocence and humility. It seems clearly established by the documents adduced at her ecclesiastical trial—a trial uncharacteristically conducted, for its time, without the use of torture or deliberate deceit—that as a child she had been inducted into the ancient rites of the mother, later crushed utterly by a patriarchal church. Certainly, she hung wreaths on the *Arbre des Dames* near her village, around which it was said the *Domines Fatales* were accustomed to gather: "fairies," we have come to call these creatures euphemistically, though "weird sisters" (as Shakespeare named them in *Macbeth*) would be a more accurate translation of their Latin title. Joan was, in short, whether or not also a saint, a witch.

—LESLIE A. FIEDLER, "The Woman as Stranger: or 'None but women left . . . ,"
The Stranger in Shakespeare (New York: Stein & Day, 1972), pp. 59–63

A. G. MOJTABAI

We all know the story, the big scenes: the Voices, the Dauphin's court, Orleans, Rheims, Rouen, the pyre. . . . It would seem foolhardy to attempt to revive these worn tales again. Yet Australian novelist Thomas Keneally has done it and carried it off with aplomb. Saint Joan lives again, robustly, in a way we have not known her before.

Jehanne is a girl who does not bleed in the way of women. In less skillful hands, this situation would border on parody or reduce to psychoanalytic cliché. There is an element of manifest compensation in Jehanne's behavior. Dressing in male attire for the first time, she thinks: "Now I'm someone else. I'm not Jacques's disappointing child. . . . No one again might ever think, there's a girl, let me father, mother, or love it." But there is more to it than that: "When she was expecting her first bleed and it was late she thought it's because I don't love anyone here enough. The house-loves and town-loves aren't sharp enough in me. She thought that she would not begin to bleed till some larger demands were made . . ."

Jehanne's blood is destined to fortify a king. Her sealed womb is merely a sign, and her jubilation on finally attaining her menarche, after wounds in battle, is gratuitous and diversionary. Surely, *this* is not the blood which matters.

The demands made upon her will be larger, and she knows it. "Jesus and the old oak king and she, Jehannette, knew the day of mid-summer when they would have to go painfully. Their blood was needed for kingship, people, beasts, earth, the cycles of things, the redemption of lost worlds."

The Dauphin Charles has a dream which meshes with Jehanne's. When Charles is 7, his nurse tells him a tale which he never forgets: " 'Now a king needs a pair, a brother-king who's king secretly. And the brother-king has to be sacrificed and the brother-king's blood feeds the power of the king himself. . . . This king is king openly.' She waggled her right index finger potently. . . . Her left index finger shifted subtly. 'This king is the king who has to be sacrificed. Like Jesus died for us and made all of us wonderful. This king never wears a crown.' "

Portrayed here is the brilliant, doomed, gala day of the mock king, who must pay the price when the sun goes down. The institution of mock kings and tempo- rary kings is familiar in many cultures and has been well documented by Frazer in *The Golden Bough. Blood Red, Sister Rose* recasts the Saint Joan legend within the framework of this broader tradition. The result is startling and, at the same time, amazingly plausible.

Keneally's use of the brother-king motif is never heavy-handed, or pushed at the expense of Jehanne and Charles as individuals. The same cannot be said of other modern versions. Shaw presented the surrounding social and theological·currents lucidly: his rendering of Joan as Protestant heresiarch is stunning. But his work reads like a tract. Joan is noble and wooden. Jean Anouilh's Joan in *The Lark* is sweet, coy, vapid—rather thin, like a wraith. Keneally's Jehanne, alone, is supple and fully dimen- sional. She is, at times, sharply nostalgic for the world of ordinary loves and lives she must leave behind. She feels herself "cut . . . out of the thick musk of her family as a vealer is cut, mourning, out of the herd." She knows she will never "grow up to be like Zabillet, ironic and fertile towards some warm oaf," a condition which sometimes seems enviable. She is quite susceptible to the ambiguous delights of sleeping be- tween de Metz and Betrand with "all her points done up." She is remorselessly physi- cal; her ankles are thick, her maneuvers at the latrine are elaborate.

The story is a tragedy, yet *Blood Red, Sister Rose* is a romp. Queen Yolande, giving the go-ahead for presentation of the girl at court, is reported to have said: " 'Although such people always abound in times of emergency it could be useful to have a prophetess on the staff . . .' " Accordingly, a subcommittee is set up for validation of the girl's virginity. When Jehanne fends off a common soldier who is making a pass at her, she reminds him of her Voices and says: "God help any man who has me." He is properly unimpressed and replies "You only want to sleep with knights."

Irreverent? Not in the final analysis. For none of this diminishes Joan. It enno- bles her sacrifice by making it real.

—A. G. MOJTABAI, Review of *Blood Red, Sister Rose, New York Times Book Review,* February 9, 1975, p. 7

THEODORE BESTERMAN

Very many very unkind things have been said about the *Pucelle,* which became widely known at this time. The most recent history of French literature, by a French university professor, refers to the 'continuous obscenity' and the 'crushing pornography' of this poem. This was by no means the contemporary view. Distinguished ladies did not hesitate to beg Voltaire for manuscripts, of which they gave readings in their drawing-rooms. Piron said that for many years Thieriot dined out on a single book of the *Pucelle*. Nor did Voltaire hesitate to send it to mme de Pompadour, who was said to have read it to the king. Mme Du Châtelet kept both works under lock and key, but thought the poem less dangerous than the *Traité de métaphysique*. The pious duchess of Saxe-Gotha preferred it to the *Orphelin de la Chine*. Even the *président* de Brosses, who comprehensively disliked Voltaire, said that 'this grotesque poem' is one of his good works, in which his epic genius is most marked. All these tributes, which could be multiplied, were written before authentic texts were available. And when Voltaire was given his great triumph on his return to Paris at the end of his life, the crowd shouted 'Vive la Henriade! vive Mahomet! vive la Pucelle!' Certainly, Voltaire's treatment of saint Joan was often condemned, but it was usually for religious and patriotic reasons, as in the Inquisition decree of 1757. This controversy has now become unreal, for whether Joan was or was not what she thought she was, Voltaire's irreverence cannot touch her. All that we are interested in is the intrinsic merit of the poem. And here I do not hesitate to assert that the literary merits of the *Pucelle* distinctly surpass those of the *Henriade*.

Voltaire started work on the *Pucelle* certainly by 1730, and possibly several years before. Manuscripts were often stolen and copied surreptitiously, circulated widely almost at once, and eventually became a considerable trade. In 1755 Voltaire said that there were 6000 manuscript copies in Paris, and independent evidence suggests that this figure may have been accurate. It would be a great anachronism to imagine that most of these copies catered to the market in *erotica*. Only those who are not aware of the substantial output of deliberate pornography at that time could imagine such a thing. Those who enjoyed the reading of 'curious' literature had no need to buy expensive manuscripts. However, it was inevitable that those of the *Pucelle* should find their way into print (1755), and increasingly corrupt texts soon proliferated. Finally, after more than twenty pirated editions had been poured out (about as many as appeared of *Candide* in a single year) Voltaire was obliged to produce an authorised version (1762).

Voltaire always maintained that the composition of the *Pucelle* was 'an amusement for the intervals between more serious occupations'. No doubt, but this does not mean that this burlesque epic is not worthy of serious examination, even if it were not by Voltaire, whose most trifling scribble deserves attention.

As the form of the *Henriade* is modelled on Virgil, so the *Pucelle* derives from Ariosto. It is in rhymed decasyllabic verse and extends to twenty-one books and about 8300 lines, thus being nearly twice as long as the *Henriade*. Nobody seems to have noticed that the *Pucelle* is unique in at least one respect: it has a complex and flexible rhyme scheme, which makes it particularly suitable for reading aloud. The effect is almost musical. Though there is no evidence that Voltaire ever read a word of Chaucer (he never mentions him and possessed nothing by him in his library), the *Pucelle* often reminds one of the *Canterbury Tales,* both in manner and matter. And Byron's *Don Juan,* in its turn, quite clearly owes a good deal to the *Pucelle.*

Before giving some account of the poem it is perhaps necessary to remind the reader that a poet's views are not to be determined by what he says in a mock-heroic epic. Voltaire more than once wrote seriously about Joan of Arc, with feeling and understanding, and those who revere Joan should realise that he was the first French historian to do so, and that she was not canonised until the present century, so that it is rather silly to call the *Pucelle* blasphemous. Voltaire wrote, for instance, that Joan's execution 'tears the heart and makes common sense shudder. It is difficult to conceive how we dare call any people barbarous after the innumerable horrors of which we have been guilty.' Nor was this revulsion of feeling unique.

Voltaire at once sets the theme and the tone:

> J'aimerais mieux le soir pour mon usage
> Une beauté douce comme un mouton;
> Mais Jeanne d'Arc eut un cœur de lion:
> Vous le verrez, si lisez cet ouvrage.
> Vous tremblerez de ses exploits nouveaux,
> Et le plus grand de ses rares travaux
> Fut de garder un an son pucelage.

Voltaire then describes the loves of Charles VII and Agnès Sorel, of whom he gives a sensually poetic description. When the king makes love to her 'La pudeur passe et l'amour seul demeure'. In the meanwhile the English are ravaging France, whose leaders hold a council at Orleans. To them appears their patron saint Denis, who announces that he intends to look round for a virgin who will liberate the country. The council laugh:

> Quant il s'agit de sauver ma ville,
> Un pucelage est une arme inutile.
> Pourquoi d'ailleurs le prendre en ce pays?
> Vous en avez tant dans le paradis!...
> Chez les Français, hélas, il n'en est plus.

The saint reaches Domremy and there finds Jeanne working in the stable of an inn. Voltaire describes her with feeling and sympathy, but his frank lines form a remarkable contrast with the painting of Agnès, even when he uses the same terminology. Compare, for instance, of Agnès:

> Téton charmant qui jamais ne reposes,
> Vous invitiez les mains à vous presser....

with this, of Jeanne:

> Ses tétons bruns, mais fermes comme un roc,
> Tentent la robe, et le casque, et le froc.

Denis arrived just in time, for the monk Grisbourdin was besieging Joan's chastity. He reveals her destiny to the girl, she is provided with armour and a donkey, and rides to find the king. She comes to the tent of John Chandos, steals his breeches, and draws three fleur-de-lys on his page's bottom. She reaches the king and apostrophises him. Charles is transported, but then asks Joan whether she is a virgin. She invites doctors, matrons, learned men, pedants, apothecaries to examine her, and is given a certificate of chastity. The king leaves Agnès and departs with the blessing of Denis.

A long satirical excursus follows, in the guise of an account of the Palace of Folly. Agnès sets out to find the king, steals Joan's armour, is captured by the English and falls into the arms of Chandos. Joan and Dunois fight the English, and Dunois resists temptation, for he knows that 'the fate of the whole nation depended on her hidden jewel'. They arrive at the château of Hermaphrodix, which gives rise to much erotic badinage, during which Joan is stripped and whipped, but Grisbourdin arrives in time to prevent the worst. The monk is transported to hell, a long description of which gives Voltaire an opportunity to debate once again the folly of Christian doctrine, which condemns all those who lived before it was possible to be saved. Hell is the

> Sépulcre où gît la docte antiquité,
> Esprit, amour, savoir, grâce, beauté,
> Et cette foule immortelle, innombrable,
> D'enfants du ciel créés tous pour le Diable.
> Tu sais, lecteur, qu'en ces feux dévorants
> Les meilleurs rois sont avec les tyrans.
> Nous y plaçons Antonin, Marc-Aurèle,
> Ce bon Trajan, des princes le modèle;
> Ce doux Titus, l'amour de l'univers;
> Les deux Catons, ces fléaux des pervers;
> Ce Scipion, maître de son courage,
> Lui qui vainquit et l'amour et Carthage.
> Vous y grillez, sage et docte Platon,
> Divin Homère, éloquent Cicéron;
> Et vous, Socrate, enfant de la sagesse,
> Martyr de Dieu dans la profane Grèce;
> Juste Aristide, et vertueux Solon:
> Tous malheureux morts sans confession.

Voltaire then spreads the net wider, and reveals that Clovis and Constantine are in hell, with great preachers, rich prelates, casuists, doctors, Spanish monks, Italian nuns, the confessors of all the kings, the inquisitors. Grisbourdin then tells the story of Joan's adventures, 'and all hell laughed at them with a good heart'.

The story then returns to earth and to the adventures of Agnès and Joan. An elaborate description follows of the temple of fame, and of the adventures of

Dunois and La Trimouille. During these picaresque scenes, in which Joan does not figure, occurs a little gem of descriptive characterisation:

Au cabaret les deux amants dinèrent;
Et ce fut là qu'à table ils rencontrèrent
Un brave Anglais, fier, dur et sans souci,
Qui venait voir la sainte Vierge aussi
Par passe-temps, se moquant dans son âme
Et de Lorette et de sa Notre-Dame.
Parfait Anglais, voyageant sans dessein,
Achetant cher des modernes antiques,
Regardant tout avec un air hautain
Et méprisant les saints et leurs reliques.
De tout Français c'est l'ennemi mortel,
Et son nom est Christophe d'Arondel.
Il parcourait tristement l'Italie,
Et se sentant fort sujet à l'ennui,
Il amenait sa maîtresse avec lui,
Plus dédaigneuse encor, plus impolie,
Parlant fort peu, mais belle, faite au tour,
Douce la nuit, insolente le jour,
A table, au lit, par caprice emportée, . . .

Even more graphic is the account of a naked duel between this Englishman and La Trimouille, during which their girls are carried off; but it is too long to quote. The two duellists pursue and recapture their mistresses. The story of Agnès Sorel is then taken up again. She finishes up in a convent, where she naturally has an amorous encounter. The English take the convent, and a fight follows between saint Denis and saint George. Joan is still wandering about naked on her donkey. The scene shifts again to the king and Agnès, who consoles herself with Montrose. At last we come back to Joan, now again dressed, who engages in single combat with Chandos, who defeats her. He is about to rape her when saint Denis again intervenes, and Dunois vanquishes Chandos.

Voltaire then describes a French banquet at Orleans, followed by a general assault against the English, Charles being encouraged by Joan. The scene of the sixteenth book is laid in heaven, where saint Peter appeases his colleagues George and Denis by promising a prize to whichever brings him the better ode. The king, Joan and their companions go mad, and are restored to sanity by the royal confessors. The next two books are filled with picaresque incidents, the most interesting passage consisting of a long excursus in which many of Voltaire's *bêtes noires* are excoriated with equal wit and bite: Frélon (the wasp, that is, Fréron), Coyon (Guyon), Chaumé (Chaumeix), Gauchat, Sabotier (Sabatier), La Beaumelle and other critics and theologians are in turn exhibited.

And so we come to the last two books of the *Pucelle,* which are again devoted wholly to Joan. The devil enters her donkey and tries to seduce her, after first addressing her in eloquent and respectful terms. Joan resists the temptation and chases the devil-donkey. Denis then replaces the devil in the ass. Joan and Dunois defeat the English, and the poem concludes:

> Du haut des cieux Denis applaudissait;
> Sur son cheval saint George frémissait.
> L'âne entonnait son octave écorchante,
> Qui des Bretons redoublait l'épouvante.
> Le roi, qu'on mit au rang des conquérants,
> Avec Agnès soupa dans Orléans.
> La même nuit, la fière et tendre Jeanne,
> Ayant au ciel renvoyé son bel âne,
> De son serment accomplissant les lois,
> Tint sa parole à son ami Dunois.
> Lourdis, mêlé dans la troupe fidèle,
> Criait encore: Anglais! elle est pucelle!

It can thus be seen that this light-hearted burlesque does not deserve automatic condemnation. Of course Voltaire could not write about religion, especially in a picaresque poem intended to amuse, without making fun of it. Nor was he in the least inclined to write with conventional respect even about a national heroine. Those who find these things shocking will be duly shocked. But all this is incidental. The main theme is a huge joke: the mystical importance attached to Joan's virginity. Voltaire found irresistibly funny the notion that the fate of France could depend on the preservation of this peasant-girl's maidenhead. And let there be no mistake about it: enormous importance *was* attached by her contemporaries to Joan's virginity. Voltaire developed this theme in fugue and counterpoint, in some of his most successful verse, pausing only here and there to sink his blade into some of man's inhumanities and stupidities. To regard the *Pucelle* as a work of pornography, that is, one intended to titillate, is a judgment a little too lumpish even from those who hate Voltaire.

—THEODORE BESTERMAN, "*La Pucelle*, 1755," *Voltaire* (Oxford: Basil Blackwell, 1969 [3rd ed. 1976]), pp. 389–96

WILLIAM SEARLE

In the period during which Twain, France, and Shaw were at work on Joan of Arc she was also undergoing a last ecclesiastical trial: the one which led to her canonization in 1924. By comparing the Catholic view of her which emerged from that trial with the skeptical views presented in the works we have studied we can gain fresh insight into the values which were at stake in the reaction against Christian fundamentalism that characterized the post-Darwinian era.

The case was first formally presented before the Sacred Congregation of Rites in 1888. At that time the promoter, or "devil's advocate," who signed his name in Latin as "Augustinus Caprara," made a sharp distinction between saintly and secular ideals of heroism. Drawing a parallel between Joan and Columbus, he pointed out that both had made great sacrifices on behalf of the faith, the one in bringing the New World under the influence of the Cross, and the other in liberating her country and consecrating it to the King of Heaven. Both, moreover, had received for this heroism the general admiration of mankind. Yet even so, Caprara argued, the virtues of both had always been regarded as purely "political." No one hitherto had attributed to Joan, any more than to Columbus, that "heroic virtue" which the Church defines as the distinguishing characteristic of the saints.

It was on the premise that "heroic virtue" is essentially spiritual rather than secular that Caprara built his case. Before a servant of God can be canonized, his supporters must prove that he achieved during his lifetime a reputation for sanctity. Caprara conceded that Joan's reputation had been great, but he argued that it had depended altogether too exclusively upon her military prowess. "Not Christian, therefore, but military was that heroic virtue which so stirred hearts and minds," he maintained. And fifteen years later his successor at the Vatican, Alexander Verde, made the same point even more succinctly: "Not her virtues but her exploits were the cause of her renown."

These remarks go to the heart of the disagreement between skeptics and believers concerning the nature of heroic virtue. They raise a question which is fundamental here: what should we value most in our heroes, pious virtues or practical ones?

For Joan's defenders in 1888, Messers Aldobrandi and Minetti, the answer to this question was not in doubt. They responded to Caprara's attack on Joan's reputation for sanctity by declaring that even in her own time she was chiefly remarkable for her kindliness, her charity to the poor, her love of prayer, and her constancy in taking the sacraments. In 1903 their successors at the Vatican actually drew from Joan's stunning success a lesson on the vanity of earthly capacity. "That in the face of such pressing difficulties," they argued, "the Maid should in four months time have overcome more people than Napoleon and have retired from battle a conqueror of scarcely less renown can only be ascribed to the glory of God who, in His inscrutable wisdom, 'hath chosen the weak things of the world to confound the things which are mighty.'" They even reasoned that, given Joan's natural infirmities, her achievement proves that she must have been virtuous, since God does not render supernatural aid to those who are not.

Our three skeptics were contemptuous of this attitude. France, to be sure, agreed with the Maid's Catholic supporters that she was more distinguished for Christian piety than for natural ability. But since he did not share their faith in divine providence, he could reconcile this view of her with her amazing success only by supposing that she had been manipulated by men who were clever enough to be able to compensate for her own incapacity. "A great deal of art," he remarks in this connection, "and even a bit of chicanery, is always indispensable in gaining credit for innocence." Shaw's Joan is so totally self-reliant that even the members of her own party accuse her of presumption: in Dunois's phrase, "she thinks she has God in her pocket." And Twain's attitude is expressed in his condemnation of the tribunal which the Dauphin established at Poitiers to inquire into the Maid's credentials as a messenger of God. "The rats were devouring the house," he makes De Conte complain, "but instead of examining the cat's teeth and claws they only concerned themselves to find out if it was a holy cat. If it was a pious cat, a moral cat, all right, never mind about the other capacities, they were of no consequence."

On similar grounds, Twain, France, and Shaw differed from the Maid's Catholic supporters in the stance they adopted toward the voices. In 1888 Caprara insisted that Joan's defense must prove that her saints had really come from God, arguing that her claim to divine inspiration could not otherwise be verified. By contrast, the question on which our skeptics base their judgment of those saints is whether they gave her sensible advice.

Naturally, their answers to that question vary with their opinions of the imagination as a source of enlightenment. Both Twain and France find fault with the voices for being either uninformative or misleading. Shaw argues that their counsel, being a reflection of Joan's common sense, was actually quite sound. The common assumption underlying both views, however, is that in the absence of supernatural aids the hero must be realistic and practical. Knowledge of divine revelation cannot help him. What he needs is knowledge of the world.

Further, in the absence of a divinely revealed law, the hero must be morally, as well as practically, intelligent. He must have better values than his fellows, and he must refer his conduct to those values rather than to an abstract moral code. In 1888 Caprara quoted from one skeptic historian a passage which, while sympathetically intended, was damaging to the Maid from a Catholic point of view:

> I venture to say (so Quicherat) that she did not always respond truthfully to the question of her judges. When all that was at issue was her own person her response was characterized by that irresistible frankness to which I have just finished paying tribute; she avowed and affirmed at the risk of a thousand deaths. But if the demand revealed the slightest tendency toward an accusation that might fall on someone else, in that case she became evasive, she hesitated, she concealed her thought, and if further pressed, she dissembled.

In denying that such mendacity may be excused by the generosity of its motive, the Church is guided by its mysticism. Since this world is merely a preparation for the next, it holds, the proper end of virtuous conduct must be not to secure worldly benefit even for others but entirely to fulfill the will of God. In 1888 Caprara explained what the Church understands by *heroic virtue:* that "it in fact reserves its highest and most exalted honors to those outstanding moral virtues which pertain to the eternal salvation of souls . . ." In a preliminary brief presented in 1874, Giambattista Minetti completed a lengthy account of Joan's life and character by denouncing those whose love for the land of their fathers makes them, in his phrase, "unmindful of the kingdom of their heavenly father." Joan's elevation, he argued, would tend to counteract that sort of patriotism which "thrives without faith or religion and even provides an excuse for crimes."

The skeptic, of course, recognizes no such transcendent allegiance. Hence his hero is a pragmatist. Just as he places his faith not in God but in himself, so also he places his hope not in a future life but in a better world. Consequently, he devotes all his energies to institutional reform; and being morally more intelligent than his fellows, he is likely to seem unscrupulous to them in the means which he uses to achieve such reform. In Twain, Joan not only sacrifices "her best self, that is, her truthfulness," to a patriotic purpose but she also justifies this course by a moral argument which her companions are too obtuse to comprehend. "Her saying had seemed shallow," De Conte declares in a canceled passage in the manuscript, "but that was because *we* were shallow; it was deep." Shaw, going even further than Twain, claims that her moral originality put her so far in advance of the conventional ethics of her time that she was driven to become a heretic in order to assert the rights of the individual conscience against institutionalized morality.

Of our three skeptics, then, only France claims that Joan was lacking in moral intelligence, and his views on the subject have more in common with those of the others than is immediately apparent. In "Virtue in France" he declares, "Virtue is not an innocent. . . . It knows how, at need, to plunge with sublime impurity into all miseries in order to solace them, into all vices in order to redeem them. It knows the nature of the great human task, and that it is sometimes necessary to soil one's hands." If, unlike Twain and Shaw, France denies such knowledge to Joan, he also indicates that it made her the ready dupe of unscrupulous opportunists.

The Church, however, refuses to approve the sacrifice of innocence to any earthly objective, however generous. Rejecting the pragmatic position taken by our skeptics, it holds that worldly success cannot be made a criterion of moral worth since, in the corrupt and uncertain condition of human affairs, such success does not always result from virtuous conduct. In 1888 Caprara argued that Joan's mission cannot really have been of God since she failed in her stated objectives of freeing the Duke of Orleans and driving the English out of France. The Maid's defense retorted that the failure of a sacred mission may be the fault not of the emissary but of those to whom he has been sent. If Joan's purpose was frustrated, they argued, it was because Charles VII too often heeded those of his counsellors who, unlike her, preferred to negotiate rather than fight. John the Baptist himself, they pointed out, had been prevented from fulfilling his goals by the wickedness and incredulity of his contemporaries.

For the Church, then, the failure of the hero is not an index of the merit of his commitment, nor does it prove that his efforts have been wasted. But to those who cannot accept the Church's mystical view of this matter the very possibility of such failure raises a poignant ethical problem. "Her folly was wiser than wisdom itself," France declares in his preface, "for it was the folly of martyrdom, without which men have not established anything either great or useful in the world." For Christians, however, martyrdom is more than a manifestation of the desire to establish the Kingdom of God on earth; it is also irrefragable proof that the martyr's love for God was greater than his love for the things of this world. To deprive his sacrifice of this mystic significance is apparently to make its merit depend upon its results. And over these he can exercise only a limited control.

France's solution to this difficulty lies in his declaration that sacrifice is beautiful in itself and that its merit is therefore independent both of its results and of the worthiness of its goals. His answer to the question, What, if not God, is the proper object of martyrdom? appears to be that the object as such does not matter. But this response is neither satisfying nor candid: it obviously matters to the martyr; it does not matter to France because he cannot imagine himself in the martyr's place. In fact, his genuine conviction appears to be that it is better to avoid martyrdom at all costs. In an essay for the *Temps*, where he describes martyrdom as a proof of fanaticism, he praises Rabelais for having avoided it.

Moreover, as Shaw points out, the glorification of sacrifice for its own sake is ethically unsound, since it encourages people to sacrifice both themselves and others unnecessarily. France's claim in "Le Cavalier Miserey" that sacrifice is beautiful even when involuntary suggests that even for him its beauty was chiefly aesthetic rather than moral. At any rate, his account of the Maid's death is far from edifying.

Shaw's treatment of this question is much more successful. Like Twain, he passes over the Catholic ideals of *caritate in deo* and *caritate in proximis* and represents Joan as having accepted martyrdom in response to an enlightened self-love. Impelled by a disinterested impulse of self-respect, he suggests, even the materialist can rise above material desires. Moreover, this idea can also be defended on pragmatic grounds, since it is only through confidence in his own intuitions that the hero can overcome the resistance which conventional people make toward revolutionary attempts at improving their lot.

Thus, like the Catholic hero's faith in God, the skeptic hero's faith in himself is at once the ground of his confidence in the future and the justification for his commitment. Perfecting himself in self-affirmation rather than in self-denial, he, unlike his Christian counterpart, makes a merit of personal pride. In the minutes of Joan's trial at Rouen, beside a passage which records one of her many defiant refusals to submit to the authority of the Church Militant, the scribe Manchon disapprovingly scrawled *"superba responsio!"* "Yes," Twain makes De Conte agree, "it was just that. For this 'superb answer' came from the lips of a girl of nineteen with death and hell staring her in the face."

—WILLIAM SEARLE, "Joan's Last Trial," *The Saint and the Skeptics: Joan of Arc in the Work of Mark Twain, Anatole France, and Bernard Shaw* (Detroit: Wayne State University Press, 1976), pp. 139–44

DONALD G. WATSON

In the first scene of *1 Henry VI* we are introduced to a fallen world, fallen heroically and historically more than morally and theologically, by the lamentations of Henry

V's brothers and uncles over his death. Three messengers announce progressively more disastrous defeats for the English in France; even the brave Talbot has been taken prisoner. The Bastard of Orleans in the next scene introduces a "holy maid" with visionary powers to accelerate this process of driving "the English forth the bounds of France" (I.2.51–54). The "overtones of the comic occur when she first appears," writes Ernest W. Talbot of Joan. "The love rhetoric of Charles is amusing in its absurdity. It also agrees with a comic conception that will place Charles and Joan in situations reminiscent of the braggart and the prostitute, as well as the ugly, rustic, brawling wench." There is never any real tension between Pucelle and Puzzel; from the beginning Joan's claim to heavenly assistance and holy chastity is undermined by the amorous dalliance, bawdy innuendo, and double-entendre. Although the comedy of Joan La Pucelle reaches its culmination in the total unmasking of the play's penultimate scene, it is openly derisive comedy all along.

Even if we set apart twentieth-century admiration for Joan of Arc, we are likely at first to think the laughter at her expense rather cheaply extracted through chauvinistic characterization. The matter, however, is more complex, for if Joan is exposed and led off to execution, Talbot, the last loyal soldier, is dead as well, and the English have sacrificed their national unity while losing their French provinces. Even this incongruity, followed by the ironic gap between Suffolk's loyal rhetoric and ambitious intentions in the last scene, cannot completely contain the comic process involved in the La Pucelle part of the play.

Part of the comedy of the Joan plot comes from simple dramatic recognition of incongruity through the superior knowledge provided by irony. This superiority, augmented by nationalistic bias, produces derisive laughter, the kind of laughter most often defined by Elizabethan rhetoricians and psychologists.

The comedy of La Pucelle begins and ends with it; what complicates the audience's response in between is the internalization of derision within the play. If we share in the English lords' mockery of Joan, her exultation over her victories and scoffing over Talbot's corpse are, if not painful, at least unpleasant, and unpleasant in proportion to the audience's identification with the English forces. One such scene occurs after Joan's capture of Rouen through the stratagem of disguising herself and her men as peasants selling corn. She and the French lords stand on the walls of Rouen, illustrating theatrically their superiority; on the stage the dying Bedford is "brought in sick to a chair":

PUCELLE: Good morrow, gallants! Want ye corn for bread?
I think the Duke of Burgundy will fast
Before he'll buy again at such a rate.
'Twas full of darnel; do you like the taste?
BURGUNDY: Scoff on, vile fiend and shameless courtesan!
I trust ere long to choke thee with thine own
And make thee curse the harvest of that corn.
DAUPHIN: Your grace may starve perhaps before that time.
BEDFORD: O, let no words, but deeds, revenge this treason!

PUCELLE: What will you do, good graybeard? Break a lance,
And run atilt at death within a chair?   III.2.41–51

It is not easy to know how to respond to the cruel humor here or later to that of Pucelle's response to Lucy's request for Talbot's body:

I think this upstart is old Talbot's ghost,
He speaks with such a proud commanding spirit.
For God's sake, let him have him; to keep them here,
They would but stink and putrefy the air.   IV.7.87–90

Lucy's rhetoric of titles is sarcastically mocked as a "silly stately style" (72), and the Dauphin's conclusion—"All will be ours, now blody Talbot's slain" (96)—is unfortunately and correctly prophetic. That York's and Somerset's unchivalric refusals to send Talbot reinforcements are more responsible for his death than Pucelle's prowess or magic further complicates the scene. The English have embarked, as Gareth Lloyd Evans says, upon a sea of "national decadence," and the French derision is justified; even the "barbs" of Joan's "searching indictment of English hypocrisy (V.4.36ff.)," as J. P. Brockbank points out, cannot "be removed by the spectacle of her converse with evil spirits." The English finally must share in the derision, and the audience's superiority is taken away. The heroism of the Talbots is at least partially cancelled by the final scenes which promise the ascendancy of Suffolk; there, Brockbank explains, in a "parody" of the "absurdities of political romance" in the "style of a professional philanderer," the "treacheries exercised in the politics of flirtation are as sinister as they are amusing—the betrayal of trust must have evil consequences in the harsh chronicle setting." The wry mockery of La Pucelle contributes to the sardonic irony of the last scene by telling truths about the faded martial glory and chivalry of the English. With Suffolk and Margaret returns the comic combination of lovemaking, politics, and warfare which characterized the first scene between Charles and Joan; only the irony has darkened. Margaret promises to succeed Joan as the scourge of England, and Henry VI's cuckolding will be an ironic counterpoint to Joan's promiscuity; the force of Talbot has given way to the fraud of France and the descent into effeminacy, cunning, and decadence is accelerating.

—DONALD G. WATSON, "The Dark Comedy of the Henry VI Plays,"
Thalia I, No. 2 (Autumn 1978): 11–12

JOHN STEWART COLLIS

We turn to *Saint Joan*. It is generally regarded as a very religious play. True, there are many clergymen in it and a lot of talk about God and much wrangling over theology, but it is very difficult to understand how Joan of Arc qualified as a saint. She was a military genius. This is very rare, even among men—can you think of a military genius during World War I? For an uneducated country girl to have possessed it is extraordinary indeed. But what has this to do with religion? The French novelist, Huysmans, has expressed the regret that Joan of Arc ever rose to wrest France from the Normans who were seeking to preserve her racial and prehistoric unity with England, and thus handed her over to Charles VII and his southerners. The advantage of the union of France and England for the world generally would have been incalculable (and incidentally, the Mediterranean population of France and the Mediterranean population of Ireland would have rendered impossible an 'Irish question'). And indeed, anyone today walking across the soil of France between Passchendaele and the Somme, knowing that beneath his feet lie nearly a million British dead who were comrades of the French, might well endorse this view. At any rate the claim seems to me by no means outrageous that when the peasant girl from Lorraine with her hallucinations galvanized into action the nerveless arms of Charles she inflicted a blow upon the progress of the modern world which may never have been exceeded.

It is hard to see exactly where her sainthood comes in. She was a martyr, certainly, to outward cruelty and inward folly. I am fond of the Epilogue because of its splendid rhetoric. But it is confusing. Near the end the various parties praise Joan. Each in turn kneels in praise. Indeed they give her a very good hand. But when she asks if they would like her to come back to earth, each makes an excuse and discreetly withdraws. We are supposed to think ill of them for this. But why should they want her back? She was not a saviour with a gospel of salvation; she was not a philosopher with a solution to the riddle of the world; she was not a moralist with a message for mankind. She was a soldier. Why should they want her back unless they had some military coup in mind? When they have all departed she has the nerve to kneel down in a holy manner and to ask God how long it must be before this beautiful earth is ready to receive its saints.

—JOHN STEWART COLLIS, "Religion and Philosophy," *The Genius of Shaw: A Symposium,* ed. Michael Holroyd (London: Hodder & Stoughton, 1979), p. 86

H. G. McINTYRE

(Anouilh's) version of the Joan of Arc story is both highly theatrical and strikingly original. The actors come on stage, pick up their props left behind from an earlier production and start discussing how they will re-enact Joan's life and trial. Her English captor, Warwick, wants understandably to proceed immediately to her trial and condemnation, but Bishop Cauchon, who presides over the proceedings, insists that "elle a toute sa vie à jouer avant". The play is effectively her trial but the initial air of improvisation is maintained by frequent flashbacks in which Joan and the other characters re-enact scenes of her past life. As in the medieval theatre—and appropriately enough, given this medieval subject—the stage is used as a single, integrated acting space where scenes can be presented in succession or simultaneously with a minimum of fuss and scenery and a maximum of imagination. It is nominally the place of Joan's trial but serves, as need arises, as Joan's home village of Domrémy, the battlefields on which she fought, the Dauphin's court at Chinon or her prison cell. Characters not directly involved in each episode often remain in the background and Joan's ecclesiastical judges intervene on occasion to question her version of events. The presentation of character is equally theatrical. Given Anouilh's wide historical canvas and the large number of episodic characters, most can only be caricatures to a greater or lesser degree. This works admirably in fact and complements the fragmented, episodic structure. These caricatures are perfectly at home in brief animated vignettes and they spring immediately to life. Even among more important characters there are no naturalistic creations. Anouilh's portrait of Joan is realistic in one sense. There is nothing of the distant, immortalized saint about her. On the contrary, she is an engagingly human and down-to-earth country girl whose plainspokenness, humour and common sense sometimes confound the theologians around her. Once or twice Anouilh uses her actual words, taken from trial records, but his portrait falls far short of documentary realism.

Joan is a theatrical heroine in another sense also. She conforms to the pattern of behaviour already established by Antigone and typical of the heroic race's rejection of life in Anouilh's plays. She defends her visions and sense of mission tenaciously until she is intimidated by the threat of torture into renouncing them and submitting to the Church. In prison she is visited by Charles and the ladies of his court and her captor Warwick. All of them commend her action and urge her to look forward to life. Joan imagines what she will become:

Jeanne acceptant tout, Jeanne avec un ventre, Jeanne devenue gourmande. Vous voyez Jeanne fardée, en hennin, empêtrée dans ses robes, s'occupant de son petit chien ou avec un homme à ses trousses, qui sait, Jeanne mariée?

Like Antigone, she rebels at this prospect of 'happiness', reaffirms her divine mission and goes to her death. L'Alouette was one of Anouilh's greatest successes but some voices were raised in a familiar protest: that once again Anouilh had debased a noble subject by subordinating it to his own preoccupations. But his greatest surprise is reserved for the end. Joan is duly condemned and the actors set about constructing her funeral pyre. Just as they have set it alight, in rushes Captain Beaudricourt, who first befriended Joan, and reminds them that they have not acted the Dauphin's coronation scene in Rheims cathedral. The pyre is hastily dismantled. An organ sounds, bells peal and the play ends with a tableau of Joan triumphant, sword in hand and banner waving, in a resplendent tableau of the coronation scene. Anouilh describes this final tableau as the kind of beautiful illustration you might find in a school prize book and his whole treatment of the subject is inspired by this view of history. ⟨...⟩

The whole of L'Alouette is a trial convened for the very purpose of contesting the authenticity of Joan's claim to be acting in the name of a cause and authority greater than herself. In the event, her moments of inspired common sense are more than a match for her learned interrogators, but her position is nonetheless undermined by a number of ironies implicit in the overall situation. Firstly the idea that God should intervene and take sides in human battles is an Old Testament concept that, despite popular legend, even a French audience cannot, upon reflection, take seriously. If, on principle, we reject Warwick's claim that "Dieu est avec le droit anglais" then we must equally query Joan's contention that God is with the French. This problem of the partisanship of God is fundamental to the meaning of the play. In *L'Alouette* all sides look to God for support and justify their actions by claiming a cause and an authority greater than themselves. The Dauphin may be cowardly and weak-willed but he has his moments of insight. Introducing Joan to the unfamiliar game of cards, he explains how an ace is more powerful than a King:

> L'as, c'est Dieu si tu veux, mais dans chaque camp.

There are, moreover, as many different interpretations of God and how his interests may best be defended as there are individuals. In the light of *Pauvre Bitos,* we suspect that these varying interpretations are the product of individual personalities. Joan's prosecutor, the Promoteur, is a caricature of a fanatic. It is not hard to see that his attacks on Joan's claim to divine inspiration are shaped by his own obsessions with witchcraft and sexuality. The sinister Inquisiteur, official representative of the Inquisition and defender of theological orthodoxy, is more interested in heresy than superstition. But he is another obsessional figure and a prototype for Bitos. His attacks on Joan's naive and unsuspecting humanism are motivated not by intellectual and theological convictions but by a morbid hatred of all humanity. The gentle and sensitive Cauchon, the most fair-minded of Joan's judges, has chosen to collaborate with the English for the sake of peace and stability. Again, his interpretation of what is in the Church's best interests is determined by his own quietist nature:

> Nous n'y pouvons rien ... Nous ne pouvons que jouer nos rôles, chacun le sien, bon ou mauvais, tel qu'il est écrit et à son tour.

The cause is not something objective, detached and external to which we harness ourselves. It is rather an expression of the deepest springs of the self. We cannot help seeing Joan's claim to be acting in a cause greater than herself in the context of all the other similar claims which surround her and we must judge them all on the same principles.

Joan's claim is further undermined by historical ironies. These are not discussed in the play but they are implicit in the blatantly contrived ending which ensures that her story is "une histoire qui finit bien" and Anouilh mentions them in his preface to the play. In reality, after her brief period of success, Joan became an embarrassment to her own side. After her death Charles and his court fell back upon "la bonne vieille politique" and eventual victory over the English was achieved by more orthodox and reasonable means: a combination of battles won, negotiations from strength and calculated compromise. Joan's only real, lasting achievement was the shining example she created and the splendid image captured in the final tableau of *L'Alouette,* which she left to posterity. Even her canonization in 1920 did not establish her claim to a divine mission. It only verified "l'excellence de ses vertus théologales". She remains "une sainte qui est morte dans une histoire politique". The story of Joan of Arc finishes well but it does not support her triumph in a cause greater than herself.

—H. G. MCINTYRE, "Heroes and Antiheroes," *The Theatre of Jean Anouilh*
(London: George G. Harrap, 1981), pp. 85–87, 96–98

ROLANDE BALLORAIN

In *Joan of Arc,* Twain brought his ideas, and his disguise pattern, to their highest achievement. Joan is first a "flawless, ideal, perfect," "entirely unselfish" person confronted with a world of curs (the King), rascals, low and debased ingrates (the English and the French), traitors (the Church). She is a peasant from a village brought to Court, like the pauper. But she is mostly a girl in a man's world; and a much better man than any man. In Twain's "Saint Joan of Arc," she is shown as having "military genius, leonine courage, incomparable fortitude, a prodigy of a mind," and also an orator's gift, an advocate's gift, a judge's gift, a statesman's gift. She was ignorant and became a commander-in-chief; she was "a cattle-pasturing peasant," and she crowned a king. Her father is the first to accuse her of "unsexing" herself. History has shown how wearing "male attire" was also held against Joan by her judges. But Twain repeats that famous accusation again and again and obviously defends her on that point in the most modern way. He even becomes her champion for that. For one obvious reason: he cannot but defend disguise. In the long tradition of misogynist literature, woman's make-up, her artifice, her love for dressing, acting, lying is constantly reviled. Not so with Twain. He emphasizes the fact that the court touched upon "the matter of her apparel," asked her to wear a woman's dress; she is ultimately reproached for "doing man's work in the wars and thus deserting the industries proper to her sex"; she is made to promise to resume "the male habit," then is reproached for not doing it. Finally when she is brought to the stake, it seems that her fundamental heresy is not her refusal to accept the law of the Established Church (and her substituting for it her own personal intuitive contact with the Deity, a belief of American Transcendentalists, by the way), but her refusal to keep to the role assigned to her by her society, by men and religion. She is burnt because she is a woman. If one sees that in Joan, her male attire is central. She is a peasant girl who dresses as a soldier in armor, and then even in prison she dresses like a man. This is the other reason for which Twain champions her. He and she think that among men, it is not only more becoming to dress like a man (in Part I, Chapter 9, a court allows her "to wear men's clothes, since she must do the work of a man and soldier"), but (since "costume makes all the difference in the world") that dressing like a man, she will become one. And an even better one than they are, for she is a better person; so she is more entitled than men to wear men's clothes. At the end of Chapter 21, she says that the Bastard and La Hire are real men, but the Council, who wish to stop her in her progress are only "disguised ladies' maids." Moreover, after all her achievements, Joan wishes to go back to her village if she could get out of prison (Part II, Chapter

7). Then, she says, she would wear her woman's clothes again; in the prison, it is impossible. They knew, Louis de Conte insists (Chapter 12), that one of the reasons was that "soldiers of the guard were always present in her room whether she was asleep or awake and that the male dress was a better protection for her modesty than the other." A very modern way of seeing the advantages of a very convenient garb. One can understand why Twain called that work "the apple of my eye."

There are other reasons. It is a pity that book has been so neglected by American readers and critics. One may guess why. It is about History; about French and English History; about a woman, and a Frenchwoman; matters of no immediate concern to Americans. They refused to follow Twain and to rehabilitate Joan as Quicherat had done, then Michelet. They decided those matters had to be irrelevant to the "best Twain" as they had decided to define him. I maintain that it is only by considering that work seriously (and *The Prince and the Pauper* as well), and not separately, but along with the other works of Twain, that one can begin, if one is interested in that writer, just begin to understand what he was really up to. Moreover one is surprised to see how well written the biography is, how elegant it is, how easily it reads from beginning to end, how even humor is smoothly mixed into it and never jars with lyrical passages, how tenderness pervades it. Clearly Twain felt very much at ease with it. Because he could harmoniously reconcile here the opposite poles of his work and find in history a confirmation of ideas important to him. History gave him the narrative line, so that the "tank" could not "run dry." History was bringing proof that the wildest dreams can come true. Already Tom Canty, who dreamed of seeing the real Prince or of becoming one himself, had started imagining in his dreams he was one, then acted being one, "organizing a royal court" in which, daily, "the mock prince was received with elaborate ceremonials borrowed by Tom from his romantic readings," an acting that worked such an effect on him that he began "to *act* the prince, unconsciously." The double meaning of "to act" shows the elaborate process of disguise and reality in Twain. To the point that Tom's personality has changed: "His speech and manners became curiously ceremonious and courtly, to the vast admiration and amusement of his intimates." When he meets the Prince for good, and in spite of himself is made to be the Prince, his dream has come true. He is metamorphosed into one. And the real Prince on English roads with Hendon—suggesting Don Quixote and Sancho, and announcing Joan and La Hire—discovers his country and tries to save his nation. All those elements are found in *Joan of Arc* too, but carried further. For Twain is aware that Tom Canty's adventure was only fabricated by him and so remained a dream for the two of them, creator and persona. But Joan, the peasant, dreamed of saving her land, of getting to the King's Court and even of crowning him; and she did it for real, in history, not in a romance! She, a girl, accomplished in reality the wildest of all the dreams of the Toms and Edwards and Sams, and she became celebrated! Tom Canty and Edward VI of England are ten; Tom Sawyer is twelve; Huck is thirteen, fourteen; Joan is sixteen to nineteen when she acts. They all are presexual. Huck, a boy, disguises himself as a girl; Joan, a girl, disguises herself as a man. All are children trespassing into the world of adults, judging it, wishing to bring order to it. In fact, only a child can be a real civilizing force, neither man nor woman; and only a villager issued from the golden age. Last, *Joan of Arc* helped Twain to put all his great ideas into action. All his prejudices against the French, against even the English, against the Church against monarchy reappear, but organized into constructive criticism. Joan's life is a demonstration of the validity of his conception of "training." Before Joan, the French had lost all courage; when she told them the necessity of urgent action, they changed; once she was gone, they became low and vile again. Joan herself, an ignorant girl, is given an army which believes in her, and thus makes her the Maid of Orléans; believing in herself (through the sponsorship of the Voices), she does accomplish wonders. Put in a man's world, she does better than any man. But once put into prison, treated as a heretic, isolated from her friends, she becomes a lonely person, "an apostate," "an idolater," a "friendless poor girl" who could only die even if in martyrdom. Those two contrasting images of the Maid correspond to the two volumes of Sieur de Conte. The last idea that Twain illustrates here is what he asserts in "What Is Man?" also. Man is nothing, all his ideas come from the outside. What could come from the outside more than the Voices? For neither in the biography nor in the essay does Twain justify Joan's extraordinary actions by the miracle of God's intervention. On the contrary, he keeps saying that there is no possible explanation for "the Wonder of all Ages," "the Riddle of the Ages": "All rules fail in that girl's case." The young man asks the old man: "Consider the man who stands by his duty and goes to the *stake* rather than be recreant to it." The old man answers: "It is his make and his training. He has to content the spirit that is in him, though it cost him his life." Ultimately then, Joan only satisfied the spirit that was in her, whether originated by the Voices of St. Catherine and St. Marguerite or by that most commendable feeling (to Twain), his last compliment, at the end of the book: "the genius of patriotism." "She was patriotism embodied, concreted, made flesh and palpable to the touch and visible to the eye."

—ROLANDE BALLORAIN, "Mark Twain's Capers: A Chameleon in King Carnival's Court," *American Novelists Revisited: Essays in Feminist Criticism,* ed. Fritz Fleischmann (Boston: G. K. Hall, 1982), pp. 162–64

PAUL DEAN

When Joan first appears in *1 Henry VI* she is tested by Reignier's pretending to be the Dauphin, a pretense she quickly exposes (I.ii.65). While she claims divine inspiration (I.ii.73–90, 113–16, 129) and is imaged as Deborah (I.ii.105), as "Astraea's daughter" (I.vi.4), and as "France's saint" (I.vi.29), she is also seen as Helen (I.ii.142), as Venus (I.ii.144), and as the focus of a number of sexual quibbles (e.g. I.ii.92–95, 111: see the notes on this passage in the New Arden). This doublesidedness culminates in her attempt to evade martyrdom by claiming to be pregnant, an explanation derided by the English as a parody of the Virgin Birth (V.iv.65). We are clearly meant to agree with the English that Joan is evil and to see in her sexual relationship with the Dauphin a symbolic joining of France to the powers of darkness. In V.iii we see her conjuring onstage "substitutes / Under the lordly monarch of the north" (l. 5ff.), devils to whom she vainly offers successively her blood, a limb, her body, and her soul (ll.14,15,18ff., 22) in return for a French victory. She then sees that her power is at an end, and the supernatural disappears until Part II.

Although Joan's methods are reprehensible, her motives are laudable and, as far as we can tell, genuinely patriotic; but in Part II Eleanor's fight is not national (against England) but personal (against the Queen); her motives are selfish and petty, and even Hume, her confederate, is privately in the pay of Suffolk and the Cardinal (I.ii.91–101). The whole atmosphere is much more sordid than in Part I. The raising of the spirit Asmoth (I.iv) to answer questions about the fates of the King, Suffolk, and Somerset is followed by the arrest of the necromancers by York and Buckingham, so the spirit works against Eleanor rather than for her; moreover his predictions, although correct, are useless not only to her but to those whose deaths they forecast, since York dismisses them as nonsense (I.iv.60ff.). In Part II the devils tell the truth: it is human beings who ignore or corrupt it.

This sketch of the supernaturalism in Parts I and II may well remind us of Dr. Faustus, whose search for knowledge through diabolic means also destroys him and gives him correct information upon which he cannot act. But unless we accept 1588 and not 1592 as the date of Dr. Faustus, we must look elsewhere for a source. Since the problem of the date is so vexed, I think we shall do better with a play whose date is fixed: Friar Bacon and Friar Bungay.

There is one striking parallel: an early proof of Bacon's powers is his seeing through the disguise of Prince Edward, the heir to the throne (scene v), just as Joan saw through the Dauphin's. Like Joan's, Friar Bacon's black magic is initially deployed for patriotic purposes, winning the King's approval by defeating the German court magician, Vandermast, in a contest treated by all present as an entertainment; his intervention to prevent the marriage of Margaret and Lacy by striking Friar Bungay mute is also more diverting than culpable. With the failure of the Brazen Head project the tone becomes more somber: Bacon admits that "I have dived into hell / And sought the darkest palaces of fiends" (xi.9ff.), that he has boasted "more than a man might boast" (xi.127). And when two students, looking into his crystal, see their fathers kill each other, whereupon they do likewise, he reproaches himself: "Bacon, thy magic doth effect this massacre" (xiii.75). But unlike Faustus, he recognizes the availability of grace for repentance and is accepted into the final festive banquet.

Shakespeare may be said to have split Bacon's attitude toward his magic into two parts: Joan dies unrepentant and cursing, Eleanor repents and is forgiven. Like Greene, Shakespeare also relates the supernatural theme to other themes in his play. For example, the Dauphin/Joan relationship is, as I noted earlier, reflective of the corruption of France; again, Joan's ambiguous nature (now saint, now witch) reflects the ambiguity of Fate in the play, the "bad, revolting stars" and "planets of mishap" (I.i.2, 4) whose government of human affairs seems arbitrary. In his emphasis on the sinister aspects of magic Shakespeare seems more akin to *Friar Bacon,* for all its prevalent festivity, than to *Dr. Faustus.*

—PAUL DEAN, "Shakespeare's *Henry VI* Trilogy and Elizabethan 'Romance'
Histories: The Origins of a Genre," *Shakespeare Quarterly* 18, No. 1
(Spring 1982): 37–39

STEPHEN WATT

In virtually every era of the Western theatre, the history play has been a hybrid genre of culturally validated serious or canonically "high" artistic matter and its opposite—namely, the sensationalistic, mundane, or canonically "low" conventions of popular drama. This was especially true of the Victorian history play, as the stage history of Victorian plays based on Joan of Arc's life indicates.

From 1871—the date of Taylor's *Jeanne d'Arc* and two subsequent *Joan* plays which allow Joan to be rescued by her lover at the last possible moment—until Shaw's *Saint Joan* in 1923, over a dozen plays or operas on this topic were produced in London. Shaw apparently saw only one of these, the American playwright Percy MacKaye's *Jeanne d'Arc* (1906), which Julia Marlowe and E. H. Sothern included in their repertory for an April 1907 run in London. More restrained than many of its predecessors, MacKaye's play nevertheless replicates several of the conventional simplifications Shaw associated with Irving at his worst: stumbling verse, an emphasis on Joan's visions which provided Sothern with numerous occasions for lavish stage-effects, and a contrived romantic relationship between Joan (Miss Marlowe) and d'Alençon (Sothern). As Marlowe's biographer Charles Edward Russell describes it, the Marlowe-Sothern production received "eloquent praise" from American critics chiefly because the play lent itself "splendidly" to "stage effects," and the parting scene between Joan and her lover was one of "poignant sorrow and truly great power." But London critics were not nearly so enthusiastic as their American colleagues. Marlowe's performance could not compensate for the play's soppy melodrama, gratuitous love interest, and at times unfortunate diction (at one point Joan is addressed as an "unvirgin thing"). Denounced by many as a mere marketable commodity with "correct" if cumbersome costumes (and Shaw echoed these denunciations), MacKaye's play and those like it *did* exert a strong influence on Shaw's *Saint Joan.*

Ivor Brown considered this influence in analyzing the success of the London production of the play (*Saint Joan* ran for 244 performances in London and 214 performances in New York). Brown suggested that some might attribute the play's success to Shaw's concession to popular taste:

The true disciples [of Shaw] must be expecting to visit a very bad play of which so much good has been said . . . The fact that she [Joan] fears no foe in shining armour has tricked the injudicious romantics into believing that Mr. Shaw has capitulated to the British theatre at last and given us the usual twaddling, romantic heroine.

Dismissing these "injudicious romantics," Brown maintains that the coats of mail in *Saint Joan* are only the trappings of Victorian "twaddle": under the coats pulse modern skin. I agree. But before examining the modern skin, I want to look somewhat more closely at the layers of tradition which covered it.

Melodrama. In assessing Shaw's indebtedness to the Victorian history play, Meisel points in particular to the similarities between Shaw's play and Taylor's *Jeanne d'Arc.* Meisel accurately identifies ways in which the plot of *Saint Joan* parallels that of Taylor's play: with the exceptions of Scene 1 (Joan at de Baudricourt's), Scene 4 (Cauchon's meeting with Warwick and de Stogumber), and the controversial Epilogue, Shaw's *Joan* follows more or less the plot construction of both MacKaye's and Taylor's plays. It might prove helpful to compare both versions of this construction:

Taylor's *Jeanne d'Arc*	Shaw's *Saint Joan*
Act I: Fairy Tree at Domremy	Scene 1: Joan at Baudricourt's Castle
Act II: Joan at Chinon—Charles' Court	Scene 2: Joan at Chinon
Act III: Joan's lodgings, at Gate of Burgundy, at Orleans	Scene 3: Joan and Dunois at Orleans
Act IV: Joan's lodging and the Cathedral at Rheims	Scene 4: Cauchon at Warwick's Tent
Act V: Court, Torture Chamber, and Market-Place at Rouen	Scene 5: Joan at Rheims
	Scene 6: Court at Rouen
	Epilogue

As this outline and Meisel suggest, Shaw deviates little from his predecessors in constructing his so-called "chronicle play." The episodes at Orleans, Rheims, and Rouen in particular afforded dramatists opportunities to juxtapose Joan's heroic innocence with the villainy both of Charles' court and Cauchon's clerics. These oppositions suit perfectly the general needs of most varieties of melodrama—an an innocent girl fighting English soldiers, sycophantic noblemen, and jealous clerics —which Shaw assiduously vowed to avoid. Though not completely successful in doing so, Shaw alters the Victorian tradition in more ways than Meisel implies.

For example, Shaw's opening scene departs from the romantic atmosphere most *Joan* plays (and Twain's *Personal Recollections of Joan of Arc*) create. Taylor, MacKaye, and Twain, to name but three, begin their histories with Joan at Domremy, enjoying with other French village girls (often her own sisters) springtime dances and songs. This kind of introductory scene allowed for the protestations of disgruntled suitors for Joan's hand and the coercions of a father suspicious of his daughter's refusal to marry. In Taylor's play and the anonymous Garrick Theatre *Joan* (1871), Joan's father returns later to betray her by accusing her of witchcraft. But as the Inquisitor in Shaw's play recognizes, stressing Joan's escapades in Domremy in effect casts her as a mere village maiden with common superstitions. For this reason the Inquisitor recommends that the prosecutors ignore Joan's activities in Domremy:

> I will ask you, therefore, to say nothing ... of these stealings of horses, and dancings round fairy trees with the village children, and prayings at haunted wells ... There is not a village girl in France against whom you could not prove such things: they all dance round haunted trees, and pray at magic wells.

In fact, most earlier Joans frolicked in enchanted forests. Also, the Domremy episodes typically produced one effect rendered superfluous by Shaw's insistence on the internal origin of Joan's voices: the creation of a climate appropriate for the appearance of one or all three of Joan's saints (and sometimes other more generic spectres like the Spirit of War in John Henderson's *Joan of Arc* [1896]). In brief, this traditional opening scene inaugurated both a series of spectacular effects and one of oppositions between an innocent country lass and villains who, in their antagonism to Joan, also stood against romance, spring, singing and dancing, and the Saints who guided Joan's actions. By omitting this kind of scene, Shaw places Joan and her ideas alone against her adversaries—and takes a good bit of the melodramatic and the spectacular, of the "romantic twaddle," out of Joan's history.

Nevertheless, as his prefatory remarks indicate, Shaw recognized that recasting his heroine would not completely rid his play of melodrama: he had to alter the traditional villains as well. Cauchon's meeting with Warwick and de Stogumber in Scene IV quite clearly serves this purpose. It constitutes, really for the first time on the London stage since Shakespeare's *1 Henry VI*, a significant explanation of the "villains' " motivations. Before Shaw, Joan's persecutors spoke only through short exchanges of dialogue and more often in snarling asides. On the Victorian stage, Joan's opponents were either dissolute French courtiers envious of her favor with Charles—La Trémouille, Flavy, and Des Chartes in MacKaye's play and L'Oislleurs in Taylor's—or power-hungry clerics like the Bishop of Winchester and, of course, Pierre Cauchon. In most *Joan* plays English military leaders play only perfunctory roles in Joan's downfall, and in Edwin Villiers' *Joan of Arc* (1871) Talbot's aide Lionel manages to rescue her from the stake. What better way to capitalize on the pro-British sentiment of much Victorian historical drama than to absolve British historical figures of complicity in Joan's burning, or to make them, in the case of Villiers' *Joan,* heroes who would risk their lives to save her?

Much more common, however, with the notable exception of MacKaye's *Joan,* are emphases on the machinations of Cauchon and his hired thugs in causing Joan's capture, ill-treatment, and execution. In these plays, as Shaw notes in his preface to *Saint Joan,* Cauchon stands as an emblem of cruelty, sadism, and unslaked villainy. One scene from Henderson's *Joan of Arc* in which Cauchon asks his henchman Loysoteur about Joan's forced confession might serve to underscore this characterization of the melodramatic villain; in his questioning Cauchon foreshadows the megalomania of, say, underworld leaders in American gangster films:

CAUCHON: Did she in your presence sign the parchment?
LOYSOTEUR: (suavely) She did—(with point)—or something like it.
CAUCHON: (with point also) Substantially the same, in fact—eh? ... Did she know and understand of what she was required to sign?

LOYSOTEUR: She cannot read or write, but I made her understand and she signed.

CAUCHON: Loysoteur, you are a gem!

In Twain's *Joan,* the narrator describes Cauchon as being "born a devil" and calls particular attention to his unnatural cruelty:

> Cauchon raged and cursed over his defeats and his impotence during seven days; then he conceived a new scheme. . . . The picture of Joan rose before me stretched upon the rack, her feet tied to one end of it, her wrists to the other, and those red giants turning the windlass and pulling her limbs out of their sockets.

While Shaw read Twain's *Joan* only after completing his own, he had seen quite enough of this sort of thing on the Victorian stage and recognized that it needed to be avoided.

Instead of raging and cursing, Shaw's Cauchon meets Warwick and de Stogumber to decide Joan's fate in a surprisingly rational, humane way. Cauchon explains the danger to the Catholic Church that Joan's personal vision and nationalism pose; he also sees in Joan a growing Nietzschean "Will to Power" that could destroy the class relations and institutional control he endorses. To his credit, Cauchon confesses his admiration of her military prowess and announces his adamant refusal to betray his anointed duty by neglecting her spiritual needs:

> I am no mere political bishop: my faith is to me what your honor is to you; and if there be a loophole through which this baptized child of God can creep to her salvation, I shall guide her to it.

A product of his society and Church's dominant ideology, his job is to "uphold the justice of the Church" and, at the same time, to "strive to the utmost" for Joan's "salvation." Warwick, too, who feels the need to preserve the feudal economy Joan threatens, expresses his sympathy for her and vows to "spare her" if he can. He cannot. Thus, in some senses Joan is executed by her admirers, men whose motives are creditable, if wrong. Scene IV of *Saint Joan* defines these motives as it illuminates Cauchon and Warwick not only as representatives of dominant ideology, but as products of it. At the same time, the scene allows Shaw to circumvent the melodramatic excesses of his predecessors.

Joan's most vitriolic adversary in Shaw's play is the blindly nationalistic John de Stogumber, a laughable caricature of British egotism and a feeble straw man for Shaw's satire to topple. Stogumber's unrelenting venom amuses Warwick and irritates Cauchon, and at base reveals the invidious depths of nationalistic bias, something Shaw had always despised—especially so after World War I. Insofar as this bias is directed at the Shavian world-historical hero, it adversely affects human history as Stogumber's outburst early in the scene confirms:

> Still, I have a feeling about it [England]; and I am not ashamed of it; . . . I will fling my cassock to the devil, and take arms myself, and strangle the accursed witch with my own hands.

Here Shaw accomplishes one clear reversal of the conventions of Victorian historical drama: passionate nationalism, the stock-in-trade of the Victorian hero, in Shaw's
play becomes a villain's weakness. Scene IV ends with each of the three "villains"
announcing his intentions in regard to Joan: Cauchon will attend to the Maid's
spiritual needs; Warwick will try to spare her; Stogumber will kill her with his own
hands.

In *Saint Joan*, then, Shaw *does* alter the melodramatic heroine-villain opposition that was so prominent both in *Joan* plays and other histories on the Victorian
stage (e.g., *'Twixt Axe and Crown, Jane Shore, The Armada, Becket,* and the like).
But, as Ivor Brown points out, Shaw's play still seems melodramatic in its presentation of an attractive heroine entrapped by powerful forces. And if the true villains
in *Saint Joan* are not historical figures, then they are institutions absolute in power
and inflexible in ideology:

> The crime of the burning cannot be washed away; if the judges were bought,
> the Church is less culpable, since basely served. If they were true, faithful
> Churchmen, then the whiter their hands the blacker the Church.

The audiences in 1923 and 1924 who attended Shaw's play seemed to find Joan's
fate poignant and responded in the same highly emotional ways Victorian audiences
responded to Wills' *Charles the First* and *Jane Shore*. Stanley Weintraub recalls that
when T. E. Lawrence attended the London production of *Saint Joan* in July of 1924
he "noticed that people in the audience, each having his own point of maximum
impact, cried at different moments in the play." Plays of ideas alone—as Shaw's
plays have often been characterized—seldom evoked tears or ran for 244 performances.

Pictorial realism. In his Preface, Shaw acknowledges and thanks those critics
who were "genuinely enthusiastic" about *Joan,* but also upbraids those "experienced" stage managers who would substitute "realistic" and "elaborate scenery" for
much of the play's rhetoric—real water in the Loire, real bridges, real horses, and
sham fights. Shaw seemed certain that these changes would be effected when he
was "no longer in control of the performing rights" to the play, implying that the
New Theatre production of *Saint Joan* did not accede to the demand for pictorial
realism. But reviews present another view of this matter, alleging that the staging of
the play at times almost overwhelmed Shaw's rhetoric.

At least in the absence of clumsy stage apparatuses and elaborate spectacle,
Saint Joan departed significantly from the excesses of Victorian spectacular drama.
This departure is most evident in the staging of Joan's victory at Orleans and in her
execution at Rouen. The siege of Orleans, as Shaw was seemingly aware, func-
tioned in most Victorian *Joan* plays as the sensationalistic climax to which the first
two acts of these plays moved. That is, in virtually every Victorian *Joan* play a long
and spectacular seige of Orleans occupied the exact middle of the text, Act III of
the conventional five-act structure. Conversely, Shaw's scene at Orleans is the
shortest in the entire play. This fact alone hints at his devaluation of the tradition he
had inherited.

Shaw's Orleans scene consists entirely of dialogue between Dunois, his page, and Joan, and thus is devoid of the trappings of spectacular drama. No heroic British soldiers (usually Glasdale, Talbot, or Lionel) appear fighting valiantly for Saint George and England. The page's puny cheer at the scene's end underscores the absence of the "big ending" to which this scene led on the Victorian stage, an ending of flag waving and loud cheering. Further, on the Victorian stage the Orleans scene was generally composed of relatively few lines of dialogue; instead, producers employed elaborate stage maneuvers to paint an intricately-detailed, enormous stage picture. In Taylor's play, for example, a fierce battle dominates the scene. Cannons on wheeled carriages fire from the wings; French troops, some of whom are "hurled" into a moat, raise ladders against the towers of the Tourelles as cannoneers and crossbowmen shoot "continuously." Finally, Joan appears on horseback to proclaim France's victory, a proclamation met with celebratory approval and wild jubilation. MacKaye's scene at Orleans proves the exception to this tradition, concluding, as Shaw's does, with a lone page cheering Joan and France.

These facts aside, the popularity of the 1924 London production of *Saint Joan* was in part due to its pictorial quality. Even Johan Huizinga, who was greatly disturbed by the comic moments of the play, praised Charles Ricketts' "realistic" stage design: "I must admit that I have never seen more convincing historical staging than this work of Ricketts. I have in mind in particular the first court entry and the tent scene. . . ." According to Huizinga, the New Theatre production of *Saint Joan* also adhered to the Victorian theatre's demand for historical accuracy by selecting an actor to play Warwick whose facial type had "clearly been copied from the gilded bronze likeness on the Earl's tomb at Warwick." Ivor Brown shared Huizinga's admiration for the production's pictorial quality and intimated that Ricketts' superior craftsmanship at times superseded Shaw's rhetoric: "Mr. Ricketts has done the decoration so handsomely that, by feasting the eye, he is in danger of putting the mind to sleep." In the final analysis, *Saint Joan*'s attractions on the stage are partly the result of a convention which Shaw despised. Without considerable concessions to this tradition, the play might never have been so well received. Yet *Saint Joan* is also much more: in its innovative dramatic form and historical implications Shaw's play helps inaugurate the tradition of the modern historical drama.

—STEPHEN WATT, "Shaw's *Saint Joan* and the Modern History Play,"
Comparative Drama 19, No. 1 (Spring 1985): 66–73

PHYLLIS RACKIN

The pattern of masculine history-writing and feminine subversion is probably clearest in *1 Henry VI*. Here Shakespeare defines the project of writing English history as an effort to preserve the legacy of English glory left by Henry V and associates it with the masculine, military struggle to secure English power in France. Michel Foucault's observation that the Greek epic "was intended to perpetuate the immortality of the hero" aptly characterizes Shakespeare's conception of history at this point in his career. In Foucault's view, the hero's death represents a kind of trade-off between the hero and his story: "if he was willing to die young, it was so that his life, consecrated and magnified by death, might pass into immortality."

The process by which human mortality is translated into textual immortality was a frequent theme for Renaissance theorists of historiography as well as for Shakespearean sonnets. However, a problem arises—as it did for historians during Shakespeare's own lifetime—when history, the second party to this trade, comes to be seen as itself subject to mutability. Various forces were conspiring in Shakespeare's time to compel a recognition that the historical past was not necessarily identical with the historiographic text. Faced with a growing sense of alienation from the past, a newly critical attitude toward texts, and an increasing reliance on physical remains to verify or refute verbal reports, the medieval union of history and myth was breaking down. Written accounts of the past were no longer accepted as authentic simply because they existed. Like the Bible itself, historical writing no longer had a direct, unequivocal relation to truth. Translated into the vernacular, subjected to different interpretations from rival Christian sects, the Bible had become a problematic document in which alternative words contended to translate the meaning of the original text and alternative interpretations contended to explicate it. In a similar way, alternative accounts of historical events and opposed interpretations of their causes and significance now threatened to disrupt each other's authority. Thus undermined, history loses its power to make the hero immortal. In such a case, the hero's death becomes meaningless, and heroism itself becomes impossible.

This is the problem dramatized in *I Henry VI*. The play begins as history itself begins, with (or immediately following) the death of the hero. The opening scene depicts the funeral of Henry V, the legendary warrior-king who was, we are told, "too famous to live long" (l.i.6); and the entire play can be seen as a series of attempts on the part of the English to write a history that will preserve Henry's fame. That conflict begins in the opening scene when the audience (along with their countrymen on stage) are confronted with reports of French victories that threaten to erase Henry's name from the historical record as surely as death has destroyed his body. Bedford's heroic invocation of Henry's ghost, implying that the dead king will occupy a place in history even more glorious than Julius Caesar's, is interrupted mid-sentence by a messenger bringing news that eight French cities have been lost.

The French action—to erase the English record—operates at two levels. Within the represented action, the French fight to drive the English from their country. At the rhetorical level, they attack both the English version of history and the values it expresses with an earthy iconoclasm that subverts the inherited notions of chivalric glory invoked by the English. Talbot, the English champion, and Joan, his French antagonist, speak alternative languages. His language reifies glory, while hers is the language of physical objects; and the play defines their conflict as a contest between English words and French things, between the historical record that Talbot wishes to preserve and the physical reality that Joan invokes to discredit it. Shakespeare departs from his sources in having Talbot bury Salisbury, one of the last English heroes of the former age, in France. The real Salisbury was buried in

England, but Shakespeare's Talbot announces that he will erect Salisbury's tomb in the "chiefest temple" of the French "Upon the which, that every one may read, / Shall be engrav'd the sack of Orleans, / The treacherous manner of his mournful death, / And what a terror he had been to France" (II.ii.13–17). Talbot's effort here, as in his military campaign to secure Henry's French conquests, is a struggle to leave an English historical record in France.

Shakespeare repeatedly calls attention to the fact that the French champion is a woman, thereby defining the conflict between England and France as a conflict between masculine and feminine values—chivalric virtue vs. pragmatic craft, historical fame vs. physical reality, patriarchal age vs. subversive youth, high social rank vs. low, self vs. other. "English Talbot" is a venerable gentleman who fights according to the chivalric code. Joan is a youthful peasant whose forces resort to craft, subterfuge, and modern weapons (a French boy sniper shoots the great Salisbury, and Joan recaptures Rouen by sneaking in, disguised as the peasant she really is, to admit the French army).

In addition to Joan, *I Henry VI* includes two other female characters—the Countess of Auvergne and Margaret of Anjou. All three are French, and all three represent threats to the English protagonists and to the heroic values associated with history as the preserver of masculine fame and glory. Like Joan, the Countess attacks Talbot; like Joan, she resorts to craft and stratagem; and like Joan she places her faith in physical reality over verbal report. The Countess says she wants to verify the reports of Talbot's glory by seeing his person: "Fain would mine eyes be witness with mine ears / To give their censure of these rare reports." What she sees—"a child, a silly dwarf. . . . a weak and writhled shrimp," in short, Talbot's physical appearance—convinces her that "report is fabulous and false" (II.iii.9–22).

The Countess's preference for physical evidence over historical report associates her with the French and female forces in the play as a threat to the project of writing English history. We see this conflict in its purest form after Talbot's death when Sir William Lucy calls for him in heroic language:

> But where's the great Alcides of the field,
> Valiant Lord Talbot, Earl of Shrewsbury,
> Created for his rare success in arms
> Great Earl of Washford, Waterford, and Valence,
> Lord Talbot of Goodrig and Urchinfield,
> Lord Strange of Blackmere, Lord Verdun of Alton
> Cromwell of Wingfield, Furnival of Sheffield,
> The thrice victorious Lord of Falconbridge,
> Knight of the noble order of Saint George,
> Worthy Saint Michael, and the Golden Fleece,
> Great Marshal to Henry the Sixth
> Of all his wars within the realm of France?   [IV.vii.60–71]

Rejecting the grandiose pretentions in the string of titles Lucy bestows on Talbot and relying on material fact to debunk the titles and attack Lucy's language, Joan replies:

Here is a silly-stately style indeed!
The Turk, that two and fifty kingdoms hath,
Writes not so tedious a style as this.
Him that thou magnifiest with all these titles,
Stinking and fly-blown lies here at our feet.   [IV.vii.72–76]

Lucy describes Talbot as history was to describe him, decked in the titles that designate his patriarchal lineage and heroic military achievements. Joan, like the Countess, insists on physical fact, rejecting the masculine historical ideals and significance that Lucy's glorious names invoke.

Joan's reductive, nominalistic attack has an obvious appeal for an audience: her vigorous language, tied to the material facts of earth, threatens to topple the imposing formal edifice Lucy has constructed with his tower of names. But in this, the first of Shakespeare's English history plays, the subversive female voice is never allowed to prevail for more than a moment, and it is tempting to speculate that at least some in Shakespeare's audience may have realized that the glorious words of Lucy, unlike Joan's fictitious speech, take their authority from an enduring historical monument, Talbot's tomb at Rouen, where they were inscribed. ⟨...⟩

This final schematic contrast between the strong bond that unites the male Talbots and Joan's denial of her peasant father completes Shakespeare's picture of Talbot and Joan as opposites and connects the various terms in which their opposition has been defined—historian vs. anti-historian, noble man vs. peasant woman, realist vs. nominalist. As Kenneth Burke has pointed out, the medieval realist conception of language had strong affinities with the medieval feudal conception of the family, for both realism and feudalism treat "individuals as members of a group" or "tribe." In direct contrast, nominalism, the subversive movement in medieval philosophy, is "linguistically individualistic or atomistic," because it treats "groups as aggregates of individuals." Realism and feudalism both imply history because both involve what Burke calls "an *ancestral* notion." A realist conception of language holds that universals precede things and "give birth" to them. Nominalism, like Joan, denies history because it denies the diachronic links that unite meaning and word like the successive generations of a great feudal family (the kind of family whose name the Talbots die to preserve). Drawing the same kind of connections, R. Howard Bloch associates the story of Abelard's castration with the fact of Abelard's nominalism: just as Abelard's intellectual position disrupted the "intellectual genealogy" of words, so too is his own physical genealogy represented as disrupted. And, although Bloch does not mention it, the castration, like the nominalism, also associates Abelard with the feminine.

Joan's sexual promiscuity, hinted from the first, is less obviously connected than her nominalism to her role as anti-historian, but it is connected nonetheless. Just as her nominalism associates her with the Countess of Auvergne, so her sexual promiscuity associates her with the third French woman in the play, Margaret of Anjou, soon to become the adulterous queen of Henry VI. Immediately linked to Joan in the audience's eyes, Margaret is introduced by being led captive onto the stage at the same time that Joan is led off it after her final capture. Moreover, we quickly learn in *2 Henry VI* that the marriage between Margaret and Henry threatens to erase history itself:

> Fatal this marriage, cancelling your fame,
> Blotting your names from books of memory,
> Razing the characters of your renown
> Defacing monuments of conquer'd France,
> Undoing all as all had never been!   [I.i.98–102]

—PHYLLIS RACKIN, "Anti-Historians: Women's Roles in Shakespeare's Histories," Theatre Journal 37, No. 3 (October 1985): 330–33, 335–36

J. L. WISENTHAL

Saint Joan was published in the year in which the Dutch historian Johan Huizinga's classic study *The Waning of the Middle Ages* first appeared in English translation. This coincidence is a reminder of an important aspect of Shaw's play. One of its main subjects is the encounter between the late Middle Ages and the beginnings of the Renaissance. Shaw claimed in the Preface to have taken care to let the medieval atmosphere blow through his play freely, and he told Sydney Cockerell that 'Ruskin and Morris and all the painters were on the job before me' in working over the historical background of the play. In a newspaper interview he went so far as to describe his play as 'a dialogue dealing with religion and with the politics of the Middle Ages'. The Middle Ages in the play, however, are the old epoch that is on the verge of giving way to the Renaissance and modernity. The encounter between one historical epoch and its successor is evident in Joan's first appearance on the stage:

> JOAN [*bobbing a curtsey*]. Good morning, captain squire. Captain: you are to give me a horse and armor and some soldiers, and send me to the Dauphin. Those are your orders from my Lord.
> ROBERT [*outraged*]. Orders from your lord! And who the devil may your lord be? Go back to him, and tell him that I am neither duke nor peer at his orders: I am squire of Baudricourt; and I take no orders except from the king.
> JOAN [*reassuringly*]. Yes, squire: that is all right. My Lord is the King of Heaven.
> ROBERT. Why, the girl's mad.   (Scene i)

In the distinction between Joan's sense of 'my Lord' and Baudricourt's we see the clash between the Middle Ages and the Renaissance, between the declining epoch and the rising one. As E. M. W. Tillyard says in *Shakespeare's History Plays* about Richard and Bolingbroke in *Richard II*, 'We have in fact the contrast not only of two characters but of two ways of life', and Shakespeare's Richard is the medieval king supplanted by the more modern Bolingbroke thirty years before the time of *Saint Joan*.

In the conflict between the Middle Ages and the Renaissance the play and its author are on both sides at once. Everyone has noticed the play's effort to be fair to the Church, and this is not simply a dramatic technique, but an expression of Shaw's historical values and judgements. Some of the dramatic strength of *Saint Joan* derives from the collision in Shaw's own mind between the Feudal, Catholic values of the Middle Ages and the Capitalist, Protestant values of the Renaissance— between the collective will of a society acting in concert and the energetic individual will that rebels against social authority. Or to put this in more biographical terms, one could say that the play reflects a conflict between Shaw's Protestant background and his exposure to the Medievalist movement of Victorian England. When the man who admired William Morris and described *Candida* as a Pre-Raphaelite play came to write a major play about the Middle Ages, he chose as his subject the breaking up of the era. Whereas the Preface, with its approving talk about the cry of 'Back to the Middle Ages', is written in the William Morris tradition, the play itself celebrates the Renaissance forces of individualism, Protestantism, and Nationalism, and dramatizes the waning of the Middle Ages as a necessary, progressive, and beneficial historical development. And the conflict is not only between the Preface and the play, but within the play itself. The play has something of the quality that Matthew Arnold attributed to the disinterested criticism which recognizes the defects of Protestantism but 'will not on that account forget the achievements of Protestantism in the practical and moral sphere; nor that, even in the intellectual sphere, Protestantism, though in a blind and stumbling manner, carried forward the Renascence, while Catholicism threw itself violently across its path'. Joan's unde- clared, unconscious mission is to destroy medieval civilization, and a production of the play should not allow us to see her only as a positive heroine, but also as a heedlessly destructive force confronting a civilization that is of value in spite of its blindness and rigidity. The Middle Ages must die, but the epoch has its dignity and beauty—a beauty that should be expressed powerfully in the sets and costumes, to remind us of the value of what is being lost.

'I really cannot keep my temper over the Elizabethan dramatists and the Renaissance', Shaw declared in writing about *Macbeth* in 1895. In the early seven- teenth century, 'every art was corrupted to the marrow by the orgie called the Renaissance, which was nothing but the vulgar exploitation in the artistic professions of the territory won by the Protestant movement'. This sounds like the voice of the Victorian Medievalist, but the next sentence begins with a reference to Protestant- ism as 'that great self-assertion of the growing spirit of man', and once again we can see both sides of Shaw's historical outlook. In *Saint Joan* the emphasis is on Prot- estantism as that great self-assertion of the growing spirit of man, rather than on the Renaissance as an orgy of vulgar artistic exploitation. In considering the play, we are less likely to think of Shaw's connection with William Morris and more likely to think of his background as he described it in the Preface to *John Bull's Other Island:* 'I am a genuine typical Irishman of the Danish, Norman, Cromwellian, and (of course) Scotch invasions. I am violently and arrogantly Protestant by family tradition.' We might also bear in mind the subtitle that Shaw suggested to his publisher for *The*

Perfect Wagnerite in 1898, 'the New Protestantism', and consider the chapter entitled 'Siegfried as Protestant', parts of which read like a description of Joan in the play. Joan's question at her trial, 'What other judgment can I judge by but my own?', is a declaration of Protestant revolt against the fundamental assumptions of the Middle Ages. Buckle called the Reformation 'neither more nor less than open rebellion': 'To establish the right of private judgment, was to appeal from the church to individuals; it was to increase the play of each man's intellect; it was to test the opinions of the priesthood by the opinions of laymen; it was, in fact, a rising of the scholars against their teachers, of the ruled against their rulers.' This is the spirit that Joan represents, and Shaw in selecting her as a Protestant heroine seems to be allying himself not only with Buckle but with Carlyle, who declared that Luther's speech to the Diet of Worms ('Here stand I; I can do no other: God assist me!') was 'the greatest moment in the Modern History of Men'.

On the other hand, Joan, as the incarnation of the Renaissance spirit, represents more in the play than the beneficial assertion of individual judgement. For one thing, she represents modern warfare. She tells Dunois that the French army cannot rely on horses but needs plenty of artillery (Scene iii), and that his medieval art of war is of no use because his knights are no good for real fighting.

> JOAN. . . . War is only a game to them, like tennis and all their other games: they
> make rules as to what is fair and what is not fair, and heap armor on
> themselves and on their poor horses to keep out the arrows; and when
> they fall they cant get up, and have to wait for their squires to come and
> lift them to arrange about the ransom with the man that has poked them
> off their horse. Cant you see that all the like of that is gone by and done
> with? What use is armor against gunpowder? And if it was, do you think
> men that are fighting for France and for God will stop to bargain about
> ransoms, as half your knights live by doing? No: they will fight to win; and
> they will give up their lives out of their own hand into the hand of God
> when they go into battle, as I do.   (Scene v)

A full response to *Saint Joan* must involve the awareness that it was written just five years after the end of the First World War, and that the War was the greatest transforming and disillusioning experience in Shaw's life. To read or watch the play without having the War in one's mind is to miss its ironic perspective, and a production should make an audience feel that Joan is a threat as well as a saint. For the fulfilment of her notions of the new warfare was manifested in the trenches of France and Belgium almost 500 years later.

Joan represents the modern warfare that made the horrors of 1914–18 possible, and also the spirit of Nationalism that led to the First World War. The play links these two post-medieval developments in that Joan's methods of warfare are in the service of a Nationalist objective. She says to Dunois in the Epilogue, when she learns that the English have now been expelled from France: 'And you fought them *my* way, Jack: eh? Not the old way, chaffering for ransoms; but The Maid's way: staking life against death ... nothing counting under God but France free and

French.' The men fight to win because they are fighting for their own nation. In *Geneva* (1936), in which we see national rivalries that will lead to a second world war, we find a different perspective on Nationalist warfare. In this play, the Secretary of the League of Nations declares that 'We need something higher than nationalism: a genuine political and social catholicism. How are you to get that from these patriots, with their national anthems and flags and dreams of war and conquest rubbed into them from their childhood? The organization of nations is the organization of world war' (Act II).

In *Saint Joan,* Joan's Nationalism is made to sound appealing, but she is not the only Nationalist on the stage. In the Tent Scene, Cauchon issues a threat to de Stogumber: 'If you dare do what this woman has done—set your country above the holy Catholic Church—you shall go to the fire with her.' The dangers of the forces that Joan represents are reflected in de Stogumber's presence in the play. He connects, in the mind of the audience, Joan's Nationalism with the fanaticism that led to and flourished during the War. Shaw wrote in the 1919 Preface to *Heartbreak House* that during the War 'There was a frivolous exultation in death for its own sake, which was at bottom an inability to realize that the deaths were real deaths and not stage ones'; this is precisely de Stogumber's attitude towards the burning of Joan, as he himself discovers to his horror near the end of the Trial Scene. Thus the play provides the audience with evidence to support the fears of Cauchon that Joan's challenge to the established authority of the Middle Ages will lead to universal war:

> CAUCHON. . . . What will the world be like when The Church's accumulated wisdom and knowledge and experience, its councils of learned, venerable pious men, are thrust into the kennel by every ignorant laborer or dairymaid whom the devil can puff up with the monstrous self-conceit of being directly inspired from heaven? It will be a world of blood, of fury, of devastation, of each man striving for his own hand: in the end a world wrecked back into barbarism. . . . Call this side of her heresy Nationalism if you will: I can find you no better name for it. I can only tell you that it is essentially anti-Catholic and anti-Christian; for the Catholic Church knows only one realm, and that is the realm of Christ's kingdom. Divide that kingdom into nations, and you dethrone Christ. Dethrone Christ, and who will stand between our throats and the sword? The world will perish in a welter of war. (Scene iv)

Joan's Nationalism, which is inseparable from her Protestant individualism, carries the threat of international anarchy.

Joan's Renaissance individualist values have also led to another modern iniquity: Capitalism. She asserts her individual will against the communal authority of the day, and Cauchon predicts that such rebellion will lead to a world 'of each man striving for his own hand' (Scene iv). The play does not anachronistically place Joan's individualism in a modern economic context, but a thoughtful, educated, twentieth-century audience might be expected to do so. Shaw himself makes such a connection in discussing the case of Galileo in *Everybody's Political What's What?*, where he sounds much closer to *Saint Joan's* Inquisitor than to the Maid herself. The case, he argues, 'is usually written of as a persecution of a great observer and fearless reasoner by a pack of superstitious, narrow-minded, ignorant priests. This is mere Protestant scurrility.' The Church had to govern simple illiterate people, and 'If Galileo were to tell the people that Joshua should have stopped the earth instead of the sun, and that the story must have been invented by somebody so unlike God as to be grossly ignorant of astronomy, their faith would be shattered; and Christendom would collapse in an orgy of selfish lawlessness.' The Church, it turned out, was quite right, as Galileo himself acknowledged. 'Sure enough, when the truth got about, what the priests feared did largely happen. The quest of salvation gave way to the quest of commercial profits; and Manchester supplanted Rome as the headquarters of civilization.' Elsewhere in this book Shaw wrote of Capitalism as a 'revolution in economic morality, fitting neatly into the great Protestant revolution called The Reformation and The Renascence', and he observed that the Wars of the Roses (which began in 1455, the year before Joan's Rehabilitation, the time of the Epilogue) exterminated the old Feudal nobility 'and gave its powers to a new self-ennobled plutocracy'.

If we look at Joan from the point of view of the declining Middle Ages, then she appears as a necessary and progressive force in history. This is the main perspective within *Saint Joan*, but the play is written for a twentieth-century audience, and from our point of view Joan represents the forces that are now the established ones in our society. Joan's independence of spirit, power of imagination, and strength of will are of enduring, timeless value as human qualities, but the play is not only personal but rather mainly historical in its focus, and the historical forces that Joan incarnates on the stage must now be superseded. Joan is the harbinger of the era that is now waning. Protestant individualism, with its economic and international political implications, is in the position now that the Roman Catholic Church and the Feudal nobility occupied in the fifteenth century. Forward-looking people in the twentieth century will look at the Renaissance in the way that Joan unconsciously looked at the values of the Middle Ages, as the old era that we must move beyond.

—J. L. WISENTHAL, "The Middle Ages, the Renaissance, and After,"
Shaw's Sense of History (Oxford: Clarendon Press, 1988), pp. 83–91

CRITICAL ESSAYS

Johan Huizinga

BERNARD SHAW'S SAINT

I. The Play and Its Performance

If there had been one miracle too few to warrant the canonization of Joan of Arc, it might have been brought forward that she has been able to wipe the grimace from Shaw's joking countenance and to force that acrobat, eternally turning somersaults about the crossbar of his ingenuity, to his knees for a moment. No one has the right to demand from the master of satiric comedy that he should refrain from every witticism and comic effect throughout a sixty-two-page Preface and a performance of three hours and a half. But, even aside from the effect of the play itself, the mere fact that this time one can read the Preface with hardly a shrug of the shoulders is proof that something unusual is happening. Shaw, in whose hands Caesar and "the man of destiny" grew small and foolish, has now experienced the power of the heroic, and whether he would or no, has written in the humble service of his incomparable subject.

The more one thinks about it, the greater the miracle seems. A person with the limitations of Shaw, that man with the utterly prosaic mind (in the good sense of the word) who appears so alien to everything that seems to us to be noblest in the Middle Ages and most essential in the history of Joan of Arc—the Catholic faith, late Gothic life, the pure, clear tone of the French spirit—what will such a person make of it all?

What he has made of it is certainly a peculiar product, and there are any number of objections, from both the artistic and the historical point of view. Meanwhile, the play is traveling through the world, and it attracts people (not only because it is Shaw), moves and affects them—and uplifts them. Shaw has once more posed a problem: this time, in spite of himself, the problem of his success. There is perhaps sufficient reason to offer a historian's marginal notes on this play

From *Men and Ideas: History, the Middle Ages, the Renaissance*, translated by James S. Holmes and Hans van Marle (New York: Free Press, 1959), pp. 207–39. First published in 1925.

that everyone has seen or read, or both. For the most part these notes have to do with Shaw's conception of the historical figure of Joan of Arc, but as a result they unavoidably touch on an evaluation of the play and its performance as well.

The task that Shaw has set himself approximates the highest task the human mind has succeeded, a few times, in accomplishing: the creation of tragedy from history. Who, aside from the Greek tragedians and Shakespeare, has actually succeeded in bringing before the eye in one close-knit image, and in its most essential and exalted significance, something that once actually happened? (Or is reputed to have happened; it makes no difference whether the subject is the Seven against Thebes, sunk into the shadows of legend, or Henry VIII, dead by Shakespeare's time no longer than a good half century.) Shaw has attempted the task, completely aware of its requirements. And attempted it with material that has increased the demands, because it is historically so extraordinarily detailed, so sharply delineated, and so fully documented, and because the mere historical account is itself so chock-full of the transcendent emotions that drama attempts to arouse: the classical combination of sympathy and fear, the shuddering admiration for the hero, the being carried away by the sweep of inevitable events, the indefinable yet so clearly conscious catharsis. In *Hamlet* all the tragic element is the work of the poet; the dramatizer of Joan of Arc may be happy if he does no more than to allow the organ tone of history itself to reverberate as purely as possible.

In constructing his tragedy, Shaw comprehended one important principle: that, in Hegel's phrase (it is rather a surprise not to find it quoted in the Preface), the truly tragic is not to be found in the conflict between right and wrong, but in that between right and right. Joan of Arc surrounded by nothing but cowards and rascals might be a romantic figure, but not a dramatic one. Yet Joan as the superior being crushed between two tremendous and necessary powers, the Church and the interests of the State, is the very personification of the tragic heroine. In its deeper foundations, history is much closer to the tragic conception of the past than to the romantic. In the historical analysis of a conflict the sense of an awesome inevitability, of the relative justness of both sides, always appears as the final result. The romantic emotion, that is to say, the polarization of the pathetic, the passionate, the personal in events, is a sentiment of a more superficial sort.

Speaking generally, then, it was not necessary for Shaw to do violence to history in presenting the judges as limited but respectable persons, and Pierre Cauchon, the bishop of Beauvais, with even a touch of greatness (whether he as a person deserved it will be discussed below); in depicting Dunois, the Bastard of Orléans, as a normal egoist of good will; and in attempting to convince us of the justness, on a lower level, of the archbishop of Reims's anxious diplomacy and the excusability of Dauphin Charles's defeatism. In doing so he could, with some justification, feel that he was the mouthpiece of history. And he is no little proud of the role. In his opinion, he has captured the historical essence of the events. The words he puts into the mouths of his personages Cauchon, the inquisitor Lemaître, and the Earl of Warwick as personifications of the Church, the Inquisition, and Feudalism "are the things they actually would have said if they had known what they were really doing. . . ." As for Saint Joan herself, the play "contains all that need be known about her." Does Shaw really think that we do not want to know anything more? Does he not understand that every word she spoke, every detail of her appearance and her actions is dear to us? If not, then he does not know the true nature of historical interest. But in the last analysis it is not a view of the past which Shaw is concerned with, but the lesson that the "case" of Joan still has to teach. "If it were only an historical curiosity I would not waste my readers' time and my own on it for five minutes." Here is the usual misconception of the nature and value of the historical sense: the things of the past, as we observe them, are of themselves nothing more than curiosities, unless a pragmatic application to the questions of today can be deduced from them. History, however, takes its revenge on Shaw.

It goes without saying that no blame is due the dramatist for his deliberate abbreviation of the reality of history, for instance, his condensation of the questioning, the sentence, the abjuration, the relapse, and the execution into one single scene. That he gave Warwick the place where the regent Bedford should have stood had good grounds dramatically, since he wished to personify the old aristocratic principle in resistance to the emergent monarchy, and for that the noble Warwick was more suitable than Bedford, a prince of the blood royal. That the honor of holding the cross before Joan, due Brother Isambard de la Pierre, is enjoyed by Martin Ladvenu will cause a twinge of pain only to a scholar at home with all the details of the story. For all his vagueness I prefer the unknown Master John Tressard, the royal secretary, who said, bitterly weeping, "we are all lost, for it was a good and holy woman that has been burned," to Chaplain de Stogumber, the jingo *avant la lettre* whom Shaw has built up out of the single phrase *quidam cappellanus Cardinalis Angliae* ["a certain chaplain of the cardinal of England"] from the record of the rehabilitation trial. But it is Shaw's perfect right to create such a character if it is necessary for the play.

Nor do inadvertent inaccuracies affect the play's worth. If Shaw thinks that it sounds better for the dauphin to say, "Anne will want new dresses," we are happy to forget that the queen's name was Marie d'Anjou, and even more so that it was not until ten years after 1429 that the Bastard of Orléans became Dunois. It is merely the schoolmaster in me who cannot refrain from mentioning such trifles.

Regarding faithfulness to history, however, Shaw pretends to much more than a painstaking accuracy in details, which he thinks of little matter. "The ideal biographer," he says (and that is, in a sense, what he considers himself), "must understand the Middle Ages . . . much more intimately than our Whig historians have ever understood them." The Middle Ages were a period "of which the thinking has passed out of fashion, and the circumstances no longer apply to active life. . . ." But Shaw knows them, thanks to the progress in the field of historical studies: "I write in full view of the Middle Ages, which may be said to have been rediscovered in the middle of the nineteenth century after an eclipse of about four hundred and fifty years. . . . Now there is not a breath of medieval atmosphere in Shakespeare's histories." Is there then, in *Saint Joan?* Here one's eyebrows rise automatically.

At this point we approach the almost bewildering questions raised by Shaw's play. For it is not only a question of the extent to which the play breathes a medieval atmosphere, but also of whether the presence or absence of such an atmosphere detracts from the play's dramatic effect and value. On this last point one's immediate response is a very definite Yes.

Today's general reader has his mind's eye too sharply focused on the differences in times for him to be able to endure any gross internal anachronism. Joan of Arc is too firmly anchored in French history of the fifteenth century to be able to serve as a timeless dramatic personage such as Phaedra or Alcestis. The drama of Saint Joan must transport us to the Middle Ages as we see them. Does Shaw's play do this? I should not dare say No straightaway, but even less so Yes. The archbishop of Reims strikes one as remarkably Anglican, and seems a cousin to the bishop in *Getting Married*. In the English production, which was rather overacted compared with the Dutch, the dauphin is all too much the spoiled Eton boy. The comic element in La Hire is quite acceptable and in no sense disturbing, but the whole tone of the dialogue, the sheerly farcical effect of the page who pounds for silence with the halberd is all too Shavian to seem medieval.

Yet is it actually the lack of a sense of the time that hampers us? Is it not rather that this lack is inseparably linked with a dramatic deficiency of a much more serious sort: the lack of a high style? I do not mean literary style, of course, but dramatic style. Shaw's play would have gained nothing and would have lost a great deal if the dialogue had been filled with archaic grandiloquence and Walter Scott-like solemnity. And it is a moot question whether that would have made it more "genuinely" medieval. The fifteenth-century *novella,* Villon, and Joan herself in her answers to her judges are testimonies enough that colloquial speech in those days could be as fluent and free as our own. What we miss is something else: the transportation of our minds into a sphere where each emotion and passion has acquired a higher potential, each word affects more deeply and resonates more fully than in everyday life. There is, says Shaw, not a breath of medieval atmosphere in Shakespeare's histories. No, perhaps not, in the technically historical sense. But there is an abundance of the high dramatic style which casts a light on the difference in times without revealing it completely. For all its mannerisms, I know no historical drama that is more real and genuine than *Richard II*. It is utterly Elizabethan, and not at all late-fourteenth-century, but even so Shakespeare, with only his knowledge from Holinshed, came closer than any chronicler to the core of the historical character of the last Plantagenet.

Tragedy may be anything but sheerly natural and realistic. Shaw shuns the romantic like the plague: it is his perfect right to do so, but by using familiarity and humor to fumigate his work of the romantic he also banishes the heroic. To dramatize the heroic virtues of Saint Joan of Arc no less a style than the stern forms of Greek tragedy or the individual genius of Shakespeare will do.[1] And that is also the reason why, before Shaw, no one else had any better success in dramatizing the Maid.

*   *   *

Once one has realized, on reading *Saint Joan,* that it is too closely akin to *Man and Superman* and the rest of Shaw to be a satisfactory dramatization of its noble subject, it comes as a great surprise on seeing it to discover that the play is not only an exciting but also an affecting and elevating experience. This is undoubtedly so, in part (to leave aside the skill of the actors), because of Shaw's vivid depiction: the excellent dialogue at the court before Joan's entrance, the conversation between Warwick and Cauchon, the Inquisitor (especially in O. B. Clarence's portrayal as a blushing, debonair graybeard in the London production). Still, the high points of the play are precisely those where the author merely presents certain essential elements of the action itself: the irresistible bravery with which Joan swept away the dauphin and the court, the simplicity of the words we know she really spoke. Shaw is at his best when he sticks closest to history. "Be you Bastard of Orleans?" This is the very phrase, Dunois testified in 1455, with which Joan first greeted him. Shaw formulated as faithfully as possible from the records of the hearings themselves all Joan's answers to the judges, among them the moving reply to the query whether she thought that she was in a state of grace: "If I am not, may God bring me to it; if I am, may God keep me in it!"

It is my impression that the play achieves its deepest effect almost beyond Shaw's own activity, as if the great theme has merely passed through him to manifest itself directly in all its gripping truth and spotless purity. Even when, at the end of the extremely questionable Epilogue, the white beam of light falling on Joan sends a shudder through us, it is not Shaw's greatness that causes it, but the greatness of the saint whose servant he there was. But what more does he want than that? In the greatest ages of drama was it not best when the truth and greatness of the subject weighed more heavily than the limited abilities of the dramatist?

Related to this is the fact that such an important part of the performance's effect is a result of ordinary stage techniques. It is as though the heroic style that Shaw was not able to give to the play has to be created in despite in him, and is ensured by the basic scenic means used. This leads me to compare the performance given by the Vereenigd Tooneel [United Theater] troupe in the Netherlands with that of the company playing the piece in London, first in Haymarket and now in the Regent Theatre.[2]

From the point of view of style, one would tend to say beforehand that the theories of Eduard Verkade here applied skillfully by Wijdeveld—a sober *mise en scène,* the historical illusion reduced to a vague impression of past forms, a sharply tempered realism—are far preferable to the trappings of historical realism which are usually still sworn by in England, though in the Netherlands they have for years been looked upon as outdated and antiquated. Nevertheless, after having seen both performances I have begun to have some doubts, and Charles Ricketts's versions lingers in my memory as much more forceful and impressive than Wijdeveld's. But that, it will be said, is precisely the mistake: the external trappings should not appeal so directly. Are they, then, no more than an indispensable husk, not to say a necessary evil? If that is so, there is something wrong with the theater. Now, that is certainly the case, but these notes do not pretend to provide fundamental solutions for such probing dramatic issues. Let us restrict ourselves to weighing the merits of the two types of staging in this particular case.

The advantage of a historical staging—providing it is designed as excellently as Ricketts's—seems to me to be that the shortcomings of the play, and in particular the lack of style, are obscured to some extent. A certain unity of acting, costuming, and *décor* develops, held together by a common degree of realism, or what can be taken for realism. This is true of the scene at court and of those in the tent, the cathedral, and the trial-hall, though not of the one in the castle at Vaucouleurs and the one beside the river. The more direct the appeal of the architecture or nature needs to be, the more all the objections to stage realism press their validity: in the London production the scene on the Loire is terrible, but the settings of gaily figured tapestries in the tent and at court go well with the costumes of the actors. In the Verkade production, on the other hand, there is a certain lack of harmony between the play, the costumes, and the *décors*. If the play had had Shakespeare's exalted style, which it is much in need of, a soberness in the setting would have been the prescribed thing, since every excessive effect would only damage and detract from the drama itself. But soberness clashes with the spirit of Shaw, and Ricketts's gay coloring has a salutary effect: without being discordant, it subdues that Shavian spirit a bit, distracts from it somewhat.

I have no illusions that I shall ever see the fifteenth century—or any other age—in the theater as I see it in my mind's eye, and as it is suggested to me by the slightest historical document, whether in word or in image. But I must admit that I have never seen more convincing historical staging than this work of Ricketts's. I have in mind in particular the first court entry and the tent scene. Not that I should like to defend the costuming throughout the play. Plate-iron armor, though it may be more accurate historically than the hinted-at mail used by Verkade, is too shiny and tinny, and hence always unacceptable on stage. Verkade's costuming is also quasi-historical (though only defectively so: all three of his prelates are post-Trent personages), yet by comparison to him what a fine harmony in variety Ricketts offers: the *Heures de Chantilly* come to life. Heraldic figures are used lavishly, but with how much care and consideration! I am constantly struck by the English eye for all the possibilities of the color red. We Dutch with our gray tradition must remember, before we turn up our nose at all this, that the period that for us begins with Jozef Israels started with the Pre-Raphaelites in England. Actually, the only colors we know, except for all the nuances of gray, are a great deal of green and some blue, and vistas and clouds rather than figures. The English eye, however, has been trained by an unbroken succession of masters who have tested all their aesthetic senses on the human figure clad in every shade and on its movement in gaily colored processions. I know that this decorative tendency in England gives birth to monsters every day—and yet when I see Ricketts following in the footsteps of William Morris and Rossetti and Ford Madox Brown I do not dare condemn.

It is risky to attempt to view art and its value as quite distinct from nationality. Is it not noteworthy that in the British production the two English characters,

Warwick and the Chaplain, are by far the best? Or perhaps the Chaplain, whom Shaw has made too much of a caricature, is really no better than Cauchon, but Warwick is unsurpassed in his appearance as well as in other things. The care that was taken for historical accuracy is best illustrated by the fact that even his facial type has clearly been copied from the gilded bronze likeness on the earl's tomb at Warwick. Happy England, which has never known a French Revolution. For Pierre Cauchon's countenance one must be content with a seventeenth-century drawing of his tombstone, long since destroyed, at Lisieux.

The very fact that, in spite of myself, the element of historical accuracy has played a greater role in my evaluation of the performance than I had suspected, I should like to consider as evidence for the correctness of my theory that the powerful effect of the play stems from the historical theme itself. There is another argument for that point of view. Sybil Thorndike has the reputation of being England's finest tragedienne; I hope I do Nel Stants no injustice by calling her a rising young player. Nonetheless, the Dutch actress's Joan was much more to my satisfaction than her more famous English colleague's, because Nel Stants could be young, spontaneous, natural, boyish—she had the same gay, laughing face Joan's contemporaries describe. In Sybil Thorndike I was put off by an excess of dramatic art—a rapturous note in her voice and gestures, a touch of high tragedy that served as a disturbing rather than a contributing factor. I have been told that in America the choice was deliberately made to train a naïve country-girl for the part. That smacks of the film. But it does serve to confirm the fact that this drama is so subject to the gravitational pull of history that the usual dramatic requirements are distorted.

It has been remarked that though any number of writers have attempted a literary adaption of the history of Joan of Arc, it was always without success. The work of art depicting her for all the ages to come does not exist. It will not be *Saint Joan,* no more than it is *Die Jungfrau von Orleans,* and very definitely not François Porché's *La Vièrge au grand cœur,* which ran in Paris (perhaps partly as a protest against *Saint Joan*) for a while, till Shaw came, was seen, and conquered, even there.

What are the great writings one reads about Joan of Arc and her life? Michelet first of all. Then one may prefer Anatole France, the skeptic (or rather the unbeliever), or Monsignor Touchet, who devoted years of labor to bringing about Joan's canonization, or Gabriel Hanotaux, who attempted to bridge the gap between rationalists and Catholics. But it is in the books that attempt to give an accurate account of the history that the reader—including the general reader—goes searching for the Maid of Orléans. Is this not some sort of indication? Should it not be assumed that there is something in the very subject that resists literary treatment, and particularly dramatization? There are subjects, such as Troy, which find their highest expression in the epic, others that flourish only in the drama. There are also some whose character lies most intimately and indissolubly contained in the historical form itself, some in which the most sublime emotions of the tragic—the fellow suffering and the catharsis—are bound to the historical account as such. Grant Clio precedence over Melpomene now and then through the ages.

II. The Figure of Joan of Arc

We have reproached Shaw that his play is too much lacking in the qualities of tragic poetry to be commensurate with the sublimity of the subject, that it is too modernly prosaic to be able to take the dramatic flight that is needed—prosaic not only in form, but also in conception. The buskin is treacherous footwear: it is much more dangerous for the best of men than skis for the beginner.

And yet, I do not know whether Shaw, whom I imagine to be the most deliberate writer there is, could have given his view the poetic passion it lacks, if he had wanted to. It is, at any rate, certain that he did not want to. For it is precisely poetry, so he argues in his Preface, which has made so much mischief in regard to an accurate understanding of the figure of Joan of Arc. A twopenny-halfpenny romanticism picturing the heroine above all a beautiful girl whose followers were all in love with her has hopelessly distorted the image of Joan. There is no other misconception that Shaw rounds on so angrily, and so justly, as this sort of cheap romanticism. But romantic sentiment is not the same thing as poetic sublimity, and it is an open question whether he has not thrown out the baby of tragedy with the bath of romanticism.

And Shaw, in his attack on the romantic view, is, as usual, exaggerating. He would like to reason away every touch of feminine charm in Joan, at whatever price. "Not one of Joan's comrades, in village, court, or camp . . ." says Shaw, "ever claimed that she was pretty." This is not true. Jean d'Aulon, the head of her military household, called her "a beautiful and well-formed girl," and Perceval de Boulain-villiers thought her "of satisfying grace." Perhaps a few details on her appearance are appropriate here. (I repeat that this article is intended as nothing more than a series of marginal notes.)

Over against the contemporaries just mentioned, Shaw can appeal to the Lombard monk who, quite some time later, briefly described her outward appearance. He spoke of her as "short of build and with a boorish countenance." But most of his evidence is of little value. Various historians have felt uneasy with the view that Joan was short of stature. Vallet de Viriville attempted to prove the opposite. Hanotaux described her as "large and strong," thus following Quicherat, who translated the *haulte et puissante* of the extremely romanticized *Chronique de Lorraine* as *grande et forte*. Whatever her stature may have been, the Lombard monk was right about another detail: that Joan had dark hair. For so she is described in a contemporary chronicle from La Rochelle, and the fact is perhaps confirmed by a black hair embedded, apparently intentionally, in the seal of Joan's letter to the town of Riom.

One might say that there is a quite general tendency to visualize Joan as being fair-haired and preferably dressed in blue. That is the way Boutet de Monvel presents her in his fine, well-known picture book. Both Sybil Thorndike and Nel Stants portray her as fair-haired. And I imagine that a survey "Do you visualize Joan of Arc as fair or dark?" would confirm their choice by a large majority. Is this a romantic notion? Ariosto paid homage to the ideal of the fair heroine. I can imagine the antiromantic Shaw expostulating with the players to avoid every element of romantic charm in the figure. No sacrifice might be made to the ideal of fairness, and even less to contemporary fashion; as the sources specify in detail, Joan's hair should be cropped close above the ears and her temples shaven, in keeping with the fifteenth-century style. But the actors point out to Shaw that his power as an author does not reach *that* far, and go their own way.

I do not know whether Shaw's passion in supporting his desire to see a portrait of Joan in the helmeted female bust in the church of Saint-Maurice in Orléans does not, in the last analysis, betray a certain chivalric sense. His argument, "If this woman be not Joan, who is she?" and his challenge to prove the negative strike one as romantic in their utter groundlessness. We have no well-substantiated authentic image of the Maid. Certainly not in the thumbnail sketch with which the greffier of the Parliament of Paris, Clément de Fauquembergue, adorned the margin of his register. (And to imagine that it would have been possible for Jan van Eyck to visit her in prison at Arras in the autumn of 1430 and draw her!)

Among the few details preserved regarding her outward appearance, the most valuable is perhaps the phrase describing her voice. At Selles-sur-Cher, in June 1429, the brothers De Laval heard her address the ecclesiastics standing in front of the church "in a very womanly voice" as she sat on the fiery black horse she had just broken. De Boulainvilliers, too, was struck by her charming, feminine voice.

To understand her personality one would like to have something of a picture of her appearance, and though one does not need to visualize her as beautiful in the usual sense of the word, a harmony in her appearance is essential. Let us attempt to combine into a consistent picture the few scanty data preserved by her contemporaries, who were little interested in personal descriptions.

She talks little. She eats and drinks sparingly. (It is still De Boulainvilliers who is speaking, in June 1429.) She delights in beautiful horses and armor, she greatly admires armed and noble men. She avoids contact and converse with the many. "She sheds tears freely; her expression is cheerful" (*abundantia lacrimarum manat, hilarem gerit vultum*). This strange combination of strength and lightheartedness with tearful emotion and an inclination toward silence provides what is perhaps the best approach to the essence of her being.

Shaw, it seems to be, has seen the basic contours of that essence lucidly, and has portrayed them clearly. I shall not paraphrase his portrayal here; everyone has it at his disposal in the play and the Preface, and I cannot do it better justice.

"In His strength I will dare, and dare, and dare, until I die." In these words, perhaps the most moving in the play, Shaw presents the essence of Joan's personality. Actually she had given herself a name that summarizes her whole personality when she heard her voices call her *la fille au grand cœur. Cœur*, in this context, should be translated as "courage," and yet such a translation would not be complete, because all the other meanings of "heart" are also there as undertones. Her courage, and her confidence—these are the most immediate elements of her nature, and the ones that give the most tangible explanation of her success. A greatness that manifests itself in a superior, irresistible, and infectious bravery. What reason could there be to doubt Bertrand de Poulengy and Jean de Metz, who took her from Vaucouleurs to Chinon, when they testify that they felt incapable of resisting her will? The very fact that they took her there proves it. Anatole France is skeptical toward the numerous testimonies in the rehabilitation trial of men who declared that they had never felt any carnal desire for her. Shaw says they were too much afraid of her to fall in love with her. One might also say that her utterly guileless concentration on one goal emanated an awe that expressed itself in a great sense of shame. A stilling of the desires in her presence is on a par with the abstention from swearing and profanity which (as the sources thoroughly document) she brought about. Whoever cannot accept the fact that an exalted personality can exert an influence on his surroundings which makes the unusual the rule will never be able to understand Joan of Arc.

The incomparably high mettle of her courage no one doubts. But there are those who question whether, aside from the great impetus emanating from her courage, her insight and military talent also played a predominant role in the deeds accomplished under her guidance: the raising of the siege of Orléans and the expedition to Reims. This is one of the most difficult problems posed by the history of Joan of Arc, and it is out of the question to go into sufficient detail on the point here. As early as the rehabilitation trial, Jean Luillier, a burgher of Orléans, gave an evasive answer to the question whether the siege was raised by means of the Maid more than the strength of the warriors. The conviction that Joan applied a natural strategic and tactical talent in deliberate calculation is based chiefly on the testimony of a comrade-in-arms, the Duke of Alençon. He praises her as being "in war . . . very expert, whether to carry a lance, to assemble an army, to order a battle, or to dispose artillery." Shaw, like Hanotaux (and Quicherat before him), tends to assume these very real talents in her. Anatole France, on the other hand, is closer to the Catholic historians on the point, though for completely different reasons. In the Catholic view the attribution of extraordinary military skill would imply a certain diminution of the supernatural nature of her mission. For France it would not tally with his thesis that Joan had been a pawn in the hands of calculating persons.

In modern military science it would certainly be unbelievable for such strategic skill to exist in a simple girl from the country. But in the uncomplicated situation of her day military talent was still largely a matter of penetrating common sense, and once one assumes the genius of her personality there seems no reason to consider impossible the presence of such a talent in Joan of Arc.

The combination of common sense and natural straightforwardness with heroic enthusiasm gave her personality the utterly unique cast that appeals immediately to everyone. At first glance she saw everything in its true form, free of any veneer of convention. Hence the ready wit of her answers, for instance, the one to the dean of the theological faculty of Poitiers, who had asked what tongue her angel spoke. "A better than yours," she said, for Brother Seguin spoke the Limousin dialect.[3]

It is worthy of attention that Joan's conceptual world lies completely outside the conventions of her time. Anyone who knows how strongly the romanticism of chivalry dominated the culture of the fifteenth century will be amazed at the fact. She knew only the *deeds* of chivalry: pleasure in horses and arms, courage and fidelity; chivalry's gaudy concepts were alien to her. Her simple spirit did not feed on the fantasy of chivalric orders and festivities and oaths; it was not directed toward the obligatory ideal of liberating Jerusalem, but toward the one close at hand, that of liberating France. All the higher culture of her century was miles removed from her. There was no conflict between her and the fashionable chivalric concepts. It is significant that even after her death literary fancy actually could find no place for her in the colorful tableau of chivalric glory. What could have been done with her? She was too real.

Also the elaborate concepts of religious life of her day were, in their details, actually alien to her. It is only when one compares Joan of Arc with other saints of the time, for instance, Saint Colette, that it becomes apparent that she lacks almost every element of mysticism, every developed sentiment of spiritual ecstasy. We find her participating in only one of the fifteenth century's many pious movements: the adoration of the name of Jesus, which she placed on her standard and had put at the head of her letters. But that is all. There is nothing to indicate that her mind was occupied by the great religious concepts of her day, the vividly colored and violently experienced awareness of the Sufferings of Our Lord, much less the shrill phantasmagoria of Death. She had no time and no place for them.

No one will ever know just how clear to Joan of Arc the forms of her conceptual world were. That they were very simple, and very forceful and direct, is obvious. And here we come to the question of the significance of her "voices."

The history of Joan of Arc—and this is another of the precious things about her—forces us to make a strict reckoning of our own convictions. The non-Catholic can understand and enjoy the story of Saint Francis or of Saint Catherine of Siena with an admiration for the Church of the Middle Ages which, though it is inevitably roused by an unprejudiced study of history, can go much deeper than purely historical and aesthetic appreciation. The story of Joan of Arc forces one to confess at once whether or not one believes in the category of sainthood in the strict Catholic sense. The person who cannot believe that the blessed souls of certain persons once known as Catherine and Margaret manifested themselves to Joan in the substance does better not to force himself to do so. The miracle does not have to stand or fall with that.

Shaw, it seems to me, has done a service by opposing violently the idea that labeling Joan's voices a morbid symptom is enough to define their significance. But in doing so he is less original than he thinks. Quicherat, though more of a rationalist than Shaw, refused to look upon Joan as a sick person. Indeed, if every inspiration that comes to one with such commanding urgency that it is heard as a voice is to be condemned out of hand by the learned qualification of a morbid symptom, a hallucination, who would not rather stand with Joan of Arc and Socrates on the side of the mad than with the faculty of the Sorbonne on that of the sane? We know that an anomaly only becomes a sickness when it has a disturbing effect on the purpose of the organism. And Joan's voices may have had a very disturbing influence on her lower purpose of enjoying life and growing old, but it is not on such things that we should like to base our conclusion. No matter how clear the psychiatric report might be, historical judgment would retain the right not to view the voices in the first place as *ces troubles . . . hallucinations perpétuelles,* as Anatole France does, but to find in them the sign of a mind occupied completely by high impulses. History has more to do with her courage and its significance than with the physiological determination of her visions.

There is another special argument that should keep us from viewing Joan's case too much in the pathological sphere. The gentlemen at Rouen in 1431 did their very best to lure Joan's thoughts onto the slippery terrain of demonology with their questions about whether Saint Michael was naked, what parts of the bodies of the saints she had embraced, and so forth. They succeeded not once. If there was anything really diseased in her mind, they would certainly have discovered it. A fifteenth-century inquisitor was just as skilled as a present-day Freudian in bringing the dregs of the soul into the open. Did Joan refer even once to the devil?

Also with regard to the form in which Joan conceived of her celestial advisers, Saint Michael, Saint Catherine, and Saint Margaret, it would seem to me that Shaw has gone squarely to the core of the matter. The form is bound to the conceptual world in which she lived. It was just as natural and logical for her to visualize the voices as saints and angels as it is for a modern man to borrow his terms from the concepts of physics. When Shaw has Joan say to the Archbishop, "even if they [my voices] are only the echoes of my commonsense," he can appeal to the hearing of March 15: "Asked how she knew it was the language of angels: replies she believed it very soon; and had the will to believe."

On the question of how Joan's mind defined and explained the concepts associated with her inspirations, I should like to go a bit further than Shaw. The writers about Joan of Arc whom I have read (only a few of the countless total) present it as established fact that she associated her heavenly commands with the figures of the archangel Michael, Saint Catherine, and Saint Margaret even at the beginning of her mission. Is that so certain? She made the association in 1431, at the trial, when she was asked to describe her visions in detail. But the witnesses in the trial of rehabilitation who had heard her speak of her voices in 1429, during her glory, do not as a rule know anything of the two saints and the archangel. It is precisely in this and because of this that they seem highly reliable. If they had merely recited what everyone knew in 1456, and what everyone wanted to hear, they would undoubtedly have mentioned Saint Michael, Saint Catherine, and Saint Margaret. It was just as natural for a person of the fifteenth century to associate a notion with a saint as for our contemporaries to use the words "mentality" and "intuition." But what do these witnesses have to say? Joan's heavenly counsel was quite without visual form, a sheer *daimonion* about which she talked with great diffidence and reticence. She speaks only of *son conseil* ["her counsel"]. When Christopher de Harcourt asked her in the presence of the dauphin whether she would "explain the manner of your counsel when it speaks to you" (*modum vestri consilii*), she blushed and replied Yes, but what she then said contains no reference to the three holy figures. And when Jean d'Aulon, one of those who were closest to her, asked her who her counsel was, she answered only: "There are three of them; one is constantly with me, the second comes and goes, and the third is the one whom the other two consult." From this it is not even clear that two of the three were female.[4]

It seems plausible to me that it was only fairly late, perhaps even only during her trial, that Joan linked her inspirations to the figures she knew best and cherished most among the saints. Even during the hearings she was very little inclined to go into detail about her visions. Asked about the great light accompanying them, she said: *passez oultre* ["pass to another question"].

Everything Joan declared regarding the spiritual state in which she heard her voices is of the utmost simplicity. It was a state of great elation, in which she would always like to be. She was filled with a feeling of knowing much more than she might or would or could express. "There is more in the books of the Lord than in yours," she said to the churchmen who examined her at Poitiers. All visionary terminology of the usual sort is utterly alien to her.

Significant is the complete skepticism she displayed toward the visions of Catherine de la Rochelle, who was able to gain access to the king as her competitor. Catherine maintained that she was visited every night by a white lady. So Joan asked to sleep with her for a night, watched until midnight and saw nothing, and then slept. When morning came she asked if the lady in white had come. Yes, while you were asleep, you could not be wakened. Then Joan slept by day and stayed awake, often asking Catherine: Will she not come? And Catherine would answer: Yes, soon!

Catherine de la Rochelle's inspirations were of a different sort from Joan's: she went through the towns with royal heralds and trumpets to summon whosoever had gold or silver or hidden treasure. That was needed to pay Joan's soldiers. Or she would go to the Duke of Burgundy to make peace with him. But Joan advised her to go back to her husband to take care of the household and her children. And there would be no peace "except at the point of the lance."

Joan of Arc was also not a true ecstatic in that she was sometimes uncertain and doubtful. Not only of her calling but also of her fate. When she went to battle she was not at all confident that she would not be slain. Her hesitation before the battle of Montépilloy led to a defeat. Her awareness that God loved certain other living persons more than her (which she testified to at the trial, without clarifying it further) is a touching thing.

Her most human traits tend only to make her greatness more vivid. Alongside her purity, soberness, and simplicity I should not want to miss in her portrait the liking for costly clothing which is only seemingly in contrast with those qualities. "And wore very noble, well-furred habits of gold cloth and silk. . . ." She wore red by preference. An order to pay thirteen old gold crowns for two sumptuous garments made for her at Orléans in June 1429, at Charles d'Orléans's expense, has been preserved, together with the receipt.

*   *   *

The picture of a historical figure does not form itself in the mind on the basis of psychological definitions. It arises seemingly without any consciously logical function, like a view of something one could not see before, or could see only vaguely. It is built up out of the arbitrary and more or less circumstantial data that tradition has preserved for us. The conviction that our picture must be accurate (or let us merely say, of value) and that the tradition is reliable develops out of the feeling, usually very difficult to describe, that though the various data are disconnected in themselves, they harmonize, they fit together. The picture of Joan of Arc emerges from the sources with an unusually high degree of homogeneity and conviction. Even among scholars of quite divergent world-views, the differences in their conception of Joan of Arc are relatively small. It is as if her personality suggested itself to everyone who testified regarding her with an immediacy that forced them merely to tell the truth in all its simplicity, unobscured by the patterns of chivalric or religious forms which usually determined their expression. To our minds all the actions and words handed down regarding Joan fit together. "The sign I have from God is to raise the siege of Orléans." "The soldiers will do battle, and God will give the victory." She carried the standard, in order not to have to kill anyone. When the women of Bourges came with rosaries for her to touch, Joan said, with a laugh toward her hostess: "Touch them yourselves. They will be quite as good with your touch as with mine." She did not like to share a bedroom with old women, and wanted only young maidens around her. Every evening at sundown she had the church bell rung for half an hour. At the peak of her happiness, shortly before the coronation at Reims, when she could not yet know that the tide was turning, came the talk on the way from Crépy-en-Valois, on August 11, 1429, while she rode between the archbishop of Reims and the Bastard of Orléans, and the populace greeted the king with glad cries of *Noël*. In the trial of rehabilitation Dunois gave testimony regarding it, testimony that was perhaps somewhat refashioned in his memory and has unfortunately been preserved only in Latin. "These are a good people!" says Joan. "I have seen none elsewhere who have shown so much joy at the coming of our noble king." And then: "Would God I might be happy enough when I shall finish my days to be buried in this soil." At which the Archbishop asked her: "Joan, in what place hope you to die?" She answered: "Wherever it may please God, I am sure neither of the time nor the place. I know no more of it than yourself. But I would it were pleasing to God, my Creator, that I might now retire, laying arms aside, and that I might serve my father and my mother, guarding their sheep[5] with my sister and my brothers, who would be greatly rejoiced to see me. . . ."

For the person who would like to take exception to the testimonies in the rehabilitation trial of 1456 as too favorable to Joan, who was then already seen in the light of a re-evaluation, the trial of 1431 presents quite the same image of unimpeachable purity. According to Brother Isambard de la Pierre and Brother Martin Ladvenu, the executioner had declared that her heart had resisted every effort to be burned. One does not have to believe it. But there is something else that is just as great a miracle, and of a more tenuous variety: all those biased persons of 1431, her judges with their dry hearts and their stiff pens, were not able to tarnish the gold of her words. Let me give only one example out of many. Asked what words she used to summon the help of her voices, she replied: "Very tender God, in honor of Thy holy passion, I pray Thee, if Thou lovest me, that Thou wilt reveal to me how I ought to answer these churchmen. I know well, as to this habit, the commandment why I took it, but I know not in what manner I ought to leave it off. Be pleased therefore to teach me. . . ."

In the testimonies of the rehabilitation trial the recollections are often fragments, rather irrelevant details reproduced by the memory with the thoughtlessness of a film image, and precisely because of that inspiring confidence: There is the talk about the carp, which Shaw makes use of, and d'Estivet's curses. There is her answer to the question whether she had ever been on the spot when Englishmen were slain: "In God's name, of course! How softly you speak!" In 1456 Thomas de Courcelles himself could recall of the sermon to Joan given by Guillaume Erard in the churchyard of Saint-Ouen only the words "the pride of this woman." He could remember but one single image of Joan's abjuration: Cauchon in conversation with some others. He stopped in the middle of a sentence, but de Courcelles no longer knew what was said. Thomas de Courcelles, in 1456 one of the lights of the Church and the University, displayed a very poor memory at the rehabilitation trial.

The picture of Joan of Arc is clear and sharply defined, but even so we cannot rigidly categorize it. Anyone who attempts to reduce it to the terms of scientific psychology will himself no doubt feel that he is violating it. That is fundamentally the case for every picture of a historical personality, but it is the more obvious the further the personality deviates from the usual norms of character and action. "The great man is unknowable," Hanotaux says rightly, and Shaw: "the superior being, being immeasurable is unbearable. . . ." For us the person of Joan of Arc, perhaps more purely than any other figure in history, lies quite utterly within the sphere of the heroic. We can seek in vain for the term summarizing her essence. "Heroine" is not satisfactory. "Genius" even less. "Saint," whether or not one understands it completely in the technical, ecclesiastical sense, is far and away the best.

III. The Opinion of Her Age

"At no single moment of her existence," says Anatole France, "was Joan known in any way but through fables, and if she set the masses in movement it was as a result of the clamor of the countless legends that sprang up wherever she went, and sped on ahead of her." The first part of this statement is undoubtedly true; the second contains a serious mistake in logic. Her effect explained as a *result* of the countless legends? But then what explains the immediate emergence of those legends themselves? Wonder-workers were nothing unusual in the fifteenth century, and many of them made a fair amount of clamor, but not one aroused the amazement, the enthusiasm, and the terror that Joan of Arc immediately brought about. Nothing is more significant in this respect than the English ordinances attempting to counteract the mass desertion to the island and the refusal to be called to the colors.[6]

The way Joan of Arc's fame developed we know best from notices in Antonio Morosini's fifteenth-century chronicle, which first attracted attention in 1895. This Venetian kept a sort of diary of the news that came to Venice regarding remarkable events of the day. He recorded the news in whatever form he was able to obtain it, and so also inserted a number of letters that Pancrazio Giustiniani, a Venetian merchant at Bruges, sent to his father, Marco, in 1429 and 1430, and also letters from another Venetian in Avignon. These letters are remarkable not so much for their factual accuracy in details as for their illustration of how, in the mind of a "neutral," the image of Joan took form from day to day of her career. Giustiniani, an Italian and a merchant living in Burgundian territory, cannot be suspected of an immoderate tendency toward ready belief in the miracle of the Maid. His reports regarding Joan begin with a passing mention at the end of a detailed account of the raising of the siege of Orléans, written around the middle of May 1429: "In the past fortnight there has been much talk about all sort of prophecies found at Paris, and other things which all together promise the dauphin great prosperity.... Many people made the most priceless jokes in the world about them, particularly those of a girl, a shepherdess[7] from Lorraine." Merchants in Burgundy had written him about the matter. He knows the rough outlines of her activities at Chinon. One of the persons writing him about her is reported to have said, "it is making me crazy." It all seems unbelievable, and yet.... In his next reference, dated July 9,[8] there is only a trace of doubt left: "These are most wondrous things if they be true, and it seems to me that they are so.... I believe that God's power is great...." Then he finds support: in his later letters, dated November 20, 1429, and January 4, 1430, he apparently knows Jean de Gerson's cautious but understanding opinion regarding Joan (to which I shall return below) and subscribes to it: "Believe what you will of it; it is said that the Maid does all these things and a thousand wonders more, which if they be true, are done by the Lord. And it is a great wonder in our days." His last word about her he wrote on November 24, 1430: *La poncela* has been sent to the king of England at Rouen;[9] John of Luxembourg has received ten thousand crowns for her. "What will follow for her is unknown, but it is feared that they will let her die, and truly these are strange and great things."

If in Morosini's tidings we have a report of Joan's activities in a crude form, a literarily colored image also developed, even in the first months. While some people who saw her simply jotted down their impressions of the Maid, as did the brothers De Laval in a letter to their mother, others make the wondrous affair a test of their style and wit, much as a modern journalist does with athletic heroes or musicians. One of the latter was Perceval de Boulainvilliers, counselor and chamberlain of Charles VII, in a Latin letter to Filippo Maria Visconti dated June 21, 1429. Another was an unknown writer, thought to be Alain Chartier, in a similar letter to an unknown prince, a month later. Now, one might expect that the form in which such authors molded Joan's image would be inspired by the chivalric concepts that so sharply dominated the minds of the day. But that was not the case. They embroidered a humanistic and hagiographic pattern with elaborate miraculous details for purposes of adornment, and quite a bit of rhetoric, so that these most original and primary sources must, remarkably enough, be considered among the least reliable.

Two of the finest and most sensible intellects of France, whose thoughts on lofty subjects had met on another terrain long before, both devoted their last work, written shortly before their deaths, to Joan's activities. Jean de Gerson wrote his *Considerations on the Fact of the Maid* on May 14, 1429, and died two months later. Christine de Pisan, spending the days of her old age in seclusion, wrote on July 31, 1429, her *ditié* of sixty-one stanzas, the last poem known from her, a bit flat and dull, but charged with an absolute faith in the mission of the Maid. Gerson, the cautious psychologist who had earlier written a long tract on how to distinguish between true and false visions, and who feared nothing as much as that all sorts of crude and cheap superstitions would gain the upper hand, wrote with a certain reserve. He is filled with sympathy for this affair that has excited all the world. The chief arguments moving him to place confidence in the divinity of Joan's mission actually fit perfectly in Shaw's picture. The very fact that her call has been able to move the king's counselors and the commanders to attack has a great deal of weight for Gerson, and rightly so. He also counts as a sign for the genuineness of Joan's mission the fact that, despite the divine order, she and the commanders who follow her do not abandon the ways of human caution. He feels, as it were, the masterly, inspired reasonability of her idea. Even if there is much in it that is natural, he goes on to say, it can still be a miracle, for also in the ancient miracles testified to by the Scriptures, those of Deborah and Judith, "something natural was always intermingled. . . . And," Gerson carefully warns, "after the first miracle everything does not always go as people expect. Hence, even if the Maid should be disappointed in all her and our expectations—far be it from me to wish it—one may not conclude that everything that has happened has been wrought by an evil spirit, or at any rate not by God."

Where there was no sincere love for France such as Gerson's at stake, the conclusion of an ecclesiastical arbiter proved to be more hesitant. There was, for instance, that of Hendrik van Gorkum, rector of a Latin school at Cologne. This same Hendrik van Gorkum is referred to by Hugo Grotius in the Introduction to *De Iure Belli ac Pacis* as one of his predecessors, on the basis of a tract *De Iusto Bello.*[10] But when in June 1429 he set side by side *Propositiones* for and against the Maid it never entered his mind that hers, too, might be referred to as a just war. His earnest objection to the genuineness of Joan's calling is that now, in the time of grace, it does not seem very probable that a spiritual mission for the advancement of a purely secular matter like the French cause against England would emanate from God. If everything was in order as regards Joan's calling, then she must be unusually holy. But that such a saintly creature should dress as a worldly warrior—how inappropriate! Judith and Esther had not done so. All of which was argued with utter logic and matter-of-factness by the good Dutchman Master Hendrik van Gorkum.

Did the archbishop of Reims, Regnault de Chartres, honestly believe even for a moment in Joan's calling? For him, the advocate of a peace by means of a *rapprochement* with the Duke of Burgundy, everything she wished to accomplish after the coronation at Reims was inopportune. As soon as she was taken prisoner by the Burgundians at Compiègne on May 23, 1430, he dropped her. He did not deny her straight out, but what he did do was worse: he cast the first stone. It was her own fault, and the reward she deserved, he wrote in a letter to the inhabitants of Reims.[11] She was unwilling to listen to advice, but did everything her own way. God had suffered the capture of the Maid because of her pride and the rich raiment she had worn, and because she had not followed His commands but her own will.

From this bit of information Shaw, in his fifth scene, worked out the figure of the Archbishop in a portrayal that is pretty much in keeping with the historical tradition. Joan's irrepressible assurance interpreted as pride and obstinacy: that was perhaps the most tragic thing in her history. Her own followers could not endure that lofty courage.

Or was it really, as Shaw would have it, crushed between the Church and the established Law that Joan met her doom as the masterly and insufferable herald of a new freedom for the individual and a new power for society? Shaw would like us to consider her trial as nothing more than the necessary defense of her age against the unknown and immeasurable danger that would destroy that age.

Undoubtedly the most exciting and most original aspect of Shaw's work is his relative rehabilitation of Joan's judges. If this dramatic argument were used for any other subject, for Caesar or even Napoleon, we might yield readily to such a view of the matter without being bothered by historical scruples. No longer to consider the trial as an infernal design to destroy Joan, but as a well-meant, regrettable mistake—it seems so logical, so understandable, so satisfactory, so historical. The countless people throughout the world who will carry with them for years to come the image of Joan of Arc as Shaw has imprinted it in them will all have made this correction of their earlier view: Pierre Cauchon was not a bribed and dishonest judge, but a decent and relatively honorable man who spared no effort to save the Maid.

Nonetheless, I believe that in this case many people who are as a rule not interested first of all in the historical course of events, but in the imaginative powers of the artist, will ask whether Shaw's view is correct.

Several points can be granted him without further ado. The proceedings of the 1431 trial of condemnation are in many respects more reliable than those of the rehabilitation trial of 1456. Indeed, as Shaw remarks with a jeer, the judges at Rouen, who after long preparations spent more than three months on her trial proper, took an extremely serious view of their task when compared with the hasty procedures we can remember from the World War. Is this at the same time proof that they were unbiased?

Shaw traces the opinion that Cauchon served the English cause and that the trial took place under pressure to a sin of romanticism. Joan was spotless, says romantic sentiment, hence her judges must have been rascals. Shaw rightly condemns such a trivial antithesis. But what if even the most serious historical research cannot lead to any conclusion but a disqualification of the judges? True, the pressure that was exerted is frequently exaggerated. It has been claimed, without grounds, that the proceedings were forged. The trial was conducted properly. Nonetheless, while he recognizes all this, Pierre Champion, more at home than anyone else in the France of the fifteenth century, refers to it as "a masterpiece of partiality under the appearance of the most regular of procedures"; it remains "odious" to him, as it was before him to Hanotaux, to Quicherat, and to a thousand other historians.

Reading through the proceedings of the trial, one does obtain an impression of relative gentleness, of a serious desire to spare Joan and to save her. But Shaw, basing his opinion on this impression, has merely become the dupe of a machination of the judges themselves. The detail and moderation of the trial had as their basis the political intent of making Joan's condemnation as unimpeachable as possible. Even the unusually large number of judges, far from proving a serious and scrupulous fairness, is suspect. They mark the trial as a political affair, a deliberate *cause célèbre*. Cauchon said even before the trial began "that it was intended to give her a fine trial...." During the deliberations of the judges as to whether torture should or should not be applied, one responded in the negative, for "it might bring disrepute upon a trial thus far so well conducted...." All the expressions of gentle admonition and sympathy with her hardened disposition can also be explained as feigned gentleness. Shaw was perhaps not aware that the words used on transferring a condemned person from the ecclesiastical court to the secular arm, "with the request to deal with her tenderly," were nothing more than a customary formula that no one expected to lead to anything but the bonfire.

As far as the bishop of Beauvais is concerned, Shaw could appeal to the sources for more than one point in his picture of Cauchon. The English accused him of being prejudiced in favor of Joan, and he answered: "You lie: by law I must seek the redemption of the body and the soul of this Joan...." The general accusation, both in contemporary chronicles and in the testimonies of the rehabilitation trial, that hatred and political intrigue had been the reasons for the acts of 1431 are not sufficient to brand Cauchon as an unjust judge, though there is a great deal that is damning against him. Even his antecedents in the service of England and Burgundy do not prove that he violated his duty at Rouen. Nonetheless, among the testimonies in 1456 there is one that it is very difficult to reject as groundless, and which is almost enough to condemn Cauchon and invalidate Shaw's view. It was made in almost identical terms by Brother Isambard de la Pierre and Brother Martin Ladvenu. When the judges had gone to see for themselves that Joan, after her abjuration, had put on man's dress again, and as a result were forced to adjudge her an obstinate and relapsed heretic, the bishop of Beauvais, on leaving the prisoner, was heard to address Warwick among a number of Englishmen. "With laughter on his lips he said in a clear voice: 'Farewell, farewell, it is done! Have good cheer!' or similar words."

If it is hard to maintain the historicity of a well-meaning Cauchon, if many of the judges were his creatures, if a few of them did raise their voices against him, none of that indicates, on the other hand, that the whole trial was sheer wickedness and conscious bias. Though she was asked cunning questions that she could not answer, though the reasoning was formalistic and one-sided, the crucial issue—whether Joan had been able to develop her amazing power owing to divine help or demonic—was a very serious one, one that, inspected on its own merits, would have been completely dubious for any other court of that day. It is perfectly understandable that ecclesiastical judges who did not share in the enthusiasm for the cause of Charles VII catalogued Joan among a host of overwrought persons who set the world in turmoil. "If it should ever come so far that the people in their rashness would rather listen to soothsayers than to shepherds and teachers of the Church, religion will be doomed. . . ." These words out of a letter from the University of Paris to the pope, the emperor, and the college of cardinals will be recognized as the basis for Shaw's sentences put in the mouth of Cauchon in Scene IV. It was a logical syllogism when her judges reasoned: a revelation from God always leads to obedience; Joan ran away from her parents and wears man's dress, both of which are evidence of disobedience; hence her revelation is not from God. Dogmatically it was quite correct that one might not believe in visions and inspirations "just as strongly" as one "believed that Christ was crucified. . . ." If only Joan had said "it seems to me" instead of "I know for certain," there was no man who would condemn her, Master Jehan Lohier, who was favorably inclined toward her, said to Guillaume Manchon. Visions such as hers are possible with God, Master Jehan Basset considered during the deliberations, but she did not support them with a miracle or with a proof from the Scriptures, hence they should not be believed. Again it was completely logical according to the formal rules of the faith.

Given the conceptual system of the day, an impartial modern judge would be able to endorse completely the conclusions of the 1431 deliberations. The judges reached the same decision a judge who did not believe in the cause of Joan could arrive at even today. Her visions were declared to be "certain fictions, conceived humanly or the work of the Evil One. . . ." She had "not had sufficient signs to believe therein and to know them. . . ." Jehan Beaupère, master of theology, who was inclined to consider the phenomena "to be not supernatural, but traceable, in part, to physical causes, and in part to imagination and human invention . . .," was not so very far from explaining them as morbid symptoms. The chief distinction between the judges of 1431 and some psychologists of today is that, while the judges needed several months, the psychologists would probably have been ready with their statement within half an hour at the outside.

The method of the judges of 1431 was utterly scholarly. They are usually reviled in the historical studies (even in Champion's) because of the weight they attached to the innocent children's games of Joan's youth at Domremy, beside the spring and under the beech tree called the Fairy Tree, which they danced around and hung wreaths upon. But they are unjustly accused of cunning and antipathy in this respect. It *was* an important point for them. If it became clear from Joan's statements that there was a link between the appearance of her "voices" and the pagan customs centered around the tree, the diabolical character of her visions would be as good as proved. Whence the urge to know whether Saint Catherine and Saint Margaret had ever talked with her *beneath that tree.*

Finally there is the question of Joan's view of the Church and her refusal to submit without reserve to the judgment of the Church Militant. Again and again the judges asked her if she would leave the decision on the nature of her deeds to the Church. They attempted to explain to her the difference between the Church Triumphant and the Church Militant. But she did not understand. "I refer them to Our Lord who sent me, to Our Lady, and to all the blessed saints of Paradise," she says. "And she thought it was all one, Our Lord and the Church, and that these difficulties should not be made for her, and asked why we made difficulties when it was all one." According to the auditor of the Rota (a court of the Roman Curia who around 1454, in connection with her rehabilitation, made a close study of the twelve articles drawn from her confessions, she had sometimes understood that her judges were the Church and sometimes merely that the Church was the building where she was not allowed to go to hear mass. To the question whether she would submit, her answer in the hearings is once recorded as only to the Church on high, and later that she would submit to the Church Militant, "provided it does not command anything impossible. . . ." The ecclesiastical court of 1431 was, indeed, from its point of view on very firm ground when it counted such an attitude heavily against her. There had to be a limit to *sancta simplicitas.*

It is not in the objective value of their decision that the infamy of the judges of Rouen lies. They could justify the decision, looked upon as a matter in itself, to the feeling of their time and to their own consciences. The most august learned body of the day, the University of Paris, had done more than anyone else to help prepare the verdict, to elicit it, and to cloak it with its authority. The University of Paris should bear the burden of memory more than the judges at Rouen. Let us hope that the rector who guided the solemn assembly of the university on April 29, 1431—Pieter of Gouda, a canon of Utrecht, born at Leiden—was an insignificant chairman. The university judged logically, bitterly, and harshly; it judged from a distance, according to the facts, and did not see its victim.

Among those who did see her, the judges at Rouen, there was more than one who became somewhat aware of her greatness and her purity and was inclined toward a more favorable judgment. But the majority could see in her only "stubborn malevolence and hardness of the heart," "a sly mind tending toward evil and devoid of the grace of the Holy Ghost," without virtue and humility as they understood them. To them it was all pride and disobedience. They thought that in her they were punishing the sin of Lucifer himself.

Can the Rouen sentence rightly be looked upon as the reaction of the Church Militant to the spirit of individual religious opinion which was to shake that Church to its foundations less than a century later? In other words, is there any historical justification for Shaw's witty toying with the word "Protestantism"?

I do not believe so. The concept of Protestantism is a composite concept. It assumes much more than merely Joan's naïve obstinacy against the Church Militant in her direct obsession with the glory of the Church Triumphant. The term Protestantism makes sense only with regard to persons who, after having tested the whole medieval Catholic concept of the Church, deliberately rejected it. If she had not become implicated in an ecclesiastical trial, the weak point in Joan's faith would never have become public. She does not testify against the Church of her own free will, but an ecclesiastical court forces her, on formalistic grounds, to a consistency that seems heretical. True Protestantism can only lie on the yonder side of the whole system of Scholastic theology; Joan's ignorant faith falls completely on this side of it—or outside it. Her spirit has nothing in common with those of Huss and Wycliffe. In her saintly simplicity she is just as Catholic as the (legendary) old woman who carried the bundle of faggots for Huss. Protestantism presupposes humanism, intellectual development, a modern spirit; in her faith Joan of Arc was in the full sense of the word a primitive. It would be regrettable if the non-Catholic world allowed Shaw's authority to lure it into denying the Catholic Church the glory of its most touching saint.

So much for Warwick's discovery: "I should call it Protestantism if I had to find a name for it. . . ." To a certain extent the same thing applies to Cauchon's countermove "Nationalism." But there Shaw is not alone. Many French authors before him have celebrated in Joan of Arc the birth of French patriotism. In a certain sense rightly so. The great love of France as a whole, concentrated on the king, became a conscious thing during (and because of) the protracted war against England. Long before Joan that patriotism had had its heroes and its martyrs, for example, the ship's captain from Abbeville, Ringois, who was thrown into the sea at Dover in 1360 because the demand that he swear loyalty to the king of England rebounded upon his "I am French." Eustace Deschamps had testified to it in many a poem thirty years before Alain Chartier interpreted that patriotic love. But Shaw means something more than mere love of country. The transformation that he would like to attribute to Joan is the assertion of national monarchy as opposed to feudal particularism, and that not only in France but also in England. *Tua res agitur,* Warwick believes. Now, this is completely incorrect. The national monarchy, both in France and in England, was from the very outset aware of its antithetical position toward feudalism, its superior task, and its superior right. In England the monarchy had had the upper hand in the conflict ever since the Conqueror, and repeatedly it was only as a result of crises and slumps that the aristocracy won ground temporarily. In France the monarchy was triumphing over the lords slowly but surely. The conflict had begun long before the fifteenth century—as early as with Louis VII and Philip Augustus in the twelfth. The elements of the modern state came into being in France in the thirteenth century under Saint Louis and Philip the Fair. In the fifteenth century Louis XI, in his struggle with Burgundy and the League of Public Weal, gained the ascendancy in what was merely a last dangerous crisis, and completed a structure it had taken centuries to build. Joan of Arc brought a new patriotic spirit, but not a new concept of the state. Her patriotic love, like her faith, was primitive, rather prefeudal than modern. To her—and not only to her—the cause of France was "the quarrel of the king of France." They are the king's faction, his loyal followers; he is their liege and France is his heritage, which an intruder unjustly contests. Joan's patriotism is built up out of utterly primitive notions. In this, too, she is sublime simplicity and sheer courage. As a result of those lofty qualities her conception of love and sacrifice could have a seminal influence on the modern notion of the state, but she did not create it. Shaw's "Nationalism" placed in Cauchon's mouth is nothing more than a brilliant touch of his wit.

Joan of Arc as the subject of a historical hypothesis, as Shaw would have it, an exponent of certain ways of thinking—there is something annoying in it. In her irreducible uniqueness she can be understood only by means of a sense of sympathetic admiration. She does not lend herself to being used to clarify currents and concepts of her day. Her own personality attracts all the attention as soon as one touches on her history. She is one of the few figures in history who cannot be anything but protagonists, who are never subordinate, always an end and never a means. And this—if I may end these marginal notes with a word of personal apology—is also the reason why there is hardly a reference to her in the work that I wrote some years ago on life in the fifteenth century in France and the Netherlands. It has been charged to me as an error. But it was a considered, deliberate omission. I knew that Joan of Arc would have torn the book I visualized in my mind completely out of balance. What kept me from introducing her in it was a sense of harmony—that and a vast and reverent humility.

NOTES

[1] I am, of course, not thinking of Joan in *Henry VI*.

[2] February 1925.

[3] Salomon Reinach attempts to take away the point of the answer, arguing that Joan cannot have meant such an impertinence, but he does not convince me. "Observations sur le texte du procès de condamnation de Jeanne d'Arc," *Revue Historique*, CXLVIII (1925), 200–23, see p. 208.

[4] According to Catherine de la Rochelle's testimony in Jules Quicherat, *Procès de condamnation et réhabilitation de Jeanne d'Arc, dite la Pucelle*, five volumes (Paris, 1841–9), I, 295, and in Pierre Champion, *Procès de condamnation de Jeanne d'Arc*, two volumes (Paris, 1921), I, 244, Joan spoke of her two advisers as "the counselors of the spring," but the testimony is unreliable.

[5] As Shaw also mentions, Joan was definitely not a shepherdess, and stressed the fact, though she had helped to care for the livestock. But the age could not conceive of a maid from the country as anything but a shepherdess, and the onus of the characterization I leave to Dunois.

[6] G. Lefèvre Pontalis, "La Panique anglaise en mai 1429," *Le Moyen Age*, VII (1894), 81–95.

[7] See note 5.

[8] In between is a brief summary of a letter dated June 4.

[9] Giustiniani was anticipating events: Joan was not yet in Rouen.

[10] The *Kirchenlexikon*, V, 1707, mistakenly states that this tract has not been published. It is the seventh piece in *Tractatus consultatorii venerandi magistri Henrici de Gorychum* (Cologne, 1503); the Royal Library at The Hague possesses a copy of this rare work.

[11] Extant only in extract.

Roger B. Salomon

ESCAPE FROM HISTORY: MARK TWAIN'S *JOAN OF ARC*

For Mark Twain as for many other individuals of the eighteenth and nineteenth centuries faith in history was a substitute for faith in God. But Twain's was always a tenuous faith—tormented by a dream of freedom and innocence outside the grip of time, shaken by his abiding sense of human sinfulness, and finally destroyed by personal suffering and a growing awareness of the oligarchic and imperialistic drift of America. Even *A Connecticut Yankee in King Arthur's Court,* ostensibly Twain's most belligerent assertion of the moral and material progress of Western Civilization, is a deeply ambivalent book and ultimately an artistic failure because of its ambivalence. It is a novel in which the conscious intentions of the author are at cross purposes with his most deeply felt imaginative insights. Clearly Twain created the Yankee in order to attack the past and defend the future; but in his personal aggressiveness, his Promethean pride ("For such as have brains there are no defeats, but only victories"[1]) and his optimism regarding the malleability of human nature and the power of technology, the Yankee comes to symbolize merely the most fatuous hopes of nineteenth-century America. He is, of course, eventually trapped in the holocaust of a collapsing civilization.

The unresolved and largely unacknowledged ambiguities of the *Connecticut Yankee* became, under the stresses of the 90's, the intellectual problems with which Twain was to wrestle for the rest of his life. On the one hand, he attempted to develop (largely but not exclusively in certain still unpublished manuscripts[2]) a cyclical theory of history. On the other, he was more and more impelled to escape imaginatively from the nightmarish implications of his own theories. *Joan of Arc* can be most fruitfully examined as a final, desperate attempt to establish values apart from the futile treadmill of sin and suffering which was the life of man on earth.

I. Joan as a Historical Phenomenon

About Joan Twain felt none of the mixed emotions which had characterized his attitude toward the Yankee. He revered her as a glorious enigma, a lonely

From *Philological Quarterly* 40, No. I (January 1961): 77–90.

exception to the laws of historical causality. The personality which made possible her amazing career, he says in an article called "St. Joan of Arc," "is one to be reverently studied, loved, and marveled at, but not to be wholly understood and accounted for by even the most searching analysis." Other geniuses were, at least in part, the product of their environment, but Joan's qualities "became immediately usable and effective without the developing forces of a sympathetic atmosphere and the training which comes of teaching, study, practice. . . ." In short, "out of a cattle-pasturing peasant village lost in the remoteness of an unvisited wilderness and atrophied with ages of stupefaction and ignorance we cannot see a Joan of Arc issue equipped to the last detail for her amazing career and hope to be able to explain the riddle of it, labor at it as we may. It is beyond us. All the rules fail in this girl's case. In the world's history she stands alone—quite alone."[3]

Thus does Twain define the historical problem presented by the Joan of Arc story and his definition is scarcely more extreme, on the whole, than that of other nineteenth-century commentators. Even the great Michelet, while he makes a perfunctory attempt to relate certain facets of Joan's life (e.g., her visions and her taking up arms) to her social background, ends his account of her in a burst of romantic and patriotic ardor; she is a "living enigma," a "phenomenon," a "marvel," a "mysterious creature."[4] Her Catholic biographers, of course, whom Twain read and from whom he occasionally borrowed source material, were authorized by their faith to abandon the yardstick of rationality completely. Actually, according to Charles Lightbody, the nineteenth-century Joan, the Joan of modern French historians and most American writing, is a creation of Armagnac tradition, "clerical, conservative or monarchist, nationalist or romantic." The Joan of this tradition is "a sweet, saintly heroine, combining the utmost in feminine charm, humanity and sensibility with the utmost in achievement in the most characteristically masculine realm. . . ." The Joan of the realistic Burgundian chroniclers—a sort of virago—was lost with the Burgundian cause.[5]

The liberal and anti-clerical Michelet responded to the clerical and monarchist image of Joan of Arc because, as an ardent patriot, he saw her (correctly) as the incarnation of the French national tradition. To Michelet's nationalism Twain, naturally, was far from responsive, though he ends his novel in a burst of rhetoric about Joan as the symbol of Patriotism—presumably a plausible enough sentiment for de Conte. But Twain's official theme rings particularly hollow if we keep in mind his lifelong dislike of the French nation. Significantly, in the "Joan of Arc" MS in the Mark Twain Papers the "Conclusion" is written in the black ink Twain was using for revisions (as opposed to the bluish-purple ink of the original text). It seems safe to assume, therefore, that this conclusion was an afterthought designed to round out the book and give it some kind of positive meaning. The original text ends with Joan at the stake, and de Conte's words on this occasion come much closer (as I shall demonstrate on the following pages) to suggesting the real meaning of the book: "Yes she was gone from us: JOAN OF ARC! What little words they are, to tell of a rich world made empty and poor" (XVIII, 282). Certainly for Michelet's occasional chauvinism Twain had nothing but contempt. In the margin of his own copy of *The Life of Joan of Arc*, for example, opposite that passage in which Michelet remarks

that an English or German woman would not have risked the journey from Vaucouleurs to Chinon because of the "indelicacy of the proceeding," Twain remarked:
"How stupid! A *Joan of Arc* would do it no matter *what* her nationality might be.
That spirit has no nationality."[6] The equally liberal and anti-clerical Twain responded
to the prevalent image of Joan both because she appealed to his romantic ideal of
womanhood and for far deeper and more complex reasons, some of which I shall
investigate in the course of this article.

Whatever his motives, Twain was thus essentially committed to the solution
of an historical problem which he freely admitted was rationally insoluble. Yet the
whole matter is further complicated by the fact that, granted the traditional Joan
was a one-sided picture, Twain could not really relate even this Joan to the Middle
Ages because he did not understand the Middle Ages in the sense that any historian
must "understand" a given period in order to interpret it correctly—that is, by
being able to re-experience or re-live it sympathetically in his own mind.[7] Twain
was largely ignorant of medieval theory and what he knew—or thought he
knew—of it clashed, of course, with his Enlightenment ideals. With medieval practices he was equally horrified. As a result, he could not relate his image of Joan of
Arc to his image of the Middle Ages; how, indeed, was one to explain the impossibly good in terms of the impossibly bad? Joan was as unique morally as she was
in her untrained genius. "When we reflect," he remarks in his Preface, "that her
century was the brutalest, the wickedest, the rottenest in history since the darkest
ages, we are lost in wonder at the miracle of such a product from such a soil. The
contrast between her and her century is the contrast between day and night" (XVII,
p. xxi). Joan's innate goodness was clearly a miraculous phenomenon. Twain had
written an historical novel whose protagonist was historically meaningless because
outside the web of historical causality.

Certain of his Catholic sources were actually on far surer logical grounds when
they treated Joan's story frankly as a saint's tale and derived from it a theological
meaning, yet it was these very writers whom Twain mocked most unmercifully for
their credulity in his marginal comments to their works. "This is the 19th century,"
he sneered at Monsignor Richard's suggestion that the Archangel Michael personally
intervened in a battle. On another occasion, Richard related an incident in which
Joan's saints refused to give her advice, and Twain noted marginally: "These saints
are merely idiots. They remind her of nothing that is valuable."[8] For the more
sentimental and pietistic Countess de Chabannes, he had even harsher strictures.
When she attempted to explain Joan's success and popularity with the common
people by arguing that it is the privilege of the poor to recognize more easily those
whom God sends because "where He chooses His instruments, He also provides
witnesses," Twain was quick to spot the absurdity. Beside the passage he wrote: "It
seems so great and wonderful that He should choose his instruments by preference
among the dull and ignorant that I marvel He does not choose cats—His glory
would be the greater and the argument is the same."[9] Twain, in short, ridiculed
miraculous explanations to certain problems he had himself defined as miraculous.
His rationalism and deep-seated dislike of Catholicism prevented him from any easy

recourse to traditional Christian interpretations of the Joan "riddle." We shall, nevertheless, observe later how close he actually came to the essential Catholic position on Joan.

Twain could scarcely conceive of Joan's taking an active part in the religious life of the Middle Ages. Where, for example, the Countess de Chabannes describes her as confessing herself several times to the Franciscans at Neufchateau during the two weeks she was there in her youth, Twain noted marginally: "Think of this heroic soul in such company—and yet nothing but this base superstition could lift her to that fearless height" (p. 25). Joan's later conflict with "this base superstition," however, Twain could comprehend and passionately sympathize with, especially since the perfect villain was at hand in the person of the Bishop of Beauvais.

Inevitably for Twain and other nineteenth-century biographers and historians of the Protestant and rationalist tradition the deeply equivocal figure of Pierre Cauchon—apparently the very incarnation of the base, subtle, and Machiavellian priest—represented a heaven-sent opportunity for the expression of anti-clerical sentiments. Even Catholic writers after the Rehabilitation were authorized to throw him to the dogs with scant explanation. For a villain condemned so unanimously Twain naturally would listen to no extenuating pleas.[10] De Conte certainly speaks for his creator when he describes the Bishop as "the cruelest man and the most shameless that has lived in this world" (XVIII, 133). Cauchon, accordingly, emerges in the novel a caricature of absolute evil. "When I looked at that obese president," says de Conte at the beginning of the trial, "puffing and wheezing there, his great belly distending and receding with each breath, and noted his three chins, fold above fold, and his knobby and knotty face, and his purple and splotchy complexion, and his repulsive cauliflower nose, and his cold and malignant eyes—a brute every detail of him—my heart sank. . . ." In contrast to this monster, Joan enters the court "a dainty little figure . . . gentle and innocent . . . winning and beautiful in the fresh bloom of her seventeen years" (XVIII, 123–124). Twain is dealing entirely in stereotypes here; the Armagnac image of Joan and the Protestant image of the fat priest merge imperceptibly into the heroine and villain of Victorian popular literature. We are asked to cheer as time and time again the frail but indomitable virgin foils the vile seducer. The diction takes on the overtones of domestic melodrama. "One wonders if he [Cauchon] ever knew his mother or ever had a sister," the agonized de Conte asks on one occasion (XVIII, 223); on another, after Cauchon and his assistants bore a hole in Joan's cell to hear her confessions: "One wonders how they could treat that poor child so. She had not done them any harm" (XVIII, 223). Twain's abysmal ignorance of the historical forces at work in the Middle Ages is never more clearly revealed than in this last remark of de Conte; he has reduced a death struggle between political and social systems to the Victorian convention of the female in distress. De Conte, of course, is the hero of the melodrama, prevented from rescuing the heroine at the point of his sword by the awkward facts of history. A note inside the cover of the Countess de Chabannes' biography suggests that Twain at one time planned to have several of Joan's playmates make an *attempted* rescue.

It remains for us to pursue further some of the implications and ramifications of Twain's idealization. If Joan's genius had flowered without training, if her moral values were antithetical to those of her brutal environment, she must have been above the pleasure-pain psychology and free from the moral sense that Twain felt to be characteristic of the human mind. Thus she was truly unselfish, in Twain's words, "perhaps the only entirely unselfish person whose name has a place in profane history" (XVII, Pref., p. xxii). She was a double miracle: unique not only for the Middle Ages but for all time, "the most extraordinary person the human race has ever produced" (XVII, 383). The next step was inevitable. From his Catholic sources (if he did not develop the idea independently) Twain perceived the similarity of Joan to Jesus, of her trial before Cauchon with that of Jesus before the Sanhedrin and Pilate.[11] Above the page in which Monsignor Richard made this explicit comparison Twain wrote in bad French: "Il y avait un charge réel contre J. C.—qu'il avail se nommé le roi des Juifs, n'est ce pas? On ne pouvait pas l'eprouver; neaumoins on a-t-il condamnè[.] L'Eglise n'apportait pas contre Jeanne que des soupçonnes et manquèe de les etablir" (p. 167). Twain seems to be saying that actually the Sanhedrin had a better case against Jesus when they turned him over to Pilate than did the Ecclesiastical Court against Joan when they released her to Warwick. By implication she was more historically "innocent"—more "unselfish" and less caught up in remorseless causality. As Twain put it in another place: "No vestige or suggestion of self-seeking can be found in any word or deed of hers" (XVII, Pref., p. xxii). But it is unwise and unnecessary for us to labor this hint of Joan's superiority to Jesus. What is important to note is that Twain consciously made the comparison, that, in fact, the two images tended to blend in his mind.

A case in point is Joan's trial at Poitiers. Twain, naturally, did not limit the expression of his distaste for Catholicism merely to attacks on the Bishop of Beauvais and his associates; they were, as I have noted above, simply particularly vulnerable targets. For the clerics at Poitiers Twain had only slightly less contempt. His feelings are abundantly evident in the savage little notes in his copy of the Countess de Chabannes' *La Vierge Lorraine,* the book which clearly was his chief source for the facts of this episode. "Persecution by these mitred donkeys," he scribbled at the head of the Countess de Chabannes' chapter describing the inquiry or, again, further on: "There the question wasn't 'Can this soldier win victories,' but 'Is he a sound Catholic' " (pp. 58, 63). This idea was given to the supposedly medieval Sieur de Conte and elaborated on in the course of his comments on the scene at Poitiers (XVII, 160).

What is more significant than Twain's gibes at the Church as an institution, however, is the manner in which he here borrowed directly from the Countess the religious overtones that continually color her description of Joan of Arc and, in particular, her implied comparison of Joan with Christ. "Assise sur un banc," wrote the Countess, "Jeanne était là devant ses interrogateurs, répondant, sans se troubler, à toutes leurs questions, déconcertant la science de tous ces sages par sa sublime ignorance..." (p. 59). Twain underlined this sentence from the word "déconcertant" to the word "ignorance" and later apparently copied the underlined part without change into his own manuscript. Altering the rest of the sentence slightly, he also added a final elaboration. His version of this scene runs as follows:

> She sat there, solitary on her bench, untroubled, and disconcerted the science of the sages with her sublime ignorance—an ignorance which was a fortress; arts, wiles, the learning drawn from books, and all like missiles rebounded from its unconscious masonry and fell to the ground harmless; they could not dislodge the garrison which was within—Joan's serene great heart and spirit. . . . (XVII, 160–161)

The Countess de Chabannes' description of Joan before the tribunal at Poitiers was clearly, as Twain noted in the margin of her book, "Christ before the doctors again" (p. 59). It was this description he chose to borrow almost intact. While rejecting the external trappings of the Catholic position regarding Joan, Twain had, in fact, like the Catholic writers, undertaken to explain her riddle by resorting to that strand of anti-intellectualism and primitivism that is such a pervasive part of Christianity. Devoid of formal training, Joan apparently derived her strength from intuitional and mystical sources—"this intoxicated child," as Twain called her in another note (p. 58). A divine spirit come to dwell among men, she was, like Christ, the more engaging because she consented to be so human. In *La Vierge Lorraine* Twain wrote after one of Joan's exchanges with her examiners: "Good incident[.] Childish but can be improved." Then he added at the bottom of the page: "No, don't improve her poor little sallies—they show what a natural human she was, and she is the more engaging for it" (p. 60). Twain's Joan is clearly a saint but, like the saints of most baffled rationalists, denatured and divorced from teleological ends.

While almost all of Joan's nineteenth-century biographers were forced by the apparent evidence to generally similar conclusions, many of them made heroic attempts to relate the ideal Joan to her base environment before falling into the attitude of awe and wonder that is called forth by the presence of the Divine. Twain, on the other hand, tries to evade the whole historical problem through the use of a narrator. With Twain, the first person point of view is a means of expressing appropriate homage to a saint without being held responsible for the implications of such homage, just as in *A Connecticut Yankee* it is a means of espousing the idea of progress and at the same time keeping it at arm's length. Instead of regarding Joan of Arc simultaneously with a medieval and a modern mind (as life on the Mississippi in *Huckleberry Finn* is viewed simultaneously with a boy's and adult's mind)—a technique which might have produced a masterpiece—Twain actually retreats first into one, then the other as the occasion seems to demand, while always *apparently* speaking in the voice of de Conte. Thus, for example, de Conte is thoroughly medieval in describing how he actually *saw* St. Michael appear to Joan,[12] and, on the other hand, thoroughly modern in his attack on the priests at Poitiers. Occasionally Twain attempts the kind of irony that might have artistically unified the two visions, but he does this only in order to exploit a humorous situation, never to give meaning to a serious one. De Conte is treated ironically, for example, when he is telling about the dragon that lived in the forest behind Domremy. Nobody has ever seen this dragon, but de Conte confidently describes it as "very big, even unusually so for a dragon, as everybody said who knew about dragons" (XVII, 7–8). When, de Conte describes his dealings with Joan of Arc, however, Twain fails to maintain the same ironic detachment, and the reader accordingly loses all sense of perspective. How are we to evaluate such scenes as the one previously mentioned in which de Conte actually comes upon St. Michael talking to Joan? The gap between Twain and his narrator has closed to such an extent that we are forced to accept the incident at close to its face value. Where the fictive elements in an historical novel should heighten and sharpen the meaning of obscure events—ideally give them both a temporal and a universal significance—those elements in *Joan of Arc* tend to obscure or blur meaning. As an early reviewer pointed out, Twain is forced to commit himself where a cautious historian would hold back.[13] But he commits himself to no good purpose except to abandon the whole historical problem. When we begin to read how de Conte saw "a *white* shadow [i.e. St. Michael; the italics are Twain's] come slowly gliding along the grass toward the Tree," we are far from the Twain who thought that Joan's saints were "merely idiots" or that one was a fool if one still imagined in the nineteenth century that St. Michael had intervened in French battles. The two positions seem hopelessly disparate and Twain, unlike some of his contemporaries, made no attempt to reconcile them.

If irony was inadmissible in dealing with Joan, so was the kind of anachronistic commentary that often elsewhere in the book makes de Conte a mere spokesman for Twain. In revising his text for publication, Twain crossed out the following lines, which were to come after the passage (XVII, 232) in which de Conte argues that the professors at the University of Paris (who had just pronounced Joan's voices to be fiends) might as easily be deceived as Joan: "Privately, I myself never had a high opinion of Joan's voices—I mean in some respects—but that they were devils I do not believe. I think they were saints, holy and pure and well-meaning, but with the saint's natural incapacity for business. Whatever a saint is, he is not clever. There are acres of history to prove it." This is on MS pp. 341–342. P. 343 is missing but de Conte's comments go on on p. 344: "...The voices meant Joan nothing but good, and I am sure they did the very best they could with their equipment; but I also feel sure that if they had let her alone her matters would sometimes have gone much better. Remember, these things which I have been saying are privacies—let them go no further; for I have not more desire to be damned than another." Twain obviously realized that the tone and sentiments of this passage, notwithstanding the final sentence, were inappropriate to de Conte. At the same time, they suggest Twain's own skepticism regarding the supernatural aspects of Joan's career and the care which he took to exclude this skepticism from his book because it had so little relation to what he felt about Joan as an individual. What was really important (and what he desperately wanted to believe in) was the basic irrationality of her life.

II. The Meaning of Joan

Clearly *Joan of Arc* is more a solution—or at least a reflection—of certain problems that were haunting Twain when he wrote it than it is a solution to the problem of Joan. The idea of progress, for example, is a distinct theme in the book; indeed, it is implied in Twain's very prejudices. In despair as he was over the nineteenth century, Twain made little attempt to understand, let alone idealize, the fifteenth.[14] In the Preface, furthermore, he suggests indirectly that moral standards have advanced from one century to another and that "judged by the standards of today, there is probably no illustrious character of four or five centuries ago whose character could meet the test at all points" (XVII, p. xxi). Finally, at one point in the book, de Conte, in an episode reminiscent of *A Connecticut Yankee,* suddenly realizes that peasants are "people." Someday they will realize it too, he says, and "then I think they will rise up and demand to be regarded as part of the race, and that by consequence there will be trouble." De Conte adds that it is only "training" which keeps "everybody" (i.e., all his contemporaries) from realizing this fact (XVIII, 65–66). In moments of disgust with the Middle Ages, Twain can thus not resist looking forward to his beloved French Revolution, even though it turns his narrator into almost as phenomenal a prophet as Joan herself. But such remarks as those he attributes to de Conte are, it seems to me, more an instinctive reaction to an age he disliked (and which he never could bring himself to equate with his own except by implication) than the fruit of a firmly held conviction which we can genuinely label a belief in progress—as we can so easily label the Yankee's ideas. They constitute, indeed, a distinctly recessive theme in *Joan of Arc.* Even Twain's remarks on moral standards are introduced simply to suggest the uniqueness of Joan. Her character, he goes on to say, "can be measured by the standards of all times without misgiving or apprehension as to the result. Judged by any of them, judged by all of them, it is still flawless, it is still ideally perfect." In other words, the locus of values in *Joan of Arc* (and this constitutes the book's chief point of contrast with *A Connecticut Yankee*) lies not in an historical epoch, but in a personality who is clearly outside the logical processes of history. "It took six thousand years to produce her," says de Conte, "her like will not be seen on the earth again in fifty thousand" (XVIII, 143).

It is not surprising that Twain groped for the miraculous during the 90's. Before *Joan of Arc* was published in 1895, the Paige typesetter had failed, the Charles L. Webster Co. had gone into receivership in the general depression that was blanketing the country, and Twain had begun his exhausting round-the-world lecture tour in an effort to pay off his creditors. He had reached, moreover, what seemed to be an artistic and intellectual as well as a financial dead end. His belief in progress was hopelessly compromised by his resurgent pessimism and the growing fear of oligarchy that he expresses in *The American Claimant.* In addition, his already fading image of the idyllic village had finally disappeared in the moral dry rot of Dawson's Landing; his dream of Eden, in the banalities of *Tom Sawyer Abroad, Adam's Diary,* and *Tom Sawyer Detective* and in the despair of old age and lost youth suggested by notes such as the one in which Twain imagined Huck as coming back "sixty years old, from nobody knows where—and crazy." He meets Tom again "and together they talk of old times, both are desolate, life has been a failure, all that was lovable is under the mold. They die together."[15] Clearly actual childhood memories and associations could no longer generate sustaining images. There was no refuge on the bosom of the river, no flight to the West, that could preserve the qualities of childhood from the ravages of life in time.

In the notebook which follows that in which Twain records the fate of Huck and Tom, however, there is the notation: "Chatto send me—Joan of Arc books."[16] He had decided to write what he himself realized would be "a companion piece to *The Prince and the Pauper*" (XXXII, 960). His imagination turned from the defeated Huck and Tom to the dream of omnipotent innocence—to that other child masquerading as absolute ruler who, like Tom Canty, had influenced history and yet was profoundly unhistorical. In *The Prince and the Pauper* Twain had accounted for "certain mildnesses which distinguished Edward VI's reign from those that preceded and followed it,"[17] not by an appeal to institutions as he did later in the *Connecticut Yankee,* but by bringing innate goodness directly and forcefully to bear on iniquity. "How his name shines out of the midst of that long darkness," Twain once wrote, at the same time arguing that Edward was the only good English ruler before Victoria.[18] The tone of this comment is close to that which Twain normally used when talking about Joan and suggests how much his later heroine was simply a feminized and somewhat more grown-up Edward and Tom. Joan brought to a brutal power struggle both an iron will that crushed all opposition and the goodness of childhood; for "she was a young girl ... and her hero-heart was a young girl's heart too, with the pity and tenderness that are natural to it" (XVII, 239).

Unlike Edward and Tom, however, Joan transcends the very images with which she is associated. She is the Christ figure, the "ideally perfect" individual who "was not made as others are made."[19] If history appeared to promise (as Satan was to demonstrate in *The Mysterious Stranger*) nothing except endless cycles of cruelty and slaughter by automatons, Twain could at least escape it emotionally and intuitively in the personality of Joan of Arc—the "intoxicated child." His phrase reveals the crux of Joan's significance for him. In her, his lifelong dream of Adamic innocence found a kind of religious sanction. Since she was, moreover, certified to be an authentic historical phenomenon by testimony taken "under oath" (as he naively boasted in his Introduction) and the authority of legions of later writers including Michelet, Twain could worship her openly and at will and yet appease, by an appeal to the record, the voice of rationality within him.

Joan of Arc, nevertheless, is a deeply pessimistic book. If it is an affirmation of the existence and power of innocence, it is also a scathing record of its betrayal. While Edward magically puts everything to rights at the end of his wanderings, while Huck (at least in *Huckleberry Finn*) succeeds in escaping to the West, Joan, on the other hand, is abandoned by her friends and burned by her enemies, and nothing Twain can do can save her. Her ultimate failure, indeed, is the central theme of a book whose real ending, as I have already noted, is the scene at the stake. Her character and her fate become a measure of the general depravity of the human race. "I believed these [reports that the King was going to ransom Joan]," de Conte notes bitterly in his old age, "for I was young and had not yet found out the littleness and meanness of our poor human race, which brags about itself so much, and thinks it is better and higher than other animals" (XVIII, 109). Only Joan's childhood companions—the other village children who followed her and formed her loyal and worshiping band—remain faithful to the end. Unlike the Huck of Twain's later fantasy, Joan manages to retain her sanity and her will but only at the cost of her freedom ("she, born child of the sun, natural comrade of the birds and of all happy free creatures" [XVIII, 124–125]) and her life. Nor did her martyrdom have the kind of positive meaning for Twain that might have led to acceptance if not faith, as Melville accepts the similar fate of Billy Budd and Faulkner does that of the Corporal. The hollow rhetoric of Twain's superimposed "Conclusion" suggests his painful awareness that for him Joan's life and death promised neither the Redemption of man nor even the enduring reality of love and goodness but simply the rise of the hated French nation. It is, in fact, but one short step from *Joan of Arc* to *The Mysterious Stranger*—from a belief in the goodness, however ultimately meaningless, of one isolated individual to a belief in the corruptibility of *all*, including specifically the young and the innocent. In his final book, indeed, Twain can only escape life in time by denying its reality, by arguing that history is literally nightmare—"a grotesque and fool dream" (XXVII, 139). For Twain as for his contemporary, Henry Adams, faith in history was to lead ultimately to a blind alley where bitterness and despair lay in wait.

NOTES

[1] *The Works of Mark Twain* (New York, 1922–25), XIV, 130. Cited in the body of the text by volume and page numbers; in footnotes cited as *Works*.

[2] Notably in "Eddypus, Books I and II" and the fragments collected by De Voto as "Letters from the Earth," catalogued respectively as Paine 42a and De Voto (DV) 33 in the Mark Twain Estate Papers (cited below as MTP). All quotations from unpublished MSS and most of the text of this article excluding the Introduction are Copyright 1957 by Roger B. Salomon and the Mark Twain Co. The author gratefully acknowledges the generous permission of Professor Henry Nash Smith and the Mark Twain Co. to make use of copyright materials.

[3] *Works*, XXII, 363–364. See also XXXVI, 186, where Twain, answering a criticism of "St. Joan of Arc," strongly reiterates this "riddle" of Joan's personality and feats. It is a "mystery we cannot master," he says.

[4] *The Life of Joan of Arc* (New York, 1887), pp. 6, 92.

[5] "Joan of Arc as Her Enemies Saw Her," in *The World of History*, ed. Courtland Canby and Nancy E. Gross, Mentor ed. (New York, 1954), pp. 190–194.

[6] P. 20 of Twain's Paris, 1873 ed. in the MTP.

[7] See R. G. Collingwood, *The Idea of History* (Oxford, 1946), p. 327.

[8] *Jeanne d'Arc, la vénérable* (Paris, n.d.), pp. 23, 213–234. In the MTP.

[9] *La Vierge Lorraine, Jeanne d'Arc* (Paris, 1890), p. 39. In the MTP.

[10] Where, for example, John O'Hagan—*Joan of Arc* (London, 1893), p. 68—one of his sources, suggests that Cauchon did not act with deliberate iniquity, Twain scrawled "Shucks" across the margin of the page. The melodramatic elements in the book have also been noted by Albert E. Stone, Jr., "Mark Twain's *Joan of Arc*: The Child as Goddess," *American Literature*, XXXI (1959), 11–13.

[11] On the page following the front cover of Countess de Chabannes' biography Twain wrote:

Several great historical trials:
   Christ before Pilate
   Joan's two trials
   That man in the time of Mary (?)

[12] *Works*, XVII, 67–76. A Catholic priest, Edward G. Rosenberger, "An Agnostic Hagiographer," *Catholic World*, CXXVII (Sept., 1938), 717–723, claims Twain created here an "accurately imagined mysticism." Rosenberger points out (though for a different purpose) what I have been stressing in this article: namely, the essential similarity of Twain's position to that of the Catholics regarding Joan of Arc.

[13] James W. Thompson, "The Maid of Orleans," *The Dial*, XX (June 16, 1896), 355.

[14] Mentor I. Williams, "Mark Twain's Joan of Arc," *Michigan Alumnus Quarterly Review*, LIV (May, 1948), 243–250 argues that Twain, escaping from a business civilization, sought for the "moral fiber, the ethical core of human society. He did not find it in the modern world. Like his contemporary, Henry Adams, he found it in the medieval world" (p. 250). There is, indeed, a basis of comparison with Adams (whose Virgin represents an escape from remorseless causality) but Williams grossly oversimplifies it because in *Joan of Arc* there is as strong a hatred of medieval life—aside from its color and spectacle—as is found in any of Twain's work. I have attempted to demonstrate that Twain loved Joan because her personality and her ideals were so very different from those of the average human being of every age—but *especially* her own. If we must identify Twain's Joan with a historical epoch, Shaw's description of her as an "unimpeachable American school teacher in armor" is far more to the point (*Nine Plays*, New York, 1947, p. 1006).

[15] Notebook No. 25 (1890–91), MTP, p. 24. Pub. In *Notebook*, ed. A. B. Paine (New York, 1935), p. 212.

[16] No. 26 (1891–92), p. 6. Twain's devotion to Joan was, of course, lifelong. His active interest in doing a biography of her, however, probably stems from the early 80's when he seems to have had a bibliography on the subject drawn up (see Paine, *Works*, XXXII, 958 and "Documents for 1892," DV 122, MTP).

[17] One of his stated purposes in writing the book as he described them to Howells (*Works*, XXXIV, 377).

[18] "Notes to Discarded Portions of the *Connecticut Yankee*," Paine 91a, MTP, p. 6.

[19] *Works*, XVIII, 215. Ironically, ten years before Twain had written in Notebook No. 21 (1885–87), p. 46: "Who could endure a French Christ." For an extended discussion of Joan's relationship to nature and childish (pre-rational) sources of knowledge and power see Stone, "Mark Twain's *Joan of Arc*," pp. 15–18.

Frank M. Fowler

SIGHT AND INSIGHT IN SCHILLER'S *DIE JUNGFRAU VON ORLEANS*

In the present century the reputation of Schiller's 'romantic tragedy' with its rhetorical pathos and its startling deviations from historical fact has fared particularly badly: there must be many today who are surprised by Thomas Mann's reference to *Die Jungfrau von Orleans* as 'dieses edelmütige, wunderherrliche Stück'[1] and few if any who would care to subscribe to Goethe's reported opinion that it is 'Schiller's best play';[2] certainly it is difficult to forget Shaw's reference to the 'witch's cauldron of raging romance'—a phrase which seems to echo Hebbel's indictment of it as 'ein hohles Überpinseln der Wahrheit mit idealer Schminke'.[3] On the other hand, even if modern producers cannot quite claim, as Schiller did of an early performance in Weimar 'Alles ist davon elektrisiert worden',[4] it must be admitted that productions of this play even in recent years have met with a remarkably enthusiastic response from the audience; despite our difficulty in coming to terms with an early nineteenth-century treatment of a medieval subject and with the depiction of a simple shepherdess as a person prone to indulge in a great deal of reflection about herself and her fate,[5] the play has still not lost all of its impact on the stage. Nonetheless, twentieth-century critics dealing with *Die Jungfrau* seem to find far more awkward problems than satisfying solutions. How could Schiller the historian forget himself to the extent of totally altering well-known historical facts? How could he in such a cavalier manner introduce into his apparently Christian material so many foreign pagan notions, which obtrude even into the speeches of his saintly Archbishop? Why should he make the divinely-inspired Johanna kill? Does the heroine's tragic guilt consist in some sort of *hubris* or in her failure to conquer her sexual urge at a crucial moment? And finally, in view of the heroine's ultimate apotheosis, is this play a tragedy at all?

It has frequently been taken as self-evident that Schiller distorts history in order to create a tragedy conforming with his particular theories and to provide a lavish demonstration of a character's attainment of sublimity—twice over, for good measure: first 'das Erhabene der Fassung', then 'das Erhabene der Handlung'. But if

---

From *Modern Language Review* 68, No. 1 (April 1973): 367–79.

this is *all* that the play has to offer, then despite its lavish display of technical brilliance it must seem hopelessly shallow when compared with the fascinating complexities of *Wallenstein*, let alone *Egmont, Iphigenie,* and *Tasso.* Is this merely a play based on one idea rather than a play of ideas? We remember the fundamental question raised in her brilliant Taylorian lecture of 1959 by Professor E. M. Wilkinson regarding Schiller's dramatic personages in general: 'Are they not chiefly concerned with the traditional problem of willing rather than with the future-orientated problems of knowing and being?'[6] Certainly a vast army of Schiller scholars would have us think so. But as long as we seek to discover in Schiller a marriage between dramatic theory and dramatic practice, that is precisely what we shall find; in fact, a relationship undoubtedly exists—but it is neither so close nor so exclusive as the ideal marriage.

In his Schiller monograph of 1959 Benno von Wiese sees the play as 'das parabolisch-legendäre Drama von der Fremdheit des Transzendenten inmitten einer eitlen, unreinen, herabziehenden Welt, von seinem tragischen Schicksal in dieser Welt und von seiner dann übertragisch vollzogenen Versöhnung und Wiedervereinigung mit dem Ursprung' (p. 375). This view, involving a considerable degree of abstraction (since the requirement of chastity is seen as having 'stellvertretende allegorische Bedeutung für die sich selbst verschließende und damit unzugängliche Transzendenz' (p. 738)), has more recently been strongly criticized by Emil Staiger, who properly points out that Schiller's audience do not require to be well-versed in philosophy in order to follow the play.[7] Certainly if we bear in mind the consideration put so firmly in *Über epische und dramatische Dichtung:*

> Der zuschauende Hörer muß von Rechts wegen in einer steten sinnlichen Anstrengung bleiben, er darf sich nicht zum Nachdenken erheben, er muß leidenschaftlich folgen, seine Phantasie ist ganz zum Schweigen gebracht, man darf keine Ansprüche an sie machen, und selbst was erzählt wird, muß gleichsam darstellend vor die Augen gebracht werden.[8]

it seems particularly unlikely that Schiller could have expected his audience to see in the requirement of chastity anything other than its dramatic function, which is as a token of selfless, single-minded dedication to a calling higher than that of ordinary men; if some of them were aware of the ancient association of chastity with strength, so much the better. It might also be objected that von Wiese's repeated insistence on Johanna's 'otherness' as opposed to her human qualities (she is, he says 'nicht von dieser Welt', 'die Fremde, die eigentlich gar nicht auf die Erde gehört' (pp. 734f.)) makes it more rather than less difficult for us to sympathize with her and also accords ill with Schiller's own identification of his heroine in the poem *Das Mädchen von Orleans* with 'das edle Bild der *Menschheit'.*

A radically different view from von Wiese's was put forward in the same year by Gerhard Storz in his book *Der Dichter Friedrich Schiller.* Storz finds any sort of 'ideologische Deutung' untenable, and instead lays stress on the dramatist's 'unermüdliche Spielfreude' (p. 355): 'Der mittelalterliche Stoff versprach neue, interessante Formen, und Freiheit im Spiel mit solchen Formen' (p. 365). But attractive though this approach may appear, it is difficult to agree with Storz when he claims that the cry

Dich schuf das Herz, du wirst unsterblich leben

in the poem *Das Mädchen von Orleans* is to be understood merely as 'ein Apell an die Unbefangenheit der Phantasie' (p. 365). And while Schiller himself expressed delight at both the quality of the Weimar performance and the reaction of the audience, he nowhere suggests (as one might expect if either von Wiese or Storz is right in his interpretation) that the audience enjoyed the play for the wrong reasons.

Emil Staiger's view of the play seems more balanced than either the philosophical approach of von Wiese or the *l'art pour l'art* theory of Storz: 'Schiller hat das Trauerspiel *Die Jungfrau von Orleans* nicht verfaßt, um den erhabenen Menschen in der höchsten Steigerung vorzuführen und dessen typisches Schicksal in einer Folge von Akten darzutun. Er hat sich der wunderbaren Gestalt und ihres heroischen Wandels bedient, um eine Tragödie zu verfassen und abermals von der Bühne herab das Mitleid und die Furcht zu entfesseln und uns durch labyrinthische Gänge unserer Leidenschaften in das Reich der Freiheit zu geleiten' (pp. 404f.). Staiger goes on to emphasize—as he had done years before in his valuable essay on *Agrippina*[9]—that Schiller is not, like some later dramatists, a 'Weltanschauungsdichter': 'Die Bühne dient nicht seinen Ideen; seine Ideen dienen ihr, die selber wieder der Freiheit dient' (p. 405).[10] Staiger's comments on the play, which are well-supported by the text and plainly not at odds with Schiller's own references to it,[11] clear away a good deal of dead wood in the way of far-fetched hypotheses; entirely eschewing the esoteric he openly admits: 'Wer nur zu hören und zu schauen vermag, der weiß, woran er ist.' (p. 406).[12] For although both early and late in his career as a dramatist Schiller insists that the poem should speak for itself, he never hesitated to equip a work with a preface when he feared that some explanation might be necessary: he did this in the case of *Die Räuber, Fiesko, Wallenstein,* and *Die Braut von Messina.* For *Die Jungfrau,* however, despite its novelty of form and treatment, of which he was fully aware, Schiller provided no such preface:[13] clearly this was for him a case in which 'the picture could speak for the artist',[14] 'the work of art providing its own justification'.[15] Bearing this in mind, we would do well to approach the play, as Staiger suggests, not as an illustrative supplement to his philosophical writings but rather as a dramatic work of art in its own proper context—that context being not theory but the theatre.

What Staiger does not take into account is whether Schiller here treats any realities of the human condition other than those dealt with in his theory of the sublime—for in Staiger's interpretation the 'traditional problem of willing' appears to be the sole central theme: Johanna chooses the path of 'Seelenfrieden' in preference to 'Sinnenglück', suffers appallingly when her sensuality asserts itself at a critical moment, but then overcomes her weakness so that we finally become witnesses of the kind of 'Aufschwung, der immer wieder in Schillers Werk, am Schluß von "Das Ideal und das Leben", des "Lieds von der Glocke", der "Nänie", alle

irdische Mühe und Qual in wesenlosem Scheine versinken läßt' (pp. 402–4). My
purpose in this article is to make clear that—despite his elaborately stylized and
even 'operatic' handling of his subject-matter—Schiller does not in this play totally
abandon reality in order to indulge either in 'raging romance' or in a mere dramatic
demonstration of the sublime; but rather that in giving his audience the experience
of tragic pity and fear he at the same time—through the use of a single dominant
and recurring theme inextricably woven into the texture of the play—comments
on the extent and limitations of man's perception. The theme is the theme of vision,
which to a great extent guides and dictates both the outer and inner action, and
which in its duality determines both the crashing discord of Johanna's crisis and its
glorious resolution. In investigating this theme we shall find—unlike those who
consider it solely as a sublime spectacle—that Schiller did not write five-sixths of his
play before 'coming to the point';[16] we shall also find that we must abandon the
traditional opinion that he distorted historical facts merely in order to make Johanna's case an example of 'das Erhabene'. Instead it will, I think, become clear that
the history with which Schiller is dealing is not a sequence of events in France
between 1429 and 1431 but rather something far nearer the whole history of the
legend of Jeanne d'Arc. Through the use of the theme of vision in his characters—
'ideale Personen und Repräsentanten ihrer Gattung, die das Tiefe der Menschheit
aussprechen'[17]—he shows mankind's long struggle to come to terms with an extraordinary figure, and finally presents an attitude amazingly close to the atmosphere of reverence to be publicly expressed—long after Schiller's death—in the
beatification and canonization of 1920.[18]

When Schiller on 18 April 1801 sent to Goethe his newly-completed manuscript of *Die Jungfrau,* he enclosed with it a prospective cast-list drawn up with the
Weimar players in mind. Hardly surprising perhaps—for surely this of all his tragedies is the one most clearly designed with a view to utilizing the total resources of
the theatre: the scenic effects of fire and storm and sunset, the acoustic effects of
thunder, background music, *and* silence, and the choreographic effects of battle
combat, regal procession, *and* motionlessness. In the text itself there are abundant
indications that Schiller was thinking throughout in terms of the theatre: in addition
to his careful distinction between instruments in the pit and those off-stage (III, 5;
IV, I), we have in this play an entire scene (IV, 6) without any dialogue at all. Even
in the Prologue, the reader is in danger of missing almost entirely—especially since
Schiller retards the appropriate stage-direction to the point at which it functions
only as a useful reminder to the producer—one of the most powerful dramatic
effects available to a playwright: the effect of a principal figure standing apart,
unmoving and unmoved for minutes on end, totally uninvolved by the very dialogue
which involves *her,* until at length she suddenly darts forward and speaks—with
words and actions symbolic of her future involvement with the community. And
here, as so often in Schiller's tragedies, theatrical effectiveness and thematic importance coincide.

In this Prologue we, the audience, see Johanna in her solitude, in her strange
remoteness from her immediate human environment, we see her refusal or her

inability to react to the very situations which bring joy and contentment to both her sisters. And simultaneously we hear the first two of many conflicting opinions on her nature and her worth—each of them based on ocular observation. Raimond's account (ll. 73ff.) of how he has watched her standing on a hillside looking gravely down on 'der Erde kleine Länder' is answered almost antiphonally by Thibaut's 'Ich sehe sie' (l. 92) introducing his report of how he has seen her sitting for hours on end under the very tree which he regards with a superstitious dread. Significantly, Thibaut refuses to accept that for Johanna the attraction might be the holy shrine rather than the druids' tree, just as a few lines later he totally ignores Raimond's reminder that he must see how she neither scorns nor fails to perform her duties to her family. In Thibaut *one* visual image of Johanna predominates, and his ambiguous dreams are interpreted by him to conform with that image. This scene thus brings the first quiet entry of the theme of vision which pervades the entire play.

The importance of the purely visual impact made by Johanna in the process of converting others to her cause is repeatedly stressed: Raoul explicitly mentions the effect which the very sight of her made both on the soldiers of Lorraine (ll. 951–3) and on the opposing army (ll. 970–2); Dunois, the practical realist who becomes Johanna's greatest champion at court has faith in her less because of her miracles than because of her *appearance:*

> Nicht ihren Wundern, ihrem Auge glaub ich,
> Der reinen Unschuld ihres Angesichts   (ll. 1115f.)

Similarly in the vitally important conversion of Burgundy to the French cause, the Duke, having at first resisted Johanna's 'süßer Rede schmeichlerischen Ton' (l. 1742), is finally convinced only when he 'schlägt die Augen zu ihr auf' and *looks* at what is before him: 'Sie trügt nicht, diese rührende Gestalt' (l. 1801). But the eye—referred to elsewhere in the play as the bringer of joy (ll. 1953ff.) and the source of lust (ll. 1824f. and 2263f.)—can deceive. For when in Act IV Agnes Sorel looks closely into Johanna's eyes, she is totally misled as to what she 'sees' there (ll. 2629ff.). And Johanna's ultimate rejection by the Archbishop in IV, 11, is brought about not by the *audible* sign of the thunder and the contrast of Johanna's silence but by her failure to give a *visible* token of her innocence:

> Im Namen Gottes frag ich dich. Schweigst du
> Aus dem Gefühl der Unschuld oder Schuld?
> Wenn dieses Donners Stimme *für* dich zeugt,
> So fasse dieses Kreuz und gib ein Zeichen.   (ll. 3026–9)

This imaginative transposition of the historical trial of Jeanne d'Arc from legal into dramatic and human terms is heralded by a double re-entry of the theme of vision; for although Thibaut cannot know it, his claim at the very beginning of his public accusation of his daughter that the French are 'verblendet' (l. 2975) follows almost immediately on Karl's first words to Johanna after his coronation—a speech which emphasizes the inevitable inadequacy of man's sight and adumbrates the situation at the end of the play:

Wenn du die Strahlen himmlischer Natur
In diesem jungfräulichen Leib verhüllst,
So nimm das Band hinweg von unsern Sinnen
Und laß dich sehn in deiner Lichtgestalt,
Wie dich der Himmel sieht, daß wir anbetend
Im Staube dich verehren.   (ll. 2964–9)

It is the fallibility of man's judgement with its constant dependence on ocular proof
which leads, then, to Johanna's banishment; and it is the explicit reconsideration of
this same point which marks the turning-point in her external misfortune, when in
V, 7, Dunois and the Archbishop reflect on the discrepancy between what they
have seen and what they thought they saw:

ERZBISCHOF: —Wer konnte
            In dieser Schreckensstunde prüfend wagen?
            Jetzt kehrt uns die Besonnenheit zurück,
            Wir sehn sie, wie sie unter uns gewandelt,
            Und keinen Tadel finden wir an ihr.
            . . . .
DUNOIS: Sie eine Lügnerin! Wenn sich die Wahrheit
            Verkörpern will in sichtbarer Gestalt,
            So muß sie ihre Züge an sich tragen!
            Wenn Unschuld, Treue, Herzensreinigkeit
            Auf Erden irgend wohnt—auf ihren Lippen,
            In ihren klaren Augen muß sie wohnen!
ERZBISCHOF: Der Himmel schlage durch ein Wunder sich
            Ins Mittel und erleuchte dies Geheimnis,
            Dans unser sterblich Auge nicht durchdringt—   (ll. 3265–82)

In this necessary prelude to Johanna's rehabilitation, then, we find a further reca-
pitulation of our theme; and at every crucial point in the text it recurs—with an
intensity and insistence equalled nowhere else in Schiller's dramatic writing.[19]

Most critics—including those who contend that Schiller's sole purpose in writing Die Jungfrau was to provide a dramatic presentation of 'das Erhabene'—agree
that this play, like Maria Stuart, cannot be understood in specifically Christian or
even purely religious terms;[20] and certainly the playwright has gone to considerable
lengths to de-christianize his material by the repeated introduction of pagan notions
which he puts into the mouths of Johanna and the Archbishop himself. Even
Johanna's prophecies, which demonstrate to the audience her exceptional capacities, can be considered a symbolic extension into the past and the future of her
unusually keen sight (see esp. ll. 3433ff.)—that strange kind of vision which has been
repeatedly attributed to various exceptional persons throughout history and which
in our own time forms the subject of serious scientific investigation. The origins of
such insight are invariably mysterious and may appear to the individual or to those
around him to come from heaven; and it seems particularly noteworthy that the
Virgin Mary appears only after Johanna's passionate prayer for the liberation of

France (ll. 1059ff.) which contains in concentrated form the essential elements of her *earthly* vision of the natural political order of the country which she expresses in the third scene of the Prologue, and which is vital for our understanding of the whole play.[21] Taking up, as it were, Raimond's description of her standing high on the hillside gazing down on 'der Erde kleine Länder', she turns from the praise of the country's natural beauty to its glorious historical tradition, and finally to a vision of a peaceful and contented France united under its own wise and benevolent king. Her vision, it is true, is of a monarchy—but with a king who protects the peasants, liberates the serfs, ensures the happiness of the burghers and aids the weak: the friend of the just who tempers justice with mercy. With this vision—which Karl by the end of the play seems highly likely to make a reality (see esp. ll. 2940–8)—is contrasted the unnaturalness of the present situation, in which the country is to be ruled by an invader from a strange land who has neither a natural love for it nor the ability to be moved by pleas put in what is to him a foreign tongue—the king whose generals are threatening to ravish every virgin in Orleans and to put to death all civilians who have attempted to defend their city.[22] Writing of this passage in the aftermath of National Socialist interpretations of Schiller, W. H. Bruford, who considers the play to be 'a rather superior *Ritterschauspiel* with a patriotic purpose',[23] states that Schiller's sympathies are clearly with Joan'. In fact it might be more appropriate to say that Schiller the artist knew that his *audience's* sympathies would be with Johanna at this point, as indeed they must be if the play is to have any appeal at all: the patriotic element is not an end in itself but a means to an artistic end. Whereas in *Maria Stuart* it was part of Schiller's purpose to illuminate from different angles the complexities of the political scene, here the English never attempt to argue their case—for they have none; even Talbot sees life as no more than an opportunity to win 'glory' (by mining a city if need be). No wonder his failure provides him with 'Einsicht in das Nichts'! In sharp contrast to Johanna's vision of what the Kingdom of France can be, we are confronted with the 'blindness' of the people (l. 802), the narrow self-centred vision of Thibaut (ll. 365ff.), the defeatism of the Dauphin (ll. 817ff.), the totally indifferent and egoistic attitude of Isabeau (ll. 1439ff.), and the severely limited view of Dunois (ll. 465ff.), who, for all his very real merits, tends like Talbot to think primarily in terms of honour rather than righteousness.

Throughout the greater part of the action the characters of the play express views of Johanna which correspond closely to the extent to which they share—or fail to share—her vision. 'Wie ich bin / So sehe mich das Auge der Welt' says Isabeau (ll. 1436f.), concerned though she is not with seeing but with the assertion of her will in the pursuit of blind and destructive instinct. But whereas Isabeau's allies perceive with ill-concealed disgust what she is, it is far less easy for those around Johanna, friend or foe, to form an adequate view. To Isabeau Johanna is an instrument of 'der Hölle Gaukelkunst', to Talbot a phantom of the imagination, to Burgundy before his conversion to the French side a 'verderblich Blendwerk' and a 'buhlerische Circe'. Then to Burgundy after his conversion, and to Agnes Sorel, she is an 'Engel'—a notion equally inappropriate to Johanna, as is made plain in IV,

2, in Sorel's lines 'Du bist der Engel ... O könntest du ein Weib sein und empfin-
den!' (ll. 2620–35)—spoken at the very moment when the heroine is suffering the
appalling anguish of mind that no angel can know. And Sorel's use of the word
'Weib' reminds us of the view of Johanna's friends at the court, who, failing to see
her as the disquieting phenomenon that she is, try so persistently to reduce her to
the status of a *mere* woman ('nichts als ein Weib') that she is finally reduced to
near-despair and has to rebuke them for their blindness (ll. 2351–4). This failure of
vision does not then begin with the ambiguous thunderclap in Act IV: it is primarily
imposed by man's unadmitted feeling of inadequacy in the presence of what he
senses to be greater than himself. It is in the brilliantly-drawn figure of Du Chatel,
whose significance so many commentators have failed to grasp, that this point is
most clearly emphasized. 'Ich sehe, was ich seh', he remarks darkly at the moment
of Johanna's evident terror in Act IV, the first of the court to express a doubt as
to the divine origin of her inspiration—and this despite the fact that Johanna has
brought him back from banishment and reconciled him with Burgundy. Du Chatel
is the first to turn against Johanna, to 'see' nothing but her present discomfiture in
Act IV, simply because the recollection of Johanna's glorious achievements in the
past is an unbearable reminder to him of his own personal failure. In Act I he had
begged the Dauphin to have him executed so as to bring about the reconciliation
of Burgundy: in this endeavour he failed where Johanna succeeded. (It is surely
significant that stage-directions in the other reconciliation-scenes instruct the actors
to embrace, whereas in II, 4, Schiller gives no indication that Du Chatel gives no
more than the necessary token response to Burgundy's 'Umarmt mich'.) Du Chatel
is of course presented as an extreme case; but the seemingly well-intentioned
efforts of all at court to interest Johanna in matrimony—despite the fact that they
have heard the very words of the Virgin—derive from a stubborn refusal to see
her for what she is: these efforts are, Johanna explicitly points out, attempts to draw
her down 'in den gemeinen Staub', where the sight of her will be easier to bear.
Like Du Chatel, all these characters see not what is before them but what they
would like to see. Only in the final scene is the exaggerated metaphor replaced by
the more appropriate simile, when Karl sees her as 'heilig *wie* die Engel'; she is now
seen neither as an ordinary creature of flesh and blood who is yet as pure and holy
as a spirit—or, as the Roman Church was to proclaim her more than a century
after Schiller's death, a saint.

　　With regard to the adequacy of Johanna's own vision, as opposed to the other
characters' vision of her, there is a good deal more to be said; but first it will be
necessary to consider the two episodes which have proved the sources of greatest
confusion to critics: Johanna's encounters on the battlefield with the weak-kneed
Montgomery and with the mysterious Black Knight.

　　The whole Montgomery episode forms a symbolic presentation, through a
character with whom the audience is able to sympathize, of Johanna's strength of
will and of the terror which this strength inspires in the enemy; the different level
on which it operates is clearly indicated by the distancing effect of the trimeter. We
have already observed with what care Schiller has presented the moral rightness of

the French cause, and we must remember that in this context Montgomery is one of the 'proud invaders' who (like Talbot himself) has voluntarily chosen to be one of the aggressors, blinded to the consequences of his decision by the vain desire for glory (ll. 1559ff.). And uncomfortable though some may feel about the episode, we cannot assert that Johanna here mercilessly kills a *defenceless* man—since he finally accepts her challenge to mortal combat with the express intention of killing Johanna and saving his country's cause, for the justice of which he has been unable to bring forth a single argument.[24] Here again the themes of sight and insight recur: Montgomery, who is at first riveted to the spot by the sight of Johanna—'Hinsehn muß ich . . .' (l. 1574)—and then discovers that she is not after all 'schrecklich in der Nähe anzuschaun' (l. 1604) is finally forced by her—'Sieh *mich* an! Sieh!' (l. 1654)—to realize that the woman before him, whom he had first taken for an invulnerable Amazon, is in fact a being mortal like himself (ll. 1655–72). What Montgomery *refuses* to see is the indisputable rightness of Johanna's cause, which she presents to him in terms close to those of her original vision of a divinely-approved order (ll. 1636–47); thus he dies bravely but stubbornly insisting on the necessity of putting an end to England's hour of need—a patriotic consideration far removed from his admitted reason for coming to France.

The more fundamental question which is often asked at this point is this: why does Schiller equip Johanna with a sword and have her instructed to kill the enemy by her own hand? But the objection to this particular alteration of the traditional story would appear to be based on a curiously unthinking sentimental approach. Does 'der tötende Täter' of Schiller's play really transgress the moral law to a greater degree than the banner-waving heroine of the picture-books who, while keeping her own hands unsoiled, constantly encourages and incites others to kill? It is difficult to see any great moral distinction here. Certainly through his deviation from the historical accounts in this respect, Schiller the 'Macher' has provided motivation for the Lionel crisis, which he could not introduce otherwise; but at the same time Schiller the realist shows us the full—and by no means pleasant—implications of the mission that Jeanne d'Arc felt herself called upon to perform. To this extent the 'romantic tragedy' focuses our attention on an aspect of the legend which most admirers of Joan would prefer to gloss over or to forget altogether.

Probably no scene in the entire play has caused more puzzlement to critics than Johanna's encounter with the Black Knight in III, 9, which some have even taken as the occasion on which Johanna incurs tragic guilt. E. L. Stahl, for example, argues in detail for the opinion first put forward by Böttiger—namely that Johanna's original guilt consists in presumption and *hubris*: 'Her love for Lionel is a consequence of her desire to transgress the limits of her mission'.[25] Stahl's argument rests on two assumptions: first that her mission is at an end as soon as the Dauphin has been formally crowned in Rheims, and secondly that the Black Knight's warning 'Geh nicht hinein!' refers not to her entry into the city but to her 'decision to continue the battle'. Persuasive though this argument is, however, it finally creates more problems than it solves. As evidence of Johanna's 'intention to go beyond the limits set by the terms of her mission' Stahl quotes ll. 2342f.:

Nicht aus den Händen leg ich dieses Schwert,
Als bis das stolze England niederliegt.

But this utterance of Johanna's appears in a completely different light if we bear in mind the parts of the divine command most closely related to it (and not quoted by Stahl): 'Dann wirst du .../Den stolzen Überwinder niederschlagen' and 'Dieses Schwert umgürte Dir./Damit vertilge meines Volkes Feinde'. It should also be observed that this argument involves a strictly chronological interpretation of the instructions given to Johanna—i.e. 'fighting first; coronation to end with'. There is, however, no unambiguous suggestion of a chronological arrangement in the words of God or the Blessed Virgin, in which the coronation may well be mentioned last because it must appear to those at court as the most glorious act which she will perform and as the pledge of the success of her mission. The audience in the theatre at any rate will scarcely be disposed to disagree with Johanna when she interprets these words to mean not that she is merely to place a piece of metal on the Dauphin's head but that she is to make him King of France in reality—a fact which cannot be achieved without the 'Vertilgen' and 'Niederschlagen' of the foreign invaders.[26] Furthermore, when considering this play on the page instead of experiencing it in the theatre we must beware of misunderstanding any utterances which may sound arrogant or presumptuous in isolation; we must never forget their dramatic context, which is that of Johanna's duty to inspire others to action, together with her own need to reassure herself during a career which—as Schiller repeatedly indicates—is utterly foreign to her natural disposition. But by far the strongest objection to the *hubris* argument is the fact that throughout the remainder of the play Johanna neither refers again to the encounter with the Black Knight, nor does she (or anyone else) at any point suggest that she had acted presumptuously in continuing the battle. In the monologue of almost one hundred lines (IV, 1), the heroine plainly identifies her sin with her love for Lionel; and her only other references to the matter tally precisely, as we shall find, with the admission of her guilt at that point—and relate throughout not to some kind of *hubris* but to the problem of vision. The Black Knight will, however, fit into the pattern of the romantic tragedy if he is seen first as a theatrical *device* designed to prepare the audience for Johanna's fall,[27] and secondly as a dramatic and visual externalization of Johanna's doubt as to her own ability to carry out her strange mission—a doubt which comes as the natural consequence of the wonderment which she expresses in II, 8, that not even all the promptings of pity which she feels within her can impede her in her necessary course of action.

Johanna's guilt, then, lies in her reaction to the *sight* of Lionel. In the scene which forms the obvious climax of the play (III, 10) Schiller provides ample stage-directions so as to present clearly to the audience the nature and force of the impact which this man's appearance makes on her. Having after only a brief combat succeeded in knocking Lionel's sword from his grasp, Johanna is about to kill her opponent—but at this very moment sees his face: 'In diesem Augenblick sieht sie ihm ins Gesicht, sein Anblick ergreift sie, sie bleibt unbeweglich stehen und läßt langsam den Arm sinken.' Averting her eyes, she urges Lionel to flee; then, when instead he approaches her again, she makes a second attempt to slay her enemy, which fails 'wie sie ihn ins Gesicht faßt'.

After this point has been reached, references to seeing and blindness abound in Johanna's speeches. In her extended monologue in IV, I, in which Johanna painfully tries to come to terms with what has happened (and even momentarily attempts to persuade herself that her sparing of Lionel was an act of mercy), this theme makes itself heard with insistent intensity, occurring at one point no fewer than six times in six consecutive lines:

> Warum mußt ich ihm in die Augen sehn!
> Die Züge schaun des edeln Angesichts!
> Mit deinem Blick fing dein Verbrechen an,
> Unglückliche! Ein blindes Werkzeug fordert Gott,
> Mit blinden Augen mußtest dus vollbringen!
> Sobald du sahst, verließ dich Gottes Schild— (ll. 2575–80)

But Johanna is not in fact extolling the virtues of blindness over sight, as lines 2590ff. soon make clear:

> Ach, ich sah den Himmel offen
> Und der selgen Angesicht!
> Doch auf Erden ist mein Hoffen,
> Und im Himmel ist es nicht!

The symbolic image of the Virgin standing for the goodness and purity of her mission and for the complete chastity (i.e. unswerving devotion to her cause) which that mission entails, has now been replaced in her mind by 'sein Bild' (l. 2554)—the image of the man with whom she has fallen in love. Her hope of 'heaven' (i.e. the successful completion of her mission by the end of her life) is now totally overshadowed by the dominating desire for another kind of life altogether. Blindness here stands for the renunciation of the selfish in favour of the selfless aim; and sight for the focusing of the vision on the lesser to the detriment of the greater good. Her first reaction was a Kleistian swoon (l. 2516), caused ostensibly by her slight wound but in reality by her inability to come to terms with a situation which even in Act IV seems to involve her in an insoluble conflict.

And yet the conflict is finally overcome. But how? By sincere repentance, with prayer and fasting in the wilderness? Apparently not: for if we pay close attention to what Johanna actually says in Act V, a rather different picture emerges. In Johanna's account of her submission to her 'fate'—

> Ich unterwarf mich schweigend dem Geschick,
> Das Gott, mein Meister, über mich verhängte (l. 3147f.)

it is possible to detect a suggestion of penance but none whatever of repentance; and it is noticeable that she has far less to say about her relationship with God (whom she does not even mention until Raimond forces her to discuss the subject) than about her relationship with nature and her new perception of herself, in which the storm and the thunder play a large if apparently mysterious part.[28] Now the motif of the storm has recurred throughout the play in both a literal and a metaphorical sense—the latter generally associated with war. It was at Bertrand's mention of 'des Donners Krachen' (referring to the mining of Orleans) that Johanna first set the helmet on her head; then in Act IV she speaks of 'des Krieges Stürme' and 'der Sturm der Schlacht'; while in V, I, the *Köhler,* describing the storm, reverses the metaphor:

> Und dieser fürchterliche Krieg dort oben . . .
> Kann unter Menschen keinen Frieden stiften—

It is in this context of the identification of the conflict of the elements with human conflict that we begin to understand how Johanna has come to gain a new insight into herself:

> Doch in der Öde lernt ich mich erkennen.
> Da, als der Ehre Schimmer mich umgab,
> Da war der Streit in meiner Brust, ich war
> Die Unglückseligste, da ich der Welt
> Am meisten zu beneiden schien—Jetzt bin ich
> Geheilt, und dieser Sturm in der Natur,
> Der ihr das Ende drohte, war mein Freund,
> Er hat die Welt gereinigt und auch mich.   (ll. 3170–7)

Johanna's vision of *'this* storm *in nature* which threatened to put an end to nature and yet finally purified it' stands in sharp contrast to her firm opposition of nature and storm in the final scene of the Prologue.[29] The nature which she so lovingly describes in the *ottava rima* is characterized as 'traulich still', fruitful, with green meadows, grottoes, cool springs, and with the hillsides echoing her song; from these 'geliebte Triften' she is being drawn away to the 'blutiges Feld' by a force which she describes as 'Sturmes Ungestüm'. Nature as seen by Johanna here (and as late as the mention of 'des stillen Berges Höh' in IV, I) is gentle, pastoral, idyllic—and entirely unreal.[30] Of its violent aspects, which cannot be unknown to her (unless we are to doubt Raimond's report of her encounter with the ferocious 'Tigerwolf') she there remembers nothing. *Now* she experiences nature in its most violent and destructive manifestation—'ein grausam, mördrisch Ungewitter'—and sees it to be not an aberration but an integral part of nature, like herself ultimately not destroying but purifying: now she can accept both the storm of battle and the tempestuous conflict within herself as an essential part of life.[31] The storm passes, having—like her own purification of the world—fulfilled a positive purpose; seeing it replaced by the setting sun, which is described as 'friedlich strahlend' (l. 3093), Johanna too finds a new serene calm: 'In mir ist Friede' (l. 3178). She now sees the setting sun as the symbol of life's essential polarity (ll. 3193ff.), for just as the storm is followed by a calm, so too the darkness will inevitably be followed by the return of the light in all its splendour.

It is this new, comprehensive vision of life that gives Johanna the strength to survive what is to be her greatest ordeal (see ll. 3225ff.). Once again she comes face to face with Lionel; but now the sight of him brings a new insight. Whereas previously the thought of any man's love for her meant 'Grauen und Entheiligung' (l. 2264), she now sees Lionel's feeling for her as something by no means evil or disturbing in itself, and—as she could never have done before—actually envisages the possibility of using it to bring about a lasting peace for both their peoples (ll. 3350ff.). Immediately after this second encounter with Lionel comes the symbolic breaking of the bonds—and appropriately, too, for Johanna has now forever rid herself of that narrowness of vision which prevented her from seeing life as a whole and from perceiving her own proper part in that whole. In her last moments Johanna sees the rainbow, the sign of the covenant established after the first great disturbance of the natural order had been ended.[32] For her—and for those around her, who have come to represent humanity finally accepting the wonder before their very eyes—this element of the earth still essentially itself, yet transformed by the last rays of the sun into a thing of indescribable beauty, is filled with significance. Johanna finally sees the Virgin Mary—that other simple girl who helped to bring about the restoration of a proper order, and with whom she has been repeatedly identified[33]—now no longer angry as she had been at Johanna's tardiness in taking up her mission (l. 1101) or as she had appeared after her weakness (ll. 2735ff.), but smiling and welcoming her into her arms. Johanna's mission is at last completed: in doing what was necessary for the welfare of others she has restored that order which—as she had seen clearly from the very beginning—had been monstrously disrupted. The play ends with a moment of reverential silence, all around being inexpressibly moved by what they have seen. Du Chatel is not present.

Although *Die Jungfrau von Orleans* is neither a specifically Christian nor a primarily patriotic drama, it cannot on the other hand be dismissed as merely a 'sublime spectacle': it is simultaneously a play about well-intentioned but blind and fearful human beings who are able to recognize and accept greatness of spirit only at the moment of its extinction; and it is the tragedy of one selfless human being of heroic stature, whose vision of herself and of life are made complete only at the hour of her death.

NOTES

[1] *Versuch über Schiller* (Berlin, 1955), p. 61.
[2] Compare Schiller's letter to Körner of 13 May 1801.
[3] Hebbel, *Werke*, edited by R. M. Werner, 12 vols (Berlin, 1901–3), IX, 267. It is, however, of interest that a later comment by Hebbel (made in 1850, when he had long since abandoned the intention of competing with Schiller by writing a play of his own on the same subject) comes surprisingly close to Goethe's view: '*Die Jungfrau von Orleans* ist Schillers höchste bewußte Konzeption, wie *Die Räuber* seine höchste unbewußte' (*Tagebücher*, edited by R. M. Werner, 4 vols (Berlin, 1903–4) III, 4863).
[4] Letter to Körner of 12 May 1803.
[5] This point is put particularly well by Hebbel when in 1859 he writes of the 'unermeßliche Kluft, welche trotz des nicht genug zu bewundernden architektonischen Baues gerade in diesem Stück zwischen der naiven Aufgabe und der sentimental reflektirenden Lösung liegt' (*Werke*, XII, 258).
[6] E. M. Wilkinson, *Schiller—Poet or Philosopher?* (Oxford, 1961), p. 30.

[7] *Friedrich Schiller* (Zurich, 1967), pp. 401–7.

[8] This passage (which concludes the essay) echoes the sentiments expressed by Schiller in his letter to Goethe of 29 December 1797.

[9] 'Zu Schillers *Agrippina*', first published in *Trivium* in 1951 and reprinted in *Die Kunst der Interpretation* (Zurich, 1955), pp. 132–60.

[10] Compare Schiller's observations on the art of tragedy in his essay *Über den Gebrauch des Chors in der Tragödie*, the relevance of which—as Staiger shows (pp. 410f.)—is by no means limited to *Die Braut von Messina*.

[11] Especially the revealing letter to Göschen of 10 February 1802 and the poem *Das Mädchen von Orleans*.

[12] Although Staiger does not explicitly mention Gerhard Kaiser's essay 'Johannas Sendung' (*Jahrbuch der deutschen Schillergesellschaft*, 10 (1966) 204–36), his argument seems to refute Kaiser's interpretation. The fundamental difference between the two approaches is that Staiger never requires us to read between the lines at the expense of the lines themselves as Kaiser does when for instance he states (p. 224) that Johanna pursues the Black Knight 'in der Privatheit ihres Hasses'. And Kaiser's extraordinary claim 'Indem Johanna *einen* Mann aus Liebe geschont hat, sind alle ihre bisherigen Tötungen zur Willkür, zum Mord geworden' (p. 266)—a statement which cannot be supported by a single line of the text—would seem to come into Staiger's category of an 'Erfindung aus der blauen Luft' (p. 404).

[13] The poem *Das Mädchen von Orleans* was published independently and never intended by Schiller as a prologue.

[14] *Erinnerung an das Publikum.*

[15] *Über den Gebrauch des Chors in der Tragödie.*

[16] Compare E. L. Stahl, *Friedrich Schiller's Drama* (Oxford, 1954), p. 128: 'Only after the coronation does the treatment of the play's major theme properly begin'.

[17] *Über den Gebrauch des Chors in der Tragödie.* Compare also the letter to Goethe of 29 August 1798.

[18] This similarity is not, of course, a miracle. For Voltaire's cynical attitude in *La pucelle* was by no means the only eighteenth-century view of the Maid: in Hume's *History of England*, which Schiller had used when working on *Maria Stuart*, he must certainly have read, as Melitta Gerhard suggests, (*Schiller* (Bern, 1950), p. 369) the description of Jeanne as 'an admirable heroine, to whom the more generous superstition of the ancients would have erected altars'. When Schiller wrote in *Das Mädchen von Orleans*

Ein edler Sinn liebt edlere Gestalten

he was celebrating the fact that such generosity of spirit was not, after all, dead. For him the canonization would have borne out his faith in humanity.

[19] The theme is, of course, present in Schiller's plays from *Die Räuber* to *Demetrius* but is most prominent here.

[20] This point is put most clearly by Gerhard Kaiser in his essay *Vergötterung und Tod: die thematische Einheit von Schillers Werk* (Stuttgart, 1967), p. 38.

[21] Compare Hume's statement: 'Her unexperienced mind—mistook the impulses of passion for heavenly inspirations'. The relevance of this point is discussed by Melitta Gerhard, *Schiller*, p. 370.

[22] Compare ll. 247–66, to which Johanna listens 'mit großer Aufmerksamkeit'.

[23] *Theatre, Drama and Audience in Goethe's Germany* (London, 1957), p. 331. The opposite view is expressed by B. v. Wiese, *Schiller* (Stuttgart, 1959), p. 734.

[24] G. Storz's presentation of the episode (*Der Dichter Friedrich Schiller* (Stuttgart, 1959) p. 355) seems to imply that Johanna kills the defenceless; she does not. Emil Staiger finds it necessary to take to task those who assume that Schiller found the killing of an enemy in a just war immoral (pp. 401f.)

[25] *Friedrich Schiller's Drama: Theory and Practice* (Oxford, 1954), p. 122.

[26] That this was her intention from the outset is made clear in ll. 305–13 of the Prologue: 'Mit ihrer Sichel wird die Jungfrau kommen ... Eh sich die Mondesscheibe füllt / Wird kein engländisch Roß mehr aus den Wellen / Der prächtig strömenden Loire trinken.'

[27] Compare Staiger, *Friedrich Schiller*, p. 406: 'Szenische Instrumentierungen sind die Wunder und Zeichen insgesamt.'

[28] Reinhard Buchwald (*Schiller*, fourth edition (Wiesbaden, 1959), pp. 752f.) draws attention to the importance of the storm; it is not, however, discussed by Storz, von Wiese, or Staiger.

[29] That Schiller saw a strong link between the Prologue and Act V is abundantly clear from his letter to Goethe of 3 April 1801 (in which he still refers to the Prologue as the first act).

[30] Compare Karl's sentimental vision of that other France beyond the Loire: 'Da lacht ein milder niebewölkter Himmel' (ll. 906ff.) as opposed to the reality of the 'rauhe sturmbewegte Zeit' (l. 796) which Johanna later enables him to accept.
[31] Johanna's natural horror of killing is expressed in ll. 1681–4.
[32] Compare Genesis I. 6–9.
[33] See esp. ll. 1084–92.

Hans Mayer

THE SCANDAL OF
JOAN OF ARC

She was probably nothing more than a marvelous and colorful byway in history, for even without Joan of Arc the English would have been driven out of France. The French monarchy would never have been endangered, even if someone other than the dauphin who had been elevated by Joan had been anointed and crowned monarch. George Bernard Shaw characterized Joan the Delinquent's embarrassing and unforthright rehabilitation in 1456, a quarter century after her burning at the stake, as an event that had nothing directly to do with her. The legality of Charles VII's coronation and the legitimacy of his reign could only be assured when it was beyond question that the girl from Domrémy who had accompanied him into the cathedral for the coronation was neither witch nor heretic.

Joan remained for centuries a historical supernumerary who was made ridiculous in invented stories, pamphlets, even in serious literary works (depending on the writer and the era): represented as obscenity personified or taken as an example of that which in the age of the Enlightenment was wont to be termed "the spirit of the dark Middle Ages." Even for Voltaire, who had written at length of the supposed virgin and her doings, the adjective *gothic* retained the universal significance 'confused, superstitious, abstruse.' Joan of Arc was for the European Enlightenment no more than a "gothic" episode.

The Renaissance and the Enlightenment were intellectually unable to come to terms with the deeds of this village maid from Lorraine. Joan was no demonic politician and far removed from a Renaissance type, not a Lucrezia Borgia or a Vittoria Colonna. Two things remained against her during the bourgeois Enlightenment of the eighteenth century: her origin as a child of farm folk and her deep, unquestioning religiosity. In the course of the centuries her undoing again and again was that she, trusting in "voices," spoke so unreservedly of her visions of faith. That was unpardonable. Even Shaw, in the preface to his *Saint Joan*, endeavors a rationalistic interpretation of the visions and hallucinations. As weird as the girl's visions

From *Outsiders: A Study in Life and Letters*, translated by Denis M. Sweet (Cambridge, MA: MIT Press, 1982), pp. 29–51. First published in 1975.

of faith appeared to her own and subsequent ages, even more so now, a half-century later, do Shaw's pacifying interpretations appear laughable when he argues in a scientific manner:

> The most sceptical scientific reader may therefore accept as a flat fact, carrying no implication of unsoundness of mind, that Joan was what Francis Galton and other modern investigators of human faculty call a visualizer. She saw imaginary saints just as some other people see imaginary diagrams and landscapes with numbers dotted about them, and are thereby able to perform feats of memory and arithmetic impossible to non-visualizers. Visualizers will understand this at once. Non-visualizers who have never read Galton will be puzzled and incredulous.[1]

Joan had offended against all of the taboos of her time: as a farm maid, as woman in arms, as virgin who forgoes marriage and motherhood, as faithful Christian. During the waning of the Middle Ages, as Johan Huizinga has called Joan of Arc's century,[2] people did not think much of prophets and those who claimed to be inspired by the Holy Ghost. The last saint whom that age was ready both to place historically and to venerate as a saint (who was, in consequence, something more than a page out of the book of golden legends) was Francis of Assisi. And he, the *poverello,* soon after his death in 1226 was transformed into a formidable entity in the art world. As early as the end of the thirteenth century Francis was, so to speak, aestheticized in Giotto's frescoes in Assisi and then later in Florence. This last saint of the Middle Ages thereafter (from Giotto and Ghirlandaio to Dürer and Rubens, on to later literary mutations in Tolstoy and Rilke) was edged out of the immediate context of burning faith and relegated to a realm of aesthetic edification.

Constricted between the age of Francis of Assisi and the striving of the counter-Reformation in the sway of Loyola, which quite consciously erected new saints by means of religious propaganda, the age of Joan of Arc runs its way as the epoch of something that is no longer and not yet. There is no longer a trust in those who are beatified through the spirit; not yet the cool *raison d'état* and *raison de foi* that created saints as later great generals and good kings would be raised on high.

When Joan appeared on the scene and began to consummate her deeds, her unremitting faith was to become the most egregious source of vexation. The inevitable collision between an inspired founder of faith and the apparatus of orthodoxy can be seen here too in the reactions of Joan's contemporaries. Her faith endangered the official faith, especially since she had won over the masses. Her inspired actions upset military conceptions and dynastic interests on both the French and English sides. Those who had been enemies for the duration of a hundred years' war finally allied themselves against her. This scheme of things surrounding Joan of Arc and her fall can be taken as a historical preview of the situation of the Parisian Commune in 1871 when Bismarck and the French bourgeoisie allied themselves against the Communards in Paris. Shaw has marvelously reconstructed this turn of events in the fourth scene of his *Saint Joan,* in the famous

French-English dialogue in the tent on points of diplomacy and ecclesiastical pre-rogative. It is only through these machinations that Joan comes to be delivered into the hands of the English—not through wily capture or military defeat. She is played into their hands. She has offended against all manner of taboo; there can be no room for clemency. Everyone bands together against this female soldier, this mili-tant prophet, this incarnation of rustic piety: the English and French courts, the feudal lords, the high ecclesiastics. The result is the well-known trial in Rouen. Joan was burned alive at the stake in the market square on May 30, 1431.

In Shakespeare's trilogy of plays concerning Henry VI, she is simply an un-polished and obscene wench. The Irishman Shaw has allowed himself a nice anti-English barb when he asserts that Shakespeare very likely first wanted to portray Joan as pure and earnest, but was kept from it by the audience and the members of his troupe: "[He] was told by his scandalized company that English patriotism would never stand a sympathetic representation of a French conqueror of English troops, and that unless he at once introduced all the old charges against Joan of being a sorceress and a harlot, and assumed her to be guilty of all of them, his play could not be produced."[3]

At the height of the French Enlightenment, La Pucelle was for Voltaire the happy excuse for a parody of older heroic epics in the form of a buffo-obscene heroic poem. Joan of Arc as well as the king's mistress, Agnes Sorel, here serve as butt for *picanteries* set to verse. Voltaire had only ridicule for Joan and so much gothic superstition. The maid of Orléans and the European Enlightenment seemed to exclude each other. Even the last of the Voltaireans in the twentieth century, Anatole France, believed he was compelled as rationalist and disciple of the eigh-teenth century to direct polemics against the supposed romanticization of this strange rustic and hallucinating French woman patriot.

What path led from Joan's execution at Rouen to her beatification in the year 1908 and to her canonization as St. Joan in 1920? To some extent an answer can be found within church history itself, in the metamorphoses of the Catholic Church on its way from the fifteenth to the twentieth century. But another question remains: how did Schiller come to elevate a figure who was the butt of Shake-speare's and Voltaire's derision to the heights of a tragic heroine? For Schiller too all those taboos against which Joan offended retained their full validity. His con-ception of women, a bourgeois one, with all its philistine aspects, is known from the poem "Würde der Frauen," and from the edifying parts of the Song of the Bell. Joan did not in the least correspond to the bourgeois ideal of a woman in the age of Goethe. On the other hand, Schiller himself, however he valued this ideal, was formed from youth onward by the Enlightenment. One can expect no understand-ing from him for Joan's visions and voices. He uses these elements in his material like so many romantic stage props. The actual tragedy of the virgin of Orléans played, as it seemed to him, outside of any religious realm.

But, then, in what realm? Schiller simply brought to sharp focus the viewpoint of a certain intellectual tradition—as much as the creative impulse was his own to take seriously and to interpret a figure of ridicule from the gothic era. The fruits of this were not gathered until, in his romantic tragedy *The Maid of Orléans,* for the first time he began to clarify those contradictions in modern man, contradictions that several years after the premier performance in Leipzig were to become the central theme of a dramatist who was a thoroughgoing opponent to Schiller, Heinrich von Kleist, who formulated the theme as *confusion of feelings.* The maid of Orléans became the heroine of an emotional conflict, precisely like Kleist's Penthesilea, Alcmene, or Friedrich von Homburg.

Thus appeared for the first time in Germany in the public consciousness a social phenomenon that had been noticed and interpreted in socially progressive France, with its centuries old and well-coalesced bourgeoisie, as early as the seventeenth century. I mean the conflict between two kinds of reason, rational thought in the narrower sense and that which Blaise Pascal had defined as "raison du coeur."[4]

Pascal had felt this duality (which he likely was the first to describe) as a tear, a rip, a gash in his being, in his daily life. He lived as a man of the world and had a prominent position as a mathematician; then came a moment of religious awakening that was to change his life. That was not new in the world, but it led in this instance to a new outcome. It did not lead, as in the comparable case of St. Augustine, to a renunciation of his previous life but to this genius's attempt at establishing, with all the means of his earlier thought, a scientific basis for the new religious realm. Pascal began to apply the full power of his mind to the defense of Christian dogma. He did so by a kind of differentiation of reason, by splitting it in two. He distinguishes— always within the rational realm—between a "spirit of geometry" and an *esprit de finesse,*[5] which one can perhaps translate 'spirit of sensibility.' This corresponds to Pascal's other famous antithesis in which he counterposes actual rational thought to the *raison du coeur,* the reason of the heart. His much quoted and much misunderstood sentence about the heart possessing its own reasons, which can often come to contradict the usual ratiocinations of daily life, has nothing whatsoever to do with sentimental illogic.[6] Pascal's thoughts rather, as a kind of rationalism for faith, proceed from the consideration that Christianity cannot be scientifically deduced by means of rational reflection. This is so since everything that Christian teaching demands of the Christian man and woman is only capable of bringing forth unpleasurable sensations. Everything preached in the Sermon on the Mount is actually "unrational" and "unnatural." One sees that with this Pascal belongs to the immediate predecessors of Kierkegaard and modern dialectical theology.

With this antithesis of rational, everyday reason to the heart's reason he had named something extending far beyond the realm of Christian theology, namely the opposition between reality and possibility in the bourgeois society that was coming into being at that time. Utopia, this transmutation toward a human/humane future supported by no social reality, became thereby a legitimate realm of inquiry.

All of this is simply going over once again the circumstance that led Schiller to take up the case of the maid of Orléans and to interpret it anew. For Schiller suffered as well from the contrast between the bourgeois reality of his age and the possibilities of man—of which he as a promulgator of the Enlightenment never tired speaking. After he had read Kant he did not attempt to reconcile—otherwise than did Pascal—the schism between human actuality and human possibility but, on the contrary, sought to tear it apart in sharp, dualistic fashion. From this come Schiller's abrupt antitheses of the joy of the senses and the peace of the soul, happiness and dignity, utility and human greatness. The tragedy of the maid of Orléans lies for him in Joan's daring to break through this dualism. In one fateful moment she attempts to change over from vision to the realm of daily life, desirous, in a word, of fulfillment instead of waiting in the realm of impersonal, historical greatness.[7]

The dramatist Schiller, in poignant contrast to Voltaire, decides to fashion a tragic heroine. But since he is incapable of taking seriously or empathizing with the real religious belief of the actual, historical Joan of Arc, he is obliged to lead his dramatic heroine into a conflict between human reality and inhuman virtuousness. Joan becomes a figure of reflection on possibility. Schiller himself imagined her as a prophet and wrote about it to Goethe on April 3, 1801: "Because my prophetess . . . stands by herself and is deserted by the gods in her misery, so is her autonomy and the title of her character to a prophet's role all the more cogent. The end of the next to last act is most theatric, and the thundering *deus ex machina* will not fall short of its effect."

This quotation from his correspondence documents the intimate alliance into which the dramatist Schiller enters at every moment of his production—an alliance between philosophical speculation and the genius of pandering to the public. The prophet Joan, but the whole apparatus of the theater as well, are all in the service of heavenly voices and dark riders from hell that are no longer believed in.

But this did not seem to suffice. The abrupt dualism between the joy of the senses and the peace of the soul, that is to say, between Joan's femininity and her prophetic mission, remained, as Schiller himself recognized, more or less purely speculative. It had to leave cold any member of the audience who had not read Kant. This is the reason Schiller, likely not even aware of it, returned to Pascal's formula of the reason of the heart. His famous poem "On Voltaire's 'Pucelle' and the Maid of Orléans," published in the *Ladies' Pocketbook* in 1802, explicitly claims this reason of the heart for Joan.

Das edle Bild der Menschheit zu verhöhnen,
Im tiefsten Staube wälzte dich der Spott,
Krieg führt der Witz auf ewig mit dem Schönen,
Er glaubt nicht an den Engel und den Gott,
Dem Herzen will er seine Schätze rauben,
Den Wahn bekriegt er und verletzt den Glauben.

Doch, wie du selbst, aus kindlichem Geschlechte,
Selbst eine fromme Schäferin wie du,
Reicht dir die Dichtkunst ihre Götterrechte,
Schwingt sich mit dir den ewgen Sternen zu,
Mit einer Glorie hat sie dich umgeben,
Dich schuf das Herz, du wirst unsterblich leben.

Es liebt die Welt das Strahlende zu schwärzen,
Und das Erhabne in den Staub zu ziehn,
Doch fürchte nicht! Es gibt noch schöne Herzen,
Die für das Hohe, Herrliche entglühn.
Den lauten Markt mag Momus unterhalten,
Ein edler Sinn liebt edlere Gestalten.

Scorning the noble image of humanity, / Mockery ground your face in the dirt, / Forever the railing mind wages war upon beauty, / And believes neither in angels nor in God, / And means to robe the heart of its treasures. / It opposes idolatry and injures faith. // Yet, as you yourself, from a childish race, / Even a pious shepherd lass like you, / Is given divine rights by poetry, / Which climbing up with you to the eternal orbs, / Encompasses you with glory. / The heart made you, you will be immortal. // The world loves to darken brightness, / And pull down nobility into the dust, / Yet fear not! There are still lovely hearts, / Which burst aflame for the sublime. / Momus entertains the market square, / A noble mind loves nobler forms.

The author of the "romantic tragedy" was perfectly serious with such theses. He wrote his publisher, Göschen, on February 10, 1802, in quite similar terms: "This work flowed out of the heart, and it is meant to do nothing other than to speak to the heart. But for that it is necessary that one have a heart, and that, unfortunately, is not universally the case."

"From the heart—may it proceed to the heart": Beethoven chose precisely this motto almost a quarter century after Schiller to characterize his *Missa Solemnis*. In both cases, however, Beethoven's connection to Schiller in the Ninth Symphony makes it apparent, the appeal to the heart is not to be understood sentimentally. It is a positing of a humanity of spirit, heart, and will; or, to put it differently, of reality and possibility, of social actuality and hope for transformation.

Schiller's version of the maid of Orléans functions unsatisfactorily and is often comic in spite of itself since it conceives as mere static antinomy unsatisfactory reality and its better possibility. Between Arcadia and the world of the philistines there were no communicating paths. For Schiller, Joan of Arc's fault occurs— grotesquely so—at the moment when she renounces her prophet's role. Her expiation can only consist in making her way as swiftly as possible back to the heroic sphere. Friedrich Schiller, a man of bourgeois affiliations, thereby identifies heroic steadfastness with success, humanity with failure. It is an identification at best questionable. Stalwart, Joan as heroine rapidly proceeds from victory to victory until her attack of woman's feelings, after which she tumbles into misery. Misery understood as her own fault, as guilt.

Posterity has sentimentalized and ridiculed no other work of Schiller's to such an extent as *The Maid of Orléans*. The reason lay in Schiller's exorbitant equating of innocence with victory in battle, of guilt with human frailty. I am going to relate a well-worn anecdote here because it shows in its own self-contained way how maliciously language is capable of doing away with heroes. Essay topic in a girls' school of yore: "Guilt and expiation in *The Maid of Orléans.*" For which one of the budding ladies wrote: "The maid of Orléans' guilt consists in having provided a young Englishman on the battlefield with his life." It is perfectly legitimate to laugh here because our schoolgirl has indeed transposed (and not parodistically, either) Schiller's tragic content into everyday life, with a linguistically quite funny connotation as well.

At the heart of it Schiller's drama is wrecked by the abrupt Kantian dualism that allows only an either/or. The reason of the heart is provided a form but simultaneously deprived of its rights. Schiller's Joan transforms herself, to make use of Schiller's terminology for certain philosophical conceptions, from a naive into a sentimental protagonist. And she does this not in any psychological development but in a point-for-point about-face as if on cue. It can come as no surprise therefore that precisely the most important critics were obliged to find the misuse of a stage figure to demonstrate philosophical antitheses as a grave shortcoming. Goethe protested heartfeltly against his friend's dramatic construction in the name of Joan's original naiveté. Hebbel, on the other hand, criticized from the viewpoint of pure reflection the girl's oddly eroticized self-knowledge in front of Lionel, her enemy. In both Goethe as well as Hebbel there was no dearth of perspicacity. Both critics hit the weak points of this play that had been so ambitiously conceived.

Schiller's depiction of the story of the maid of Orléans seems to have lost in the running to Shaw's *Saint Joan.* Nowadays it is scarcely possible for anyone to put out of mind for the entire length of the production that Joan did not receive a mortal wound on the battlefield—as in Schiller's drama—then deliver after the battle several prophetic and gripping verses while dying, whereupon the banners of her king are dipped, in her honor, as a last military farewell. The actual Joan of Arc was publicly burned to death as a heretic on the market square of Rouen. The dramatic problem connected with this singular human life and destiny does not develop—as in Schiller—out of love and war, freedom and necessity. Instead, it has to do with the historical occurrence completely omitted by Schiller, namely with Joan's trial. It was no accident that this exciting historical event remained entirely irrelevant for Schiller whereas Shaw guided his play precisely toward it. Not only Shaw did that: following him has been the French dramatist Jean Anouilh in his play *The Lark* and Brecht in his stage adaptation of a radio drama by Anna Seghers entitled *The Trial of Joan of Arc at Rouen, 1431.*

What captured Shaw's attention is not difficult to guess. In the Joan of Arc story he found material that in his eyes demonstrated an English political crime. Reason enough for an Irish patriot and Fabian socialist once again to lay bare on the stage the obtuseness and brutality of the English ruling classes, as he had done in *Widowers' Houses, Major Barbara, Heartbreak House,* and many other of his "unpleasant plays." In *Saint Joan*[8] this theme is represented in the deeds and opinions of the Earl of Warwick and, additionally, by the Chaplain de Stogumber, an aristocratic and dyed-in-the-wool Englishman.

It seems most important for Shaw to have found in Joan of Arc one more figure who allowed the development of another of the themes he loved so well.

I mean the superiority of female reason in contrast to all the economic, political, military (and, I might add, scientific) undertakings of the male world. In Joan, Shaw reached the apex of his earlier heroines Cleopatra, Candida, and Eliza Doolittle, who were so impressive for their rationality and for their *raison du coeur*. Joan combined in herself the political instinct of Cleopatra with the plebeian vigor of the flower girl Eliza. And thus did Shaw compose his figure: a subject matter hostile to the English; superiority of feminine reason; and then adding two elements that were consciously anachronistic, but which for Shaw (as he explains in the preface) were decisive for an understanding of his Joan figure: Protestantism and patriotism. The anti-English Irish patriot Shaw has Joan appear as an anti-English French patriot. For her English counterparts in the play, this is the central crime. Warwick, in the tent scene, sees expressly therein "the Maid's secular heresy," and accuses the French cardinal, Cauchon, of certain sympathies with this heresy of a political nature. Cauchon protests, defining the matter at hand with the word *nationalism,* since "I can find you no better name for it." But even this French cardinal characterizes such French patriotism as "essentially anti-Catholic and anti-Christian."

Warwick had just ingratiated himself to the Church by offering the following explanation of Joan's central spiritual sin. "It is the protest of the individual soul against the interference of priest or peer between the private man and his God. I should call it Protestantism if I had to find a name for it." In Shaw's dramatization Joan is presented as a patriot *before* the existence of a French fatherland or any other fatherland. The bourgeois nation of the nineteenth and the early twentieth centuries is projected back into the first half of the fifteenth. Joan is furthermore a protestant *before* Luther. With this, a dramatic constellation is provided parallel to the intellectual one. Joan is superior to her mortal enemies and the plotters against her in three ways: as woman, as farm maid, as precocious model for humanity's later historical development. She is filled with Pascal's reason of the heart. Blaise Pascal had himself aspired to a synthesis of the spirit of geometry and the spirit of the heart; Schiller had postulated a radical antinomy incapable of synthesis of a heroic world versus the pragmatism of daily life; it was Shaw who represented the reason of the heart incarnated by Joan as a superior attitude toward life that is perfectly capable of realization. All of Joan's adversaries are pragmatists in their actions and consequently are hemmed in. Joan's reason of the heart guides her to the correct actions—from the viewpoint of the future, to be sure. She simply came too early and therefore had to die. Joan's death in Shaw is anything but a tragic event, however.

It is for this reason that in the trial scene in Shaw there is only a fleeting moment of something like a confusion of feelings. Joan recants when for an abrupt interlude she no longer gives heed to the reasoning of the heart—her voices—but goes over to the side of "commonsense" pragmatism: "I have dared and dared; but only a fool will walk into a fire: God, who gave me my commonsense, cannot will me to do that." But the ensuing complementary pragmatism of her adversaries, who intend to imprison her for life, forces her heart's logic to triumph. Joan recants the recantation, recants her confession: "My voices were right." With that she has triumphed as an individual, or, to use Shaw's words, she has triumphed as a "Protestant," but is, at the same time, condemned to death. She had come too early, this Joan of Arc, an impotent possibility amid a reality that appeared to know nothing of utopia as a reasoning of the heart.

Through her death, so Shaw intimates, Joan becomes a historical personage of continuing significance, "Saint Joan" to be exact. More is meant to be expressed in this than the mere fact of canonization. The skeptical English earl has the last word in the trial scene. The executioner assures him, "You have heard the last of her." To which Warwick answers, "The last of her? Hm! I wonder."

Shaw appended an epilogue to the history of Saint Joan. The idea is a master stroke: his intent was to loosen the case of Joan of Arc from its historical foundation and to view it from the perspective of posterity. But Shaw refrains from taking the simple way and having contemporaries from the year 1920 discuss the case of the maid from Domrémy. His Irish love of contrariety once again produces the exact opposite of the expected, and this is well and good. The epilogue is situated in the period immediately succeeding Joan, in the year 1456, after her rehabilitation at the behest of the French king, whose interests, of course, lay in that direction. Instead of having figures from the fifteenth century appear in the Europe of 1920, Shaw has a Vatican spokesman from 1920 appear amid the figures of 1456, causing them, by his dress and mentality, a good deal of hilarity.

This Shavian epilogue ends in Dostoevsky's sense in the talk between Christ and the Grand Inquisitor. Everyone is more than willing to venerate the incinerated farm girl as martyr and saint, under the condition that she does not return. Her reason of the heart must not disturb everyday pragmatism. Joan and her reason of the heart—that is for Shaw the spirit of contrariety. One could also call it the spirit of progress, skepticism, or resistance. Shaw chose the expression "Protestantism" and did not mean Luther or Calvin with it, but the spirit of protest. Reason of the heart and the spirit of protest: these are, to a great extent, identical for him. It is on this account that in the year 1920 Joan must be made a saint: so that her spirit of contradiction can be socially integrated and, with that, rendered innocuous. Wherefore such an epilogue. How could it be otherwise but that it concludes with a question addressed to God and the world that can have no answer?

Bertolt Brecht, a younger contemporary of Shaw, thought much of him. An appreciative review like the "Ovation for Shaw," which was written for Shaw's seventieth birthday, is certainly a rarity in the works of the young Brecht.[9] He applauds above all what he calls Shaw's "terrorism." "The Shavian terror is unusual, and it makes use of an unusual weapon, namely humor." Brecht does not offer an analysis of individual works; yet one senses an easy familiarity with them, especially with the Salvation Army piece, *Major Barbara*. Certain reflexes and reactions to and from it can be ascertained in the Black Straw Hats in Brecht's *Saint Joan of the Stockyards*.

At the conclusion of his "ovation," Brecht distances himself from Shaw's biological, evolutionary credo; but on the other hand he subscribes to what he at least holds to be a Shavian "evolutionary theory": "At any event, his belief that humanity is infinitely capable of improvement plays a decisive role in his works. One should bear in mind that it comes to the same thing as a sincere ovation for Bernard Shaw when I admit without reservation that I ... blindly and without qualification subscribe to this Shavian theory."[10]

Perhaps Brecht took this nearness to Shaw—but scarcely to Shaw's Fabian socialism—as a certain stimulus to demonstrate in a treatment of the Joan of Arc story both his distance from Schiller and his criticism of social reformism. It was something that, by the very nature of the themes chosen, had to bring him into opposition with German classicism and the so-called culinary theater of the late bourgeois period. In opposition at once to Schiller and to Shaw. His *Saint Joan of the Stockyards* was meant to provide a synthesis of his critical occupations with Marxism. It was on this account that Brecht conceived for it a material rather than a formal dramatic technique. The action is not built up around the elements of the story—for it is not its concern to relate a story at all. The events are "quoted" from the very first and, through the reference to Saint Joan, stripped of all the usual and traditional elements of tension. One knows at the start how a story about a Saint Joan has to end: badly. Therefore there is no dramatic action that might be inspired by the behavior of the characters or by a rising and falling turn of events, but only representation of an economic state of affairs. The dramatic course of events is to be guided by the economic cycle of crisis and prosperity. It is a well-known fact, expressly mentioned by Brecht himself, that he endeavored to represent the process of the circulation of capital in the play.[11] This was the dramatic event of each scene, and it followed Karl Marx's analysis as found in the second volume of *Capital*. When "classical" writers are mentioned in Brecht's plays and poems, the classical writers of Marxism are the ones always meant. Only their ideas had for Brecht the authenticity of classical texts. And now in *Saint Joan of the Stockyards* the classical ideas of Karl Marx and Friedrich Engels are juxtaposed in a thoroughly malicious manner with texts that were viewed in the German bourgeois world as classical: Schiller, Goethe, and in one place even Hölderlin. Let me start by citing the last-mentioned episode. In the tenth scene Graham, with all the flourishes of classical rhetoric, provides one of those accounts of battle so familiar from *The Maid of Orléans*. But in this case the account is of a battle at the stock exchange. The corpses littering the ground are not those of actual people but of artificial people, namely corporations. Graham reporting on the repercussions in the price of beef: "To the prices namely / it was given from quotation to quotation to fall / as water thrown from crag to crag / deep down into infinity." That is Hyperion's song of fate mutated, simultaneously quoted and parodied, to represent an occurrence at the Chicago stock exchange.

A further example: In Schiller's final scene, Joan's banner is extended to her at the king's bidding as she lies dying on the battlefield. The final verses of the romantic tragedy are spoken, after which Schiller adds the following stage directions, meant to exploit advantageously the theatric effect: "The banner falls from her grasp; she sinks down dead upon it. Everyone stands for a long time in speechless emotion. At the king's faint gesture, all the banners are gently touched down to her so that she is completely covered over with them." Whoever reads Brecht's *Saint Joan of the Stockyards* finds a thoroughly familiar line in the last scene: "Give her the flag." This is what the king had commanded in Schiller. In Brecht the line is spoken by Pierpont Mauler, the meat-packing king of Chicago. The flag is passed to her and falls out of her grasp as she dies. Mauler's parodistic, Goethe-like aria ensues, whereupon we come across more lines familiar from Schiller: "Everyone stands for a long time in speechless emotion. At Snyder's gesture all the flags are gently touched down to her so that she is completely covered over with them. The scene is lit with a rosy glow."[12] This time it is not the king but the major of the Salvation Army who commands that the flags be lowered—the Salvation Army flags, namely those of the Black Straw Hats. The rosy glow at this juncture is Bertolt Brecht's imaginative contribution.

It is evident what is going on. Brecht is confronting in the body of his work the classicism of the bourgeoisie with the classicism of socialism. The material events roll along according to Marxist analysis. The events taking place in the characters' consciousness, however, are represented—at least seemingly so—through the means of idealist drama. All characters of the ruling order, starting with Mauler, declaim in classical intonation. Mauler's first few sentences at the very beginning are intended as conscious parody of a classical exposition, namely the hero's dialogue with the one who has his trust. For Brecht it does not suffice to have the crudest deals declaimed in a high pomp verse; he at the same time situates this pomp verse as bourgeois ideology, that is to say as false consciousness. Mauler and his broker Slift not only speak in blank verse, they also ostentatiously pluck here and there the most famous and best loved expressions from Goethe and particularly from Schiller:

> Ach der Mensch in seinem Drange
> Hält das Irdische nicht aus
> Und in seinem stolzen Gange
> Aus dem Alltäglichen
> Ganz Unerträglichen
> In das Unkenntliche
> Hohe Unendliche
> Stösst er übers Ziel hinaus.

> Woe, that man cannot abide / in his stress the earthly bond / and that in his haughty stride / from the daily grind / that breaks his mind / toward an unknown / infinite throne / he hurtles far, above, beyond!

Joan Dark's monopoly-minded antagonist is presented at the end—after the demise of Saint Joan of the stockyards who now in rosy light is made out to be a saint—as a Faust from Chicago with the famous two souls passage:

> Denn es zieht mich zu dem Grossen
> Selbst- und Nutz- und Vorteilslosen
> Und es zieht mich zum Geschäft
> Unbewusst!

I'm drawn to what is truly great/free from self and the profit rate/and yet impelled to business life/all unawares!

Quotation and parody are used here not merely as dramatic techniques but as the elements of an ideological critique that is grounded in the substance of the work. To put it bluntly, one would have to say that Brecht interprets German classicism, in particular Friedrich Schiller, as the ideological superstructure of bourgeois business dealings. In doing this he allows no distinction between the superstructure of a society with an ascending bourgeoisie and a later, bourgeois-monopolistic form. As later in *The Good Woman of Szechuan,* in his adaptation of Lenz's *The Tutor,* and finally in the comedy about intellectuals dealing with Turandot and the Congress of Whitewashers, Brecht takes up battle with Immanuel Kant's bourgeois philosophy, particularly with the categorical imperative, and with Friedrich Schiller's Kantian drama. *Saint Joan of the Stockyards* is explicitly set up as a counterversion to *The Maid of Orléans.* And with that the title figure comes to be interpreted in a decisively different fashion. Brecht has conceived his Joan Dark at once against Schiller and Shaw. For the first time in one of his main works a title-figure is presented who will serve as a demonstration of false behavior. Brecht has written his play against Joan, just as he later undertook to demonstrate the false behavior of Mother Courage, of Shen-Te, of Galileo, and probably even of Schweyk.

The fundamental error of this Joan Dark, in the eyes of the author of the piece, is precisely that attribute of character that provided her in Schiller with the dignity of a tragic heroine, in Shaw with the superiority over all her adversaries; I mean of course the *raison du coeur.* In Brecht as well as in Schiller and Shaw, Joan trusts in her inner voice and seeks to help, to mediate, to relieve material distress. The voice can do no wrong. She is taken in by everything that is presented convincingly. If she reads in the newspapers that the stockyards are going to be reopened, that the lockout is over, she believes it and asks: "Why shouldn't it be true if these gentlemen say it is so? You can't joke around about such a thing." To which the wife of the fallen worker, Luckerniddle, responds: "Don't talk so stupidly. You have absolutely no idea. You haven't sat here long enough in the cold." Joan Dark comes from a middle class family and is unfamiliar with the life of the poor. Therefore she trusts the newspapers and assurances of the bourgeoisie. She wants to decide with her heart and resists both "cold" ideological criticism and the use of force. She objects to the workers' decision to offer resistance:

Halt, lernt nicht weiter!
Nicht in so kalter Weise!
Nicht durch Gewalt
Bekämpft Unordnung und die Verwirrung!

Stop! no more lessons/so coldly learned!/Do not use force/to fight disorder and confusion.

But the turn of events has produced a confusion of feelings in her as well. She no longer trusts her own "warm" humanity because she has begun to feel the inconsequentiality of such virtue. In a monologue she postulates: "I'm going to leave. What's done by force can't be good. I don't belong to these people. If hunger and the tread of misery had taught me force as a child, I'd belong to them and ask no questions. As it is, I've got to leave."

Here the contrary between Brecht and Schiller is driven to its limit. Kant had postulated that there is nothing in man that unreservedly could be called good but goodwill. Karl Marx poked fun at that and said it was but an expression of immature German social conditions that Kant had appraised mere goodwill so highly. Brecht here too follows Marx. And so he wrote his play against Joan's goodwill and against her reasoning of the heart. Such goodwill was simple immediacy. It reflected real conditions, but it did not reflect *on* them, which is to say grasp them by intellect in their social context. Schiller led his Joan from a naïve frame of mind and frame of acting to a sentimental one. Brecht too, composing a counterversion to idealistic tragedy, has his Joan Dark go through a "change of character" in the sense of classical drama.

The main character of a later play, Mother Courage, goes along pulling her canteen cart, remaining unchanged in her complete lack of insight. Brecht's Joan Dark, however, dies transformed. Transformed to be sure from idealism to materialism. Her last lines therefore are not at all sad, but are an angry renunciation of the *raison du coeur* and the simple, unreflected will to be good. She says,

> I've learned one thing and I know it on your
> behalf, dying myself:
> how can it be that there is something in you
> that won't come out! WHAT do you know in your knowing
> that has no results?
> I, for example, have done nothing.
> Let nothing be counted good, although, as always, it may seem
> really helpful, and nothing henceforth be considered honorable
> except what changes this world once for all: it needs it.
> Like an answer to their prayers I came to the oppressors!
> Oh, goodness without results! Unnoticed attitude!
> I have altered nothing.
> Swiftly, fruitlessly vanishing from this world
> I say unto you:
> Take care that when you leave the world
> you were not only good but are leaving
> a good world!

Here in Brecht's interpretation of Joan there is added a third Marxist element. To the drama's layout, constructed according to the rules of Marxist political economy, to the ideological criticism of philosophical idealism and its classical representatives in German literature, comes the criticism of that school of politics that would like to act in the whole social order much as Joan Dark, that is, inspired by *raison du coeur*, harmonizing, mediating. Joan had joined the Black Straw Hats, but the play does not have to do with the Salvation Army as does Shaw's *Major Barbara*. Brecht is not at all concerned with the badness of monopoly owners and the heroism of the proletariat. Both are of little consideration in the play. Mauler possesses—at least this is my personal impression—a character one can warm up to. There is just under the surface a partiality for each other between Joan and Mauler. The workers, as so often in Brecht, are presented as poor miserable wretches so that Joan is forced to say that Mauler did not demonstrate the badness of the poor to her, but only their impoverishment.

If the play demonstrates anything at all, it has to do with the function of those who desire to mediate and smooth over matters between classes in the name of universal humanitarianism. Where that leads is the subject of some of Joan's final words: "How handy I was for the oppressors!" In so far as she gave heed to her reason of the heart and joined the Black Straw Hats, whose function of political pacification is shown quite maliciously by Brecht, Joan herself became an instrument of repression.

It is common knowledge that Brecht was expressing a criticism of reformism within the German workers' movement of 1930 in the manner in which he has Joan Dark act. This play, like many a poem and so many of Brecht's tracts of the same time, deals with the Marxist opposition between social reformism and revolution. To reduce this Joan Dark to a logical formula: Goodness without effect equals wishfulness for harmony, equals idealistic apologetic, equals contribution to repression.

As so often in Brecht's writings of his first Marxist period, there is here—and this is a fact that must not be lost sight of—a radical reaction into a kind of mediated inhumanity. Brecht places the blame on Joan Dark for her lack of dialectical thinking, yet he himself offends here by a black and white, undialectical breaking apart of ends and means, struggle for reform and struggle for absolute and complete change. In the poems from the period of exile much of what here is still undialectical antinomism is taken back. There is ineffectual social reform, and there is just as surely ineffectual revolution. The relationship between the author Brecht and his figure of Joan Dark is a commentary on both.

In *Saint Joan of the Stockyards* he had chastened his lead figure and forced her to a metamorphosis in the Aristotelian sense with which he had broken. But that does not suffice for the dramatic figure of Joan. At the end of Brecht's career it became clear that he had occupied himself with this figure from a mere historical episode to an extraordinary extent—more so than with any other historical personality. Even Julius Caesar had not provided him so many ideas and so much difficulty to work out as had this girl from Lorraine. One has today in Bertolt Brecht's collected dramatic works three attempts at sorting out the phenomenon of Joan of Arc. In addition to *Saint Joan of the Stockyards*, there is the play *The Visions of Simone Machard*,[13] written in the period of exile and inspired by his friend Lion Feuchtwanger's report about certain events connected with the French military collapse in June 1940. And there is finally, as adaptation for the Berlin Ensemble in East Berlin, the stage version of Anna Segher's radio play about the trial of Joan of Arc.

Simone Machard is a child. Brecht specifically calls for the stage role to be filled by a little girl. Simone experiences first-hand the behavior of the French bourgeoisie and civil service when the German troops of occupation march in: treason, collaboration, compromise, at best impotent rage. In her favorite storybook she had read the history of Joan of Arc, how she rose up and drove out the enemy, crowned the king, and was in the end convicted by an ecclesiastical court and bound over to the civil arm for execution. And so too do dreams and visions come to Simone Machard. As in Gerhart Hauptmann's *Hannele's Ascension,* the girl clothes her dream figures in the features, clothes, and characteristics of the persons familiar to her. That includes the angel who gives her her orders:

Daughter of France, Joan: something must be done
Or our great France will perish before two weeks have run.
The Lord our God has looked around for aid
And now His eyes have fallen on His little Maid.

It is the very familiar angel in the very familiar church, left of the altar, his robe at the sleeve having, as Simone says later, "peeled off the tiniest bit." To put it bluntly, an angel of the poor. With that everything is said and decided. Simone Machard was the France of the people; in her dreams she saw the rising up of the poor and felt their power to drive out the enemy. The rich, however, behave in June 1940, in actual fact and in Brecht's play, just as the nobles and ecclesiastics did in Shaw's tent scene. They league together to make common cause against the masses and against Joan, the little Simone Machard who has become a threat. She is bound over to the nuns of a cloister to be kept in custody. Before she is taken away her angel speaks once more to this little saintly Joan of June 1940, alone:

Daughter of France, don't be afraid.
None will endure who fight the Maid.
The Lord will blast the arm
That does you harm.
Where they take you it matters not
France is wherever you set foot.
The day will soon be coming when
Glorious France will rise again.

This is a different tone and a different interpretation of the Joan of Arc story. In *The Visions of Simone Machard,* which likely never was put into its final form as a theater piece, Brecht discovered something of the original scandal surrounding the historical person of Joan of Arc. For so long before that he had simply drawn Joan in opposition to Schiller and Shaw. Now there was a Joan who offended against taboos, unpardonably against two above all: that she wanted to make history though she came from the lower classes and that she possessed visions and utopias that reached far beyond the dogmas dictated by the officials of State and Church.

In Brecht's adaptation of *The Trial of Joan of Arc at Rouen, 1431,*[14] Joan is likewise understood as a representative of the masses. She dies, but the girls of

France burst into song, a song with the refrain: "Fight on, Frenchmen, for French soil, you who till it." The concluding words of the peasant Jacques Legrain (who has a name reminiscent of the peasants' rebellions, the Jacqueries, and in which the word *grain/corn/seed* occurs) are a comment on this song: "they are singing it now in both Frances, here and over there." What Brecht must have meant with that when he produced the play for the "Theater on Schiffbauerdamm" at the beginning of the fifties is manifest. He had found his way back to Joan, to the adversary of religious and state authoritarianism, to the breaker of taboos.

The *Optimistic Tragedy* of Vsevolod Vishnevskii was written in 1932, two years after Brecht's *Saint Joan of the Stockyards.*[15] Vishnevskii was born in 1901, had served as a machinegunner in the Red Army as a nineteen-year-old, and had experienced at first hand the establishment of the Red Navy. It was this experience that provided the historical context of the *Optimistic Tragedy.* Since the writing of his first drama, the *First Cavalry Corps* in 1929, he had been essentially a playwright. It has been ascertained that in 1932 he did not know of *Saint Joan of the Stockyards.* Neither had he read *The Maid of Orléans,* either before then or in the years thereafter, as he has observed to me in conversation.[16] The *Optimistic Tragedy* thereby becomes an all the more singular continuation of Western European dramatic *and* social constellations. What otherwise would have been simply an interesting example in literary history of the continuity of a particular theme suddenly takes on an altogether different quality. It is a new, namely postbourgeois coming to terms with the scandal of Joan of Arc.

In Vishnevskii too the lead figure is the woman with a weapon. She kills in the manner of Joan or Judith. At the first confrontation on the ship commandeered by anarchists between the woman commissar, a member of the Bolsheviks who had been sent by the government in Moscow, and the anarchist delegates from the sailors, one of these libertarian potentates, despising Bolshevism, commissars, and women in uniform, starts a shoving match. She shoots him on the spot. Judith defends her honor; Joan kills her class enemy.

The commissar has no name: she incorporates an idea, a party, a mission. The lonely outsiderdom of the maid of Orléans, even that of the transformed Joan Dark in Brecht, finds its logical conclusion here. The female member of the party feels herself the equal of, and on an equal footing with, any other member, male or female. Schiller's heroine lived in the antinomy of her own feminine individuality and her historical mission. The one had to give way to the other, but it was the task of the "romantic tragedy" to demonstrate both sides of the alternative. Vishnevskii's commissar writes home to relatives. Curiously enough, our Bolshevik dramatist has given her only relatives, no husband or children. "Nicht Männerliebe darf dein Herz berühren / Mit sündgen Flammen eitler Erdenlust ..." ("The love of men must not move your heart / With the sinful flames of vain earthly pleasure ..."). So spoke Joan's voices in Schiller's *Maid of Orléans.* We see that the taboo in the antinomy of feminine existence and action as woman with a weapon is carried over into a tragedy no longer bourgeois (and therefore "optimistic").

This tragedy's optimism, which in the final scene—precisely as in Schiller—is laid out in state with the commissar dying on the battlefield, is derived from two premises. They are premises based upon a certain hope and philosophical understanding of the processes of history. To wit: socialism brings to a close a proto-historical epoch of man; the life of the fallen commissar was a part of socialism, therefore her death served the realization of historical necessity. Vishnevskii's artificial dramatic figure was herself of this same understanding. To a fainthearted comrade she once explained: "Don't you know that even death can be a task for the good of the party?" That could just as well be a line in Brecht—in *The Measure Adopted.*

The second premise of this tragic optimism means to provide a cure for isolated individuality's suffering and mortality. The cure is collectivity, which integrates and transcends all individual suffering—and which itself outlives its parts. Within the framework of a thoroughly similar optimism, one of the most famous and most widely propagated works of Soviet literature was conceived; I mean the frankly autobiographical novel *How the Steel Was Tempered* by Nikolai Ostrovskii. Vishnevskii, of course, knew the work. His conception of tragic optimism coincides with the philosophy of life and survival of the suffering Pavel Korchagin in Ostrovskii. The final scene of the *Optimistic Tragedy* shows the dying commissar. Vishnevskii's stage directions are far more than mere guidelines for a director when he writes: "The sailors stand frozen a moment, out of breath, bewildered; the old sailor, the boatswain, the commander stand at attention and salute; one after another the sailors salute their dead commissar, even the wounded, finally Alexei. They surround the dead commissar in a mighty living ring."

Here the individual representative and activist of an idea died. But the idea and the organization carry on. The apotheosis is not consummated in any "speechless emotion" as in Schiller, but it takes place as preview, as anticipation of a future order of men.

Brecht had parodied *The Maid of Orléans* and the Kantian system of ethics that Schiller had adopted. In *The Tutor* he made the Kantian Paetus the butt of derision. Vishnevskii's *Optimistic Tragedy,* on the other hand, he produced in his Schiffbauerdamm theater, even arranging the staging himself. The piece's dialectical relationship both to Schiller and to his own *Saint Joan* had not escaped him. In a Brecht text dating from 1954, one finds the following lines concerning the drama of social realism, in which Brecht, though probably not in full agreement with such a realism, makes use of the sanctioned terminology: "The social-realist work of art shows characters and events to be historical and changeable . . . and to be contradictory. This signifies a great about-face."[17]

Brecht died in 1956, exactly 500 years after the first opportunistic and disconcerted rehabilitation of Joan of Arc. He never quite came free of the story of the girl from Lorraine despite his threefold attempt. As little as did Catholic dramatist Paul Claudel or the commercial playwright Jean Anouilh. This phenomenon of never quite coming free of Joan touches on the reasons that led Schiller to ignore Joan's trial whereas Shaw, Claudel, Anouilh, and Seghers/Brecht took great pains to make the trial and execution come alive. Schiller's demurral, however, can only be seen as a complement to the other writers' insistence. He wrote at the high tide in Germany of the bourgeoisie's Enlightenment optimism. Joan is the Idea incarnate, at the price of surrendering not only her femininity but also her individuality. Only forty years later Friedrich Hebbel set up against Schiller a newly individualized and newly "feminized" counterversion in his *Judith* and in his plans for his own version of the story of Joan of Arc.

Shaw and Brecht grasp Joan as an exception who gives the lie to all the trivial rules of political, ecclesiastical, and familial routine. And so they are obliged to bring to a clear focus her state of existence as outsider, and the trial with its turning point of recantation, and recantation of the recantation, if extraordinarily well suited to that. In this way Joan becomes an actualizer of utopia. She practices Pascal's *raison du coeur;* she incorporates Protestantism in herself before Luther; without books and in the stockyards of Chicago she imbibes the lessons of class struggle: Joan of Arc as permanent scandal—consequently as permanent actual, concrete moment of utopia.

This development from Schiller to Vishnevskii is comparable to a Hegelian triad. In *The Maid of Orléans* is postulated an idea that through abstraction is removed from the actual, concrete reality of its carrier. In Shaw and Brecht the idea and all idealistic confidence and conviction are negated through confrontation with a nonideal reality. This is brought home in the actual figure meant to incorporate the idea. In Vishnevskii the transcendence is postulated of all opposition between idea and negation of the idea in a new reality. The idea is made concrete in the Bolshevik party. The antagonism between society and individual dissolves in the dialectical energy field of the collective. The commissar has been delegated. There is consequently no longer an autonomous Joan of Arc.

This synthesis by Vishnevskii in 1932, however, marks the beginning of a new dialectical process. The days of the collective and party from the heroic age of war and civil war at the beginning of Soviet history are long gone. The situation has changed. The political premises of "optimism" have been consigned to the ash heap, and so too have the aesthetic premises of an optimistic tragedy. A Joan of Arc has become thinkable who is a negation of that collective. History and literary history know the names: that of the poet Anna Akhmatova, that of Nadezhda Mandelshtam. The scandal will not end.

NOTES

[1] George Bernard Shaw, *Saint Joan: A Chronicle Play in Six Scenes and an Epilogue* (New York: Penguin Books, 1958), Preface: Joan, a Galtonic Visualizer.
[2] Johann Huizinga, *The Waning of the Middle Ages* (London: E. Arnold, 1924).
[3] Shaw, *Saint Joan,* Preface: The Maid in Literature.
[4] Pascal, *Pensées,* in *Oeuvres complètes,* ed. Jacques Chevalier (Paris: Bibliothèque de la Pléiade, 1954).
[5] Ibid., pp. 1091–92: "Dans l'esprit de finesse, les principes sont dans l'usage commun et devant les yeux de tout le monde. On n'a que faire de tourner la tête ni de se fair violence; il n'est question que d'avoir bonne vue, mais il faut l'avoir bonne. . . ."
[6] Ibid., p. 1221: "Le coeur a ses raisons, que la raison ne connaît point; on le sait de mille choses. Je dis que le coeur aime l'être universel naturellement, et soi-même naturellement, selon qu'il s'y adonne; et

il se durcit contre l'un ou l'autre, à son choix...." (Pensée 477). See Pensée 479 as well: "Nous connaissons la vérité, non seulement par la raison, mais encore par le coeur; c'est de cette dernière sorte que nous connaissons les premiers principes, et c'est en vain que le raisonnement, qui n'y a point de part, essaye de les combattre." In the trial this conflict is to be felt everywhere—to be sure as the contrast between subjective convictions, while Pascal is postulating here objective givens.

[7] The analysis is based on materials in volume 9 of the National Edition of Schiller, ed. Benno von Wiese and Lieselotte Blumenthal (Weimar: H. Böhlaus Nachf., 1948). On the history of its development, p. 401ff. On the history of its reception, p. 438ff.

[8] Shaw, Saint Joan, Scene IV.

[9] Bertolt Brecht, Ovation für Shaw (July 15, 1926), in Gesammelte Werke in acht Bänden, vol. 7 (Frankfurt: Suhrkamp, 1967), pp. 96ff.

[10] Ibid., p. 101.

[11] See the fragments and variants to Die heilige Johanna der Schlachthöfe in vol. 427 of the edition Suhrkamp series (Frankfurt, 1971).

[12] Brecht, Die heilige Johanna der Schlachthöfe, in Gesammelte Werke, vol. 1, p. 785. [Verse translations are taken from Saint Joan of the Stockyards, trans. Frank Jones (Bloomington, Ind.: Indiana University Press, 1970).]

[13] Brecht, Die Gesichte der Simone Machard, in Gesammelte Werke, vol. 2, pp. 1841ff. [Verse translations are taken from The Visions of Simone Machard, in vol. 7 of Bertolt Brecht, Collected Plays, trans. Ralph Manheim and John Willet (New York: Random House, 1973).]

[14] Brecht, Der Prozess der Jeanne d'Arc zu Rouen 1431 nach dem Hörspiel von Anna Seghers, in Gesammelte Werke, vol. 2, pp. 2499ff.

[15] The analysis is based on Friedrich Wolf's German translation and edition of The Optimistic Tragedy (Berlin, 1948).

[16] The source here is a conversation with Vsevolod Vishnevskii at the German Writers' Congress in Berlin in October 1947.

[17] Brecht, "Sozialistischer Realismus auf dem Theater," in Gesammelte Werke, vol. 7, p. 935.

Paul Hernadi

RE-PRESENTING THE PAST:
SAINT JOAN
AND *L'ALOUETTE*

"**W**ell, if you will burn the Protestant, I will burn the Nationalist." So says the Earl of Warwick to Bishop Cauchon about the title character in the fourth scene of George Bernard Shaw's *Saint Joan* (1923). During the entire conversation, Joan's principal opponents express their misgivings in clearly anachronistic terms. In the summer of 1429, just before the coronation of Charles VII by The Maid, no language had words for "protestant" and "nationalist." Nor is it likely that any of Joan's contemporaries perceived her as representing what Warwick describes as "the protest of the individual soul against the interference of priest or peer" with the private person's relationship to God and the state (1971:107). But Shaw's preface to the play defends the conceptual anachronism of his dialogue with a remarkable argument: "It is the business of the stage to make its figures more intelligible to themselves than they would be in real life; for by no other means can they be made intelligible to the audience." In order to secure "sufficient veracity," the playwright must incur a "sacrifice of verisimilitude" and portray his characters as saying "the things they actually would have said if they had known what they were really doing" (52–53).

This line of thought has far-reaching implications not only for historical drama or the craft of playwriting at large. It points to the inevitable hindsight involved in any re-presentation of past events. The skillful historian will convey a sense of how certain men and women of a past period understood themselves and their relationships to each other. Yet he or she will also suggest certain patterns of cause and purpose of which the participants in the narrated events could not have been fully aware. In short, the historian will try to make us see the past both from within and from without—as evolving drama and as the fixed target of distanced retrospection. Such a dual mode of vision is, of course, sustained by the historian's favored verbal medium: narrative discourse. Historiography typically turns the untold *dramas* of history, in which many a disconcerted player "struts and frets his hour upon

From *Interpreting Events: Tragicomedies of History on the Modern Stage* (Ithaca, NY: Cornell University Press, 1985), pp. 17–37.

the stage," into intelligible *tales.* These tales may well be "full of sound and fury" but escaped Macbeth's charge of "signifying nothing" (V.v. 24–28) by being channeled through a narrator's unifying consciousness. Indeed, most readers are inclined to doubt the reliability of historians providing verbatim reports of what was said or thought on a given occasion—a practice for which even Thucydides (1928:1, 39) felt called upon to offer a somewhat apologetic justification:

> As to the speeches that were made by different men . . . it has been difficult to record with strict accuracy the words actually spoken, both for me as regards that which I myself heard, and for those who from various other sources have brought me reports. Therefore the speeches are given in the language in which, as it seemed to me, the several speakers would express, on the subjects under consideration, the sentiments most befitting the occasion.
> [I.xii.i]

By using a narrative rather than dramatic mode of communication, modern historians conspicuously refrain from pretending to mirror what they in fact mediate. When they indulge in the mimetic luxury of direct quotation, they usually quote written documents postdating the events under consideration, and such documents themselves are verbal mediations of largely nonverbal events. In pronounced contrast to the narrative historian's predilection for *indirectly presenting envisioned action,* the author of dramatic work is engaged in *directly representing action.* Except for the "side text" of stage directions, the playwright is typically absent from the linguistic surface of his play. In the colorful words of young Stephen Dedalus, he remains, "like the God of the creation, within or behind or beyond or above his handiwork, invisible, refined out of existence, paring his finger-nails" (Joyce 1916:252). In performance, even the stage directions (as well as such clearly authorial utterances as prefaces and postscripts) become submerged. From staged historical drama, therefore, an obviously imaginative version of what happened in the past can emerge without any overt intervention by a present consciousness. The result is a paradoxical relationship between historiographical narrative and historical drama. While the dialogue form of history plays and the documentable content of history books claim to offer unmediated insight into what really happened, the imaginative content of drama and the narrative form of historiography typically acknowledge that the re-presented events have been produced, or at least reproduced, in a human mind.

Beyond Verisimilitude

Shaw's concern for "veracity" as opposed to "verisimilitude" highlights the generic tension between the dialogue form and the imaginative content of earlier dramatizations of history. Generally speaking, serious historical drama before the late nineteenth century attempted to conceal rather than betray, let alone flaunt, the playwright's imaginative role in re-presenting the past. Shakespeare's debased and Schiller's romanticized Joan of Arc, for example, presumably reflected their authors' view of the character. But the iambic pentameters of neither Joan—one speaking in English, the other in German to boot—strike us as pointing to an authorial stance outside the imaginative worlds evoked in *Henry VI* or *Die Jungfrau von Orleans*. By contrast, Warwick and Cauchon in *Saint Joan* discuss the Maid in frankly anachronistic language, and Shaw's dreamlike Epilogue—of which more will be said later—relies completely on authorial hindsight.

In *The Lark* (1953), Jean Anouilh made an even bolder attempt to combine retrospective vision with the prospective orientation of the represented characters. As his Cauchon orders Joan's coronation of King Charles to be performed *after* the scene at the flaming stake, the King (rather than, as in Christopher Fry's English version, Cauchon himself) has the dubious privilege of explaining why:

> The real end of Joan's story . . . the end which they will always tell, long after they have forgotten our names and confused them all together: it isn't the painful and miserable end of the cornered animal caught at Rouen: but the lark singing in the open sky, Joan at Rheims in all her glory. . . . Joan of Arc: A story which ends happily.   [227/103]

Remarkably enough, the modern playwright's overt departure from historical veri-similitude does not interfere with our willing suspension of disbelief as regards his representation of past events. Quite to the contrary: when Schiller's Joan dies on the battlefield, *history* is felt to be violated; but when Anouilh explicitly disrespects the only possible chronology (coronation before death) of two very historical occurrences, most readers and spectators are pleased to contemplate his *story* of Joan, with its happy "real end," from the bird's-eye view of a retrospective authorial perspective.

The same applies to Shaw's Epilogue, in which Joan, twenty-five years after her death, discusses her recent rehabilitation with half a dozen characters from the play and with a "clerical-looking gentleman in black frockcoat and trousers, and tall hat, in the fashion of the year 1920" (159). Much to Joan's surprise, this Gentleman announces her canonization by the Catholic church. Much to Joan's grief, however, her offer to "rise from the dead, and come back . . . a living woman" provokes general rejection or evasion for a number of all too human reasons. Bishop Cau-chon's plea must exasperate her the most: "Mortal eyes cannot distinguish the saint from the heretic. Spare them" (162). In 1456 as in 1920, the world can live with Joan's statues—the one in Winchester Cathedral and the one in front of Rheims Cathedral even become visible through the window of Charles's bedchamber. But as a "living woman," who might once more act as an early (and thus too early) proponent of the future, she would have to be burned, crucified, or otherwise disposed of all over again. Since the burning of Joan we have seen many a victory of Protestantism and nationalism, but as a renewed incarnation of whatever at a given time struggles to become the order of the day, she must forever forgive or despair. This is why Shaw makes her speak some of the last words of Jesus ("Father, forgive them; for they know not what they do" and "My God, my God, why hast thou forsaken me?") in characteristically revised version: "They were as honest a lot

of poor fools as ever burned their betters" (153) and, at the very end of the
Epilogue,"O God that madest this beautiful earth, when will it be ready to receive
Thy saints? How long, O Lord, how long?"(164).

Such an epilogue fully defies the principle of verisimilitude. Upon her aston-
ishing entrance Joan tells King Charles that she is but a dream of his; yet this
"psychological" explanation for Shaw's complete departure from the quasi-realistic
tradition of historical drama is no doubt offered tongue in cheek. Joan significantly
remains on stage after Charles and the other characters have disappeared. Her
presence in the final "white radiance" and her concluding appeal to God (just
quoted) clearly indicate that she is not Charles's dream but Shaw's. Only as a
figment of the playwright's historical imagination, which he endeavors to share with
us, can the Maid emerge from the Epilogue as the unwanted harbinger of the time
to come, another genius cast by the less gifted bulk of humanity in the gloriously
thankless role of the crucified Messiah.

Anouilh's Joan, too, is a harbinger of daybreak: she is *l'alouette,* the lark. But
Anouilh refuses to see her as championing any particular cause (such as Shaw's
"Protestantism" and "Nationalism," for example). In a note for the program of the
first French production, quoted here from the unnumbered pages preceding the
play in Christopher Fry's translation, he declared:

> The play that follows makes no attempt to explain the mystery of Joan. The
> persistent effort of so-called modern minds to explain mysteries is, in any case,
> one of the most naive and foolish activities indulged in by the puny human
> brain since it became overstocked with shallow political and scientific notions,
> and can yield nothing, in the long run, but the nostalgic satisfaction of the small
> boy who discovers at last that his mechanical duck was made up of two
> wheels, three springs, and a screw. The little boy holds in his hands three
> springs, two wheels, and a screw, objects which are doubtless reassuring, but
> he has lost his mechanical duck, and he has usually not found an explanation.

Privileging the historical imagination of collective memory over the latest findings of
scholarly research, Anouilh holds fast to the popular image of Joan as "haggard and
thin (yes, I know she was a big healthy girl, but I couldn't care less)." At the same
time, his own imagination attempts to penetrate deeper layers of the past than his
(or anybody else's) notion of what actually happened. For example, King Charles,
his mistress Agnes Sorel, and Queen Yolande, the delightfully unconventional
mother of his lawful wife, visit Joan in her prison. As with Shaw's Epilogue, it *could*
be argued that their obviously pseudohistorical conversation takes place in the mind
of one of the characters. Once again, however, a much more natural location
suggests itself: the playwright's and the reader's or spectator's minds contemplating
subliminal aspects of historical causation and motivation.

JOAN: Take care of Charles. Let him keep his courage.

AGNES: Of course he will, silly girl. I am working at it the same as you. Do you
think I want to be the mistress of a poor little king who is always being

beaten? You shall see, I will make our little Charles a great King yet, and
without getting myself burnt for him.   [206/92]

What most pre-twentieth-century historical plays occult and what even
Shaw's *Saint Joan* merely suggests becomes explicit in *L'Alouette:* the present
mode of existence of men and women of the past belies our ordinary frame-
works of space, time, and personal identity; it is a complex mode of becoming
by dint of being imaginatively re-called in a retrospecting consciousness. The very
structure of Anouilh's play is designed to evoke not an actual sequence of past
events but their imagined presence in *memory*—be it the playwright's memory
and the spectator's or the memory of each and every stage figure. To Warwick's
urging, "The sooner she is found guilty and burned the better for all concerned,"
Anouilh's Cauchon replies: "But, my lord, before we do that we have the whole
story to play: Domrémy, the Voices, Vaucouleurs, Chinon, the Coronation" (9–
10/1). So the play of Joan's life, as recalled in the course of a playfully staged trial,
is ready to commence:

JOAN: May I begin wherever I like?
CAUCHON: Yes.
JOAN: Then I'll begin at the beginning. The beginnings are always the best. At
      my father's house, when I am still a little girl. In the field where I am
      looking after the sheep and hear the Voices for the first time.   [12/2]

From this early point on, the almost bare stage will serve to represent many
places, and the spacial simultaneity of different locations is paralleled by Anouilh's
stress on the synchrony of all remembered time. In a play like *L'Alouette,* therefore,
anachronism—whether intended or unintended—cannot be an issue. Shaw's Joan
nonpluses the medieval Captain Baudricourt, who has dismissed her voices as
merely coming from her imagination, with this postromantic answer: "Of course.
That is how the messages of God come to us" (69). By contrast, Anouilh's Joan
replies to "Who is going to play the Voices?"—a question shouted at her from the
crowd of as yet unidentified actors—"I am, of course" (13/2), and proceeds to
speak "in the deep voice of the Archangel [Michael]" (15/3) whenever the occasion
arises. The difference between the two playwrights' respective approaches to
Joan's calling could hardly be more pronounced. To be sure, Shaw's principle of
veracity makes him represent his characters as saying "the things they actually
would have said" had they known what, in the playwright's retrospective estimation,
they were really doing. Yet Anouilh's memory play expressly fuses the multiple
perspectives of the little girl in the field and the young woman on trial with those
of Joan's judges, chroniclers, and her more or less skeptical present and even future
admirers into a single acoustic phenomenon within the massive here and now of
every performance: Joan's voice and Joan's Voices are emphatically identified as the
voice of the actress playing the part.

The counterpoint of voices within a remembered event is particularly suggestive when it allows Joan to interiorize the future opinion of others. As the

following "exchange" implies, genuinely interior dialogue and the assessment of the self by fellow human beings can converge in a single stream of consciousness:

> JOAN: You see, holy St. Michael, it isn't possible; they won't ever understand. No one will. It would be better if I gave up at once. Our Lord has said that we have to obey our father and mother. (*She replies in the voice of the Archangel.*)
> —But first you have to obey God.
> —But if God commands the impossible?
> —Then you have to attempt the impossible, calmly and quietly.... He doesn't ask the impossible of everybody, but He does ask it of you. He thinks that nothing is too difficult for you. That's all. (*Joan rises and says simply.*)
> —Well, I will go.
> A VOICE (*from somewhere out of the dark background*): Arrogant girl!
> JOAN (*disturbed*): Who is calling me arrogant? (*After a pause, in the voice of the Archangel.*)—It was you, Joan. And when you have begun to do what God is asking, it will be what the world calls you.   [48–51/18–19]

It should be sufficiently clear by now that Shaw and Anouilh deviate from the standard of verisimilitude in two essentially different directions. The main thrust of Shaw's deviation is sociological. To quote once again from his Preface, *Saint Joan* is intended to make us see "not only the visible and human puppets, but the Church, the Inquisition, the Feudal System." Pulling the strings behind the stage of the puppet show, those institutions seem to Shaw "more terrible in their dramatic force than any of the little mortal figures clanking about in plate armor or moving silently in the frocks and hoods of the order of St. Dominic" (51). Anouilh's characters, too, have certain strings attached to their visible limbs. But they are manipulated, so to speak, from within their psyches.

When, for instance, Cauchon's indulgent treatment of Joan promises to result in her compromising willingness to recant, the Inquisitor falls to his knees, oblivious of all around him, and expresses what is best understood as an unconscious psychological motivation for his institutional orthodoxy:

> O Lord! It has pleased You to grant that Man should humble himself at the eleventh hour in the person of this young girl.... But why has it also pleased You to let a shameful tenderness be born in the heart of this hardened old man who was supposed to judge her? Will you never grant, O Lord, that this world should be relieved of every trace of humanity, so that at last we may in peace consecrate it to Thy glory alone?   [200/89]

Anouilh thus attributes the Inquisition as an aggressive social institution to a self-consuming urge, reminiscent of Freud's "death drive" (*Todestrieb*), in its human representatives. By contrast, his Joan's psyche appears to propel her toward death by an existential impulse to be what she is: Anouilh's Joan steers away from public repentance and proceeds to the flames because of her strong sense of personal identity and the concomitant fear of entering what, for her, would be an inauthentic mode of existence. In talking to Warwick she verbalizes that fear, as far as the style of the speech is concerned, very much in character; yet her words express what is, strictly speaking, the playwright's rather than Joan's own psychological insight into why she is about to revoke her previous recantation:

> My life isn't lavish like yours, my lord, running orderly and smoothly between war, hunting, divers pleasures, and your beautiful fiancée. . . . What will be left for me when I am not Joan any longer? . . . Can you see Joan . . . set free, perhaps, vegetating at the French Court on her small pension? (*Almost laughing, yet sadly.*) Joan accepting everything, Joan with a big belly, a glutton. . . . Can you see Joan all made up, entangled in her gowns, busying herself with her little dog or with a man courting her, or who knows, Joan getting married?
> [214–15/96–97]

Veracity as Composite Vision

Just as it is the case with Shaw's institutional puppeteers ("The Church, the Inquisition, the Feudal System"), the existential-psychological motives stirring Anouilh's "visible and human puppets" are, of course, ultimately mobilized by a master puppeteer—the playwright. T. S. Eliot once remarked that we discern such manifestly poetic lines of drama as Macbeth's speech beginning "To-morrow and to-morrow and to-morrow" as if they were spoken by the character and the playwright "in unison" (1954:34–35). The last sentences just quoted from *The Lark* seem to call for an analogous observation except that the authorial voice heard in them becomes audible in a quasi-narrative rather than Shakespeare's quasi-lyrical register. "Can you see Joan. . . ?": Joan is being heard here as referring to her imagined, inauthentic future self in the third grammatical person characteristic of storytelling. And she addresses her interpretation of her historical prototype's unconscious motivation to Warwick, if not indeed to each member of the audience, as a narrator would appeal to the "dear reader"—in the second person. Along with the deliberately conspicuous use of anachronisms, which Anouilh shares with all the playwrights under present study, such quasi-narrative rhetoric makes us perceive clairvoyant *figures of drama* as capable of intellectually penetrating (rather than simply embodying) the *historical characters* whose lives are being supposedly re-presented on the stage.

Instead of saying what the "real" Joan, Warwick, and Cauchon could have said, heard, or at least thought in their actual historical situation, the dramatic figures in both *Saint Joan* and *The Lark* give verbal expression to the playwright's vision of the action of the persons they are invoked to represent. As Shaw explains in the Preface, his characters should make intelligible not only "themselves"—that is to say, their historical prototypes—but also the institutional imperatives of history governing their way of thinking and their manifest behavior. "Obviously," he adds, "the real Cauchon, Lemaître, and Warwick could not have done this: they were part of the Middle Ages themselves, and therefore as unconscious of its peculiarities as of the atomic formula of the air they breathed" (53). Much of what his characters are made to *say* is really *meant* by the playwright, whose vantage point is that of a different and presumably better-informed era. For the most part, however, Shaw appears to abide by the verisimilar convention of historical drama. Despite what may be called a newly added sound track, what Shaw's characters do up to the Epilogue remains, roughly speaking, in the realm of that which could have been filmed by a candid camera *avant la lettre*. By contrast, Anouilh's entire play evolves along lines similar to Shaw's Epilogue, in which all pretense of historical "verisimilitude" is sacrificed in the author's search for historical "veracity."

Consider the two playwrights' respective dramatizations of a well-known sequence of supposedly miraculous events. Having recognized the Dauphin among his much more lavishly dressed courtiers, Joan succeeds in persuading the insecure young man to allow her to lead the army, against the will of his overbearing councilors, to beleaguered Orléans. This theatrically effective scene, transmitted in Joan's legendary history, is dramatized by Shaw and Anouilh in rather similar fashion. But Shaw forestalls the supernatural interpretation of Joan's prodigious success merely through an anachronistically enlightened exchange about the nature and function of miracles (79–80) between the Archbishop ("nourish their faith by poetry") and La Trémouille, commander of the army ("Poetry! I should call it humbug"). By contrast, Anouilh makes a laughing Warwick comment on and thus defuse the impressively represented events (I quote Christopher Fry's delightful, though far from literal, English version):

> In point of fact, that wasn't exactly how it happened. They called a meeting of the Council, and discussed the matter for hours. In the end they agreed to use Joan as a sort of color-bearer at popular demand. An attractive little mascot, well qualified to charm the general public into letting themselves be killed.
> [131/56]

Their different treatment of Ladvenu, the Dominican friar who appears to have shown sympathy for Joan during the 1431 procedures, also manifests the same contrast between the approaches taken by the two playwrights: while Shaw introduces his "veracious" hindsight mainly in the realm of diction, Anouilh permits the composite vision required for any re-presentation of the past to permeate all dramatic action. In response to Warwick's remark about Joan's execution, "I am informed that it is all over," Shaw's Ladvenu "enigmatically" declares: "We do not know, my lord. It may have just begun." Even when Warwick asks him to elaborate, Ladvenu continues to anchor the playwright's retrospective "prediction" of the future in a reasonably verisimilar account of what has just happened:

> When the fire crept round us, and she saw that if I held the cross before her I should be burnt myself, she warned me to get down and save myself. My lord: a girl who could think of another's danger in such a moment was not inspired by the devil. When I had to snatch the cross from her sight, she looked up to heaven. And I do not believe that the heavens were empty. I

firmly believe that her Savior appeared to her then in His tenderest glory. She called to Him and died. This is not the end for her, but the beginning. [147–48]

Anouilh's Ladvenu in turn interrupts the reenactment of an early scene from Joan's life, the savage disciplining of the young girl by her father, who is enraged because she wants to join the army to save France. Joan's defender at the court proceedings sets out to defend her, prematurely, in her home town against her father: "Stop him right away! He is hurting her!" Cauchon, likewise disrespecting chronology, puts the preposterous intruder in his—Ladvenu's—chronological "place": "We can do nothing, Brother Ladvenu. We don't get to know Joan until the trial. We can only act our parts, each his own, good or bad, as it is written, and each in his turn. And soon, you know, we shall do worse things than this to her" (41/15).

Such passages, informed by the interplay between the personal core and figural circumference of Anouilh's major characters, highlight the dialectic between history's past "text" and any subsequent "reading" of it. The quotation marks around the key words of the last sentence are, of course, required by the circumstance that history (the "text") is always fleeting and largely nonverbal while its imaginative reconstruction (the "reading") is made permanent by being verbalized: historians, historical playwrights, and dramatic figures expressing the unspoken attitudes of their historical prototypes all translate, so to speak, from a shadowy "original version"—the world of events forever past—into the idiom of a continually present discourse. Thus it may seem surprising that neither Shaw nor Anouilh attempted to stay very close to the language of the extant documents concerning Joan's trial. After all, the re-presentation of the past would have required relatively little "translation" from the medium of occurrences into the medium of words in the case of such a "dramatic" and predominantly verbal event. The "natural affinity between drama and trials" (Lindenberger 1975:21) has indeed appealed to many modern playwrights with documentary or otherwise realistic ambitions. Even Peter Weiss, whose *Marat/Sade* (1964) is far from being a docudrama in any sense of the word, based his next play, *Die Ermittlung* (1965; *The Investigation*, 1966), almost verbatim on selected excerpts from the 1963–65 Frankfort trial of eighteen former staff members of the Auschwitz concentration camp. By contrast, Shaw and Anouilh are allied with the Weiss of *Marat/Sade*, of *Trotzki im Exil* (1970), and of *Hölderlin* (1971) in refusing to conceal the editorial, retrospective aspect of the production, transmission, and any later use of such historiographical materials as trial transcripts and archival records. As a result, their plays unmistakably dramatize history by turning private acts of *envisioning action* into public events of *enacting vision*.

Let me clarify the italicized terms by elaborating on some implications of my earlier study, *Beyond Genre: New Directions in Literary Classification* (1972), where I contrasted Action and Vision as two poles between which the sparks of imaginative literature are generated. I used proverbs and realistic conversational dialogue as my respective literary examples for the thematic presentation of vision and the dramatic representation of action. I have also noted, however, that vision and action interconnect even in those relatively "pure" thematic and dramatic modes of discourse, and that predominately narrative and lyric texts or passages integrate vision and action—those organizing principles of predominantly thematic and dramatic texts or passages—into the presentation of envisioned action and the representation of enacted vision, respectively (cf. esp. pp. 156–70).

I wish to stress now what I merely implied a dozen years ago: only methodological considerations warrant the privileging as "basic" of any one (or two or three) among *four* constitutive dimensions of human life and consciousness out of which, in addition to much else, four distinct yet combinable modes of discourse have evolved. These dimensions are the (protodramatic) continual interaction between self and other, the (protolyric) instantaneous awareness of what is happening both within and outside the evolving self, the (protonarrative) molding of all experience including imaginative experience into sequential patterns, and the (protothematic) systematizing of all experience including imaginative experience into more or less explicitly articulated world views. The four dimensions intersect in all human activity, but their respective prevalence can be seen, to use a homely set of illustrations, in each player's interaction with other players during a ball game, the radio announcer's "blow-by-blow coverage" of the game and of his emotional response to it, the Monday-morning quarterback's sequential account of what was going wrong and what ought to have been happening on the field, and the bookmaker's (or some other well-informed gambler's) systematic overview of recent game scores and of additional factors affecting the odds in a proposed wager.

It is clear that historical chronicles re-present past events primarily from the Monday-morning quarterback's vantage point of envisioned action and that a great deal of historical drama is aligned with documentary plays in appearing to represent action as if directly from the unmediated points of view of the interacting "players." To continue with the same analogy, annals offering a year-by-year account of frequently unrelated occurrences (for example, "720. Charles fought against the Saxons. 721. Theudo drove the Saracens out of Aquitaine. 722. Great crops") approximate within their larger chronological framework the structure of the sportscaster's highly selective running commentary; and philosophers of history as well as those historians who attempt to explain or even quantify events by subsuming them under general laws aspire to the systematic coherence underlying the predictive operations associated with bookmaking. It should also be clear, however, that each of those approaches to history can and usually does include in its favored structure of re-presentation features favored by the others. How else, indeed, could its practitioners hope to avoid impoverishing their understanding of human life and consciousness, which, as I have suggested, always involve continual interaction, instantaneous awareness, sequential orientation, and systematic overview? It is by adding lyric, narrative, and/or thematic components to their primarily dramatic orientation that playwrights moderate the demand of "strict" drama for unmediated interaction among the characters with the respective compensatory demands of "subjective" experience, "objective" historiography, and "pure" philosophy for intense awareness, structured progression, and systematic theorizing. It takes a different set of verbal strategies for most historians to temper their predilection for presenting envisioned action in the objectifying narrative pattern of unilinear time. But historical playwrights and narrative historians alike enact their present, future-bound vision of the past by always placing received history in a new context of authorial hindsight concerning the present and future significance, as they see it, of past words and deeds. As Goethe's Faust points out to his literal-minded assistant Wagner:

Mein Freund, die Zeiten der Vergangenheit
Sind uns ein Buch mit sieben Siegeln.
Was ihr den Geist der Zeiten heisst,
Das ist im Grund der Herren eigner Geist,
In dem die Zeiten sich bespiegeln.

To us, my friend, the ages of the past
Are like a book with seven seals protected.
What you the spirit of the ages call
Is but the scholars' spirit, after all,
In which the ages are reflected.   [575–79]

Must we share Wagner's presumably great discomfort with this state of historical affairs? I think not. Precisely because history as we can ever hope to know it is "reflected" in human minds, it can teach us important lessons about the mind's method of critically translating the sealed book of How It Really Was into the anthology—still incomplete, always to be revised—of How It Shall Be Remembered.

The Erotics of Retrospection

The most pervasive shared trait of such "translations" is, perhaps, that they are mostly stories that, in terms of plot structure, character delineation, and audience response, invite the kind of analysis that is applied by literary critics to works of both drama and narrative fiction. It is worth remembering that Shaw himself rejected some historical accounts of Joan that were casting her in the role of "melodramatic heroine" while making her antagonists look like "villains of melodrama" (7); his own play had been intended, rather, to combine "The romance of her rise, the tragedy of her execution, and the comedy of the attempts of posterity to make amends for that execution" (46). In another set of comments on aspects of genre within his play, Shaw claims that, since Joan was burned "by normally innocent people in the energy of their righteousness," her death resulted from one of those "pious murders" whose inherent contradiction "brings an element of comedy into the tragedy: the angels may weep at the murder, but the gods laugh at the murderers" (52). Of course, Shaw's risible divinities can amuse themselves not only at the expense of Joan's antagonists, whose attempt to stay the progress of history was doomed to eventual failure. The "law of God," which Shaw's Preface defines as "a law of change" (39), prompts its apostles always to engage in uphill battles against the social establishment of their day. Many such battles will be lost because, as a friend points out to Joan, "God is no man's daily drudge, and no maid's either. . . . For He has to be fair to your enemy too: don't forget that" (114–15). In this most tragicomic of his tragicomedies, Shaw seems to be implying that the frequent frustration of "progressive" saints entails, as a corollary, the temporary fulfilment of some of humankind's more conservative, less inspiring, but by no means less human aspirations.

Shaw was, of course, neither the first nor the last person to generalize about historytelling in this fashion. Ancient rhetoricians, as well as modern philosophers of history, have often been characterizing remembered or recorded historical occurrences as "tragic," "farcical," and the like. In the next two chapters I shall have more to say about a large variety of generic moods that plays, as well as other representations of human events including historiographical narratives, convey to their responsive readers. At this point I merely wish to suggest that the often-noted resemblance between stories and histories invites contrary interpretations. We may assume that life itself has such qualities as epic breadth and tragic depth, and that therefore the structure of history has given rise to literary genres. Or else we may assume that all narratives follow the generic patterns of myth and literature, and that therefore the structures of historiography ultimately stem from the human imagination. Let me sidestep the question of temporal priority between stories and histories. Why argue which came first and smash both the chicken and the egg under the spinning wheels of just another history that may turn out to be fiction? It should be more rewarding to consider whether storytellers and historytellers are not closely allied agents of what might be called the erotics of retrospection; in other words, whether our reactions to events evoked by historiographical narratives and to events evoked by imaginative literature are not in fact determined by similar strategies of desire.

In recent decades there has been much discussion of the marked contrast between historiography as an essentially *narrative* endeavor and the more readily *quantifiable* findings of natural or even social science. At the same time, historical research has usually been assimilated to scientific inquiry on the basis of their presumably shared capacity to yield knowledge. It is true, of course, that all knowledge is being generated for some purpose, and Jürgen Habermas (1971) has plausibly distinguished three kinds of motivation for knowledge as the "human interest" in, respectively, our (technological) domination over nature, our (hermeneutic) participation in culture, and our (self-consciously critical) alteration of the very framework of human nature and culture (cf. esp. 301–17). It seems to me, however, that the connection between human interest or desire and historical knowledge is far more intimate than Habermas and most other writers on the subject appear to assume. Indeed, to the extent that historiographical narratives share with overtly imaginative works of literature their quasi-mythic narrative focus on the fulfillment and/or frustration of human projects, they are primarily answerable to the principle of desire rather than the principle of knowledge. Sure enough, different stories will be found in greater or lesser agreement with "historical evidence" as the latter is extracted from other, perhaps earlier and more rudimentary stories about the past. But the primary reason why we tell and listen to such stories does not lie in their presumed truth value.

Why, indeed, should we want to know the kinds of things histories are about? The slim chances of using—and thus plausibly validating—such knowledge hardly warrant the vast effort required to reach what is a tentative, and probably rather distant, approximation of it. To be sure, the most inclusive scientific theory is only hypothesis awaiting additional corroboration, and even the most profound insight into an intimately known mind or object leaves further depths unplumbed. Yet the application of a basically appropriate theory or of a roughly adequate insight tends to follow more or less generalizable methods of technological or sociopsychological "engineering." In contrast, the historian never knows just how far he is from a comprehensive understanding of all pertinent occurrences or the ultimate under-standing of a single life or event. His only advantage over theoretical scientists and over such interpreters of individual people as practicing psychoanalysts and prac-ticed poker players is that he need not even strive for complete coverage and complete penetration. Precisely because total knowledge of the Every and total knowledge of the Each conspicuously elude the historian, his stories may claim assent on the basis of reasonable probability about the Many and persuasive plau-sibility about the Some. In other words, the historian can, and his readers will, be satisfied if he shows, for instance, that *many* successful revolutions were started by active minorities or that *some* people would have thought and acted the way he suggests (but cannot prove) Luther or Napoleon thought and acted in particular moments of their lives. Even under the best of circumstances, however, the his-torian's appeal to the Many (rather than the Every or the All) can promise only very imperfect knowledge of a statistical kind, and his appeal to the Some (rather than the Each or the One) should make us expect of him such very partial verdicts as juries render in response to courtroom rhetoric.

The persistent concern of historiographers and their readers with the past can thus be explained much more plausibly in terms of another question, namely, *Why is it that we enjoy telling and hearing or reading histories?* One answer to this question is suggested by the recognition that storytellers and historytellers avail themselves of comparably structured narrative forms and that the correspondence between the moods conveyed by such forms and the desire for self-asserting entertainment and self-transcending commitment can help us to understand why we "like" both literature and historiography. But even a secondary reason for the popularity of historytelling has more to do with the conative motives of cognition than is generally supposed. The very notion that the human agents of a story I am contemplating actually existed allows me to react to the already determined fate of other people with the survivor's sense of superior vitality and increased hindsight. Even when I follow fictive representations of actions, my attitude is not unlike that of the unobserved observer standing behind a one-way mirror. But such privileged status over people actually believed to have existed will enhance my self-esteem even if—or rather, especially if—I am made to admire them. To the extent that a historian *persuades* me that he has understood the life and times of Luther or Napoleon, he offers to share with me both his (presumed) intuition of what it felt like to be Luther or Napoleon and his (presumed) hindsight into more than what Luther or Napoleon could fully grasp about his own situation. The ego trip involved hardly requires commentary. But it testifies to the reality of pleasure rather than to the pleasure of reality because, clearly, the rhetorical effectiveness of a historiographical work is hardly evidence for its mimetic accuracy.

Many people will, of course, object to a view of historical knowledge as tentative supplement—now you believe it, now you don't—of hard and fast literary pleasure. One powerful objection runs as follows: even the pleasures of great fiction are ultimately pleasures of a deeper insight into the same reality whose surface is traced by historiographers. Arguments based on that objection tend to invoke Aristotle's remarks about the pleasure we derive from any truthful representation and his favorable view of the poet's mimesis of actions as "more philosophical" than the historian's (cf. *Poetics,* chaps. 4 and 9). But can we really claim that the acquisition of nonpractical knowledge—a "knowing that" without bearing on some "knowing how to"—is in fact pleasurable? Learning a new skill—learning to ride a bicycle, for instance, or to play a difficult piece on the piano—many indeed give me a great deal of pleasure. Yet I rather suspect that whenever a piece of new but, in practical terms, inapplicable information fills me with unadulterated pleasure (rather than with the agony accompanying the process of any conversion against the grain of one's mental fabric) I have either acquired additional confirmation for a preconceived conclusion—new ammunition for shooting at an old target—or only abandoned tenets that, subconsciously at least, I had wished to abandon in the first place. Thus the satisfaction derived from an actual or imagined increase of knowledge by means of both literature and historiography requires a more plausible explanation than the alleged pleasure of coming face to face with reality, and I will graft such an explanation on my ensuing consideration of audience response to dramatic works, only some of which claim to offer insight into history.

WORKS CITED

Anouilh, Jean. *L'Alouette.* Paris: Le Table Ronde, 1953.
———. *The Lark.* Trans. Christopher Fry. New York: Oxford University Press, 1956.
Aristotle. *Poetics.* Trans. Leon Golden. Commentary by O. B. Hardison, Jr. Englewood Cliffs, N.J.: Prentice-Hall, 1968.
Eliot, T. S. *The Three Voices of Poetry.* New York: Cambridge University Press, 1954.
Goethe, Johann Wolfgang von. *Faust.* Trans. Walter Arndt. Ed. Cyrus Hamlin. New York: Norton, 1976.
Habermas, Jürgen. *Knowledge and Human Interests.* Trans. Jeremy J. Shapiro. Boston: Beacon, 1971.
Hernadi, Paul. *Beyond Genre: New Directions in Literary Classification.* Ithaca: Cornell University Press, 1972.
Joyce, James. *A Portrait of the Artist as a Young Man.* London: Egoist, 1916.

Shaw, [George] Bernard. *Saint Joan.* Ed. Stanley Weintraub. Indianapolis: Bobbs-Merrill, 1971.

Thucycides. *History of the Peloponnesian War.* Trans. Charles Forster Smith. London: Heinemann; New York: Putnam, 1919. Reprinted and revised for the Loeb Classical Library (1928).

Gabriele Bernhard Jackson

WITCHES, AMAZONS, AND SHAKESPEARE'S JOAN OF ARC[1]

Glory is like a circle in the water,
Which never ceaseth to enlarge itself
Till by broad spreading it disperse to nought.
With Henry's death the English circle ends;
Dispersed are the glories it included.

—*I Henry VI,* 1.2.133–37[2]

This wonderfully evocative description of the everything that is nothing, an exact emblem of the rise and disintegration, in Shakespeare's first tetralogy, of one new center of power after another, is assigned to Joan of Arc, the character whom most critics agree in calling a coarse caricature, an exemplar of authorial chauvinism both national and sexual, or at best a foil to set off the chivalric English heroes of *I Henry VI.* Her portrait, says Geoffrey Bullough in his compilation of Shakespeare's sources, "goes far beyond anything found in Hall or Holinshed or in the Burgundian chronicler Monstrelet."[3] Bullough ruefully lauds Shakespeare's mastery in discrediting the entire French cause through Joan; many subsequent critics have shared Bullough's admiration, although not his compunction, over the skill with which Shakespeare delineated an "epitome of disorder and rebellion" to pit against the "epitome of order and loyalty," the English hero Talbot: "She is absolutely corrupt from beginning to end," rejoices the author of one book on Shakespeare's history plays.[4] When the play was presented in 1591 or 1592, English troops were once again in France, once again supporting a claim to the French crown, a claim by another Henry—their religious ally Henry of Navarre. "A play recalling the gallant deeds of the English in France at an earlier period . . . would be topical," Bullough rightly says.[5]

The portrait of Joan, by this calculus of relation between drama and social context, takes it place among "English attempts to blacken the reputation of Joan of Arc"[6]—an easy task in the Elizabethan period, when women "who refuse[d] the

From *English Literary Renaissance* 18, No. 1 (Winter 1988): 40–65.

place of silent subjection" could, like Shakespeare's Joan in Act 5, be carted to execution as witches.[7] By this reckoning, the character of Joan of Arc becomes a regrettable sign of the times.

Neither the content nor the form of Joan's words about glory easily supports such a reading. Joan's image of the circle in the water is not only the most poetically resonant statement in the play, it is also specifically borne out by the action. The eloquence of her recognition that all human achievement is writ in water, one of the play's thematic pressure points, sorts ill with a lampooned character "coarse and crude in language and sensibility."[8] Yet *I Henry VI* does contrast English chivalry, especially in the figure of heroic Talbot, with the pragmatism of the French, especially Joan, and Act 5 does dispel both Joan's power and her pretensions to divine aid in a series of progressively less dignified scenes.[9]

First she vainly offers diabolical spirits her blood and sexual favors in exchange for continued French success; subsequently captured, she rejects her old father to claim exalted birth; finally, faced with the prospect of death by burning, she claims to be pregnant, shifting her allegation of paternity from one French leader to another in response to her captors' insistence that each of these is a man whose child should not be allowed to live.

Perhaps it is a reflection as much on accepted critical standards of aesthetic unity as on the gullibility of individual critics that several have read this last scene as Joan's admission of sexual activity with the whole French camp. Ridiculous as such a reading is, it does at least integrate Act 5 with what precedes, undercutting Joan's claims to virginity just as her conjuring undercuts her claims to divinity. Such an interpretation of Act 5 makes it synchronic with previous acts in meaning; only the revelation of that meaning is postponed. Similarly, Joan's claims to divine mission, which she never mentions again after her introductory speeches in Act 1, become in such an interpretation synchronic with the action which follows them. In the long central section of the drama, according to such a unified interpretation, Joan's prior assertion of godliness struggles against Talbot's repeated assertions of diabolism until Act 5 vindicates Talbot. The unstated premise of this kind of reading is that temporally multiple suggestions of meaning collapse finally into an integrated pattern that transcends the temporal process of dramatic presentation. In this final pattern, all suggested assignments of value are reconciled and each plot line or character allotted its proper plus or minus sign *sub specie unitatis.* The individual incident or dramatic effect has no more final autonomy than a number in a column for addition has in the sum below the line. These assumptions are very clear in Riggs' influential 1971 summation of Joan's character: "Beneath these postures, Joan is generically an imposter. . . . Hence the scenes in which she is exposed and burnt as a witch, like the stripping of Duessa in *The Faerie Queene,* serve a formal expository purpose that supersedes any need for a controlled, sequacious plot."[10]

Now of course the typical Shakespearean play does have a very powerful sense of ending, partly brought about by a "formal expository" resolution of difficult issues. I want to emphasize, however, that it is equally typical of Shakespeare to present unexplained and suggestive discontinuities. One might remember the complete reversal of Theseus' attitude to the lovers in *Midsummer Night's Dream:* having backed up Hermia's coercive father in Act I by citing the unalterable law of Athens, Theseus reappears in Act 4 (after a two-act absence) to overrule the same father and the same law with no explanation whatever. A more subtle version of this kind of turnabout occurs when Othello, calmly superior in Act I to the accusation that he has used sorcery in his relationship with Desdemona, informs her in Act 3 that the handkerchief which was his first gift to her is a magical talisman. In these instances, the critic's expectation of unity forces interpretive strategy back on unspoken motivations and implicit character development, raising such questions as whether Othello deliberately lied to the senate in Act I, or when exactly he gave Desdemona the handkerchief. I want to propose that these are unsuitable strategies and questions for a phenomenon that has little to do with unity of character and much to do with the way in which a character is perceived by the audience at a particular moment of dramatic time. I would argue that in Act I, Othello had not given Desdemona a magic handkerchief as his first gift, but in Act 3 he had. It is a matter of the character's consonance with the key into which the movement of the play has modulated.

This is not the place to make a detailed case for such an interpretive approach or to try to identify for these examples the reasons—external to a concept of character as coherent selfhood—that direct a change in Shakespeare's presentation. Applying such an approach to the problem of Joan's significance, however, permits us to recognize and give individual value to the phases of her portrayal, which, not untypically for Shakespeare, is partially continuous and partially disjunct. The changing presentation allows Joan to perform in one play inconsistent ideological functions that go much beyond discrediting the French cause or setting off by contrast the glories of English chivalry in its dying moments.[11] As Bullough long ago suggested, the play's ideology is topical, but in what way and to what end cannot be answered as simply as he or some of the play's subsequent critics have believed.[12] To characterize its main military hero, Talbot, the play alludes specifically to the contemporaneous French expedition led by Essex, as John Munro first suggested, but it incorporates far more ideologically ambiguous detail than has been recognized. Similarly, for its presentation of Talbot's national and sexual opposites, the three Frenchwomen who are the play's only female characters, it draws heavily on the current controversy about the nature of women and on the interrelated types of the Amazon, the warrior woman, the cross-dressing woman, and the witch, all figures that—for a variety of reasons—were at the end of the sixteenth century objects of fascination both in England and on the continent.

It is now generally accepted that the play dates from 1591/92, when English troops under Essex had been sent to France for the particular purpose of besieging Rouen; the play unhistorically dramatizes that city's recapture from the French. Actually, Rouen had never been retaken, nor was it after this hopeful piece of stagecraft. But the parallel does not remain general and wishful. The play explicitly links Talbot to the current effort through a neatly turned compliment to Queen Elizabeth which has, oddly, been deflected by critics to Essex alone. Bearing away the fallen Talbot and his son, the English messenger declares: "from their ashes shall be rear'd / A phoenix that shall make all France afeard" (4.7.92–93). The phoenix was one of Elizabeth's emblems; Shakespeare uses it again in *Henry VIII*. She had not up to this time fulfilled the messenger's prediction: early military success against French forces in Scotland had been completely cancelled by a disastrous occupation of Le Havre in 1563. The vaunting compliment can only refer to the most recent French expedition. Its leader—the dashing young popular favorite, Essex—would be an eminently suitable candidate for the role of Talbot redivivus.[13] In 1591 the becalmed campaign was serving as backdrop for his exploits, one of them mimicked by another of the play's departures from its sources. Encamped before Rouen, "Essex sent a challenge to the Governor of the town daring him to fight either a duel or a tournament," which was, not surprisingly, declined.[14] In *I Henry VI*, Talbot similarly challenges Joan and her supporters as they stand victorious on the walls of Rouen (2.2.56ff.).[15] He is contemptuously rebuffed by Joan in one of those moments when English chivalry confronts French pragmatism: "Belike your lordship takes us then for fools / To try if that our own be ours or no" (3.2.62–63). A critic guided by the play's obvious national sympathies could plausibly feel that Joan's reply, however momentarily amusing, lacks magnanimity.

A closer look at the topical link between Talbot and Essex, however, suggests a more complicated ideological situation. Both the expedition and its leadership were controversial. Henry IV had broken his promise of reinforcements for a first set of troops, sent in 1589, and Elizabeth sent the second army with misgivings, putting the hot-headed Essex in command with a reluctance well justified by the results. "Where he is or what he doth or what he is to do," she wrote angrily to her other officers, "we are ignorant."[16] Halfway through the expedition she ordered her uncontrollable deputy home, although he talked her into sending him back. A likely rescripting of this sequence of events appears in Act 3, where Talbot interrupts his conquests to go and visit his sovereign "with submissive loyalty of heart" (3.4.10) and receives acclaim, reward, and a commission to return to battle (3.4.16–27, 4.1.68–73). In the second of these scenes, Talbot strips a coward of his undeserved Order of the Garter and makes a long speech about the value of "the sacred name of knight" (4.1.33ff.)—another touchy subject after Essex's temporary recall, for he had just knighted twenty-four of his do-nothing soldiers. Lord Treasurer Burghley kept this news from Her Majesty as long as he could; Elizabeth was notoriously stingy with new titles—holding, in fact, rather the attitude expressed by Shakespeare's Talbot. She had wanted to deny Essex the privilege of dubbing knights, and remarked caustically on hearing of the twenty-four newcomers to fame unsupplemented by fortune, "his lordship had done well to have built his almshouses before he had made his knights."[17]

Are these portions of Talbot's behavior and speech, then, aligned with the latest news from France in order to celebrate Essex?[18] Or do they obliquely defend him by rewriting his indiscretions in more acceptable terms, sympathetically dramatizing the "real" meaning of his grand gestures? Or do Talbot's loyal actions, on the contrary, undercut the play's apparent endorsement of Essex by showing how a truly great champion acts? The answers are not at all clear.[19] What is evident is that the play situates itself in an area of controversy easily identifiable by its audience, an area of growing ideological conflict in which a "war party" contested, if it did not openly confront, the Queen's favored policy of negotiation, delay, and minimal expenditure. Far from playing down the controversial aspects of Essex's command, the drama singles them out for reenactment, but presents them in such a manner that either side could claim the play for its own. In light of the play's tendency to go both ways, Joan's sardonic reply to Talbot's challenge acquires an integrity of its own, sounding surprisingly like the voice of Her caustic Majesty Queen Elizabeth. Is the play, then, lauding chivalry or correcting it? Is it pro-war or not? This irritable reaching after fact and reason that Keats found so uncharacteristic of Shakespeare is not soothed by the parallels between Talbot and Essex or by the tone of Joan's voice. The coexistence of ideologically opposed elements is typical of the play's dramatic nature and foreshadows the mature Shakespeare.

Critical examination of the play's three women has not proceeded on this assumption. The perceived dominance of patrilineal and patriarchal ideology in Shakespeare's era and in the play's action has been the basis of most interpretations, whether feminist or masculinist.[20] The three women have been seen as a trio of temptresses,[21] of threats to male and particularly English hegemony and to the chivalric ideal,[22] as incarnations of what Marilyn French calls the "outlaw feminine principle."[23] This kind of negative reading, like the purely positive reading of the play's military expedition, has support in the action. All three women are in different ways unconventionally strong and all three threaten the English with losses. Coppélia Kahn's claim that Shakespeare is here exposing, but not sharing in, male anxieties about women is surely counsel of desperation.[24] Fortunately, it is not the only alternative to pathological or paternalistic Shakespeare. Like the positive militaristic reading, with which it is closely connected, the negative misogynist one neglects both the play's topicality and the historical moment's ideological complexity.

The nature of women had long been under discussion in western Europe in a semi-playful controversy that became especially active in sixteenth-century England. Contributors to this controversy buttressed or undercut female claims to virtue by citing *exempla,* worthy or unworthy women chosen from history, the Bible, and legend. As Linda Woodbridge's recent account of this literary sub-genre in England points out, "The formal controversy did not always appear full-blown, in carefully developed treatises; it was sometimes sketched in cameo, with the names of a few exemplary women stamped on it like a generic signature."[25] The 1560s had seen a spate of plays about individual *exempla* in the controversy. By the time *I Henry VI* appeared, the controversy had already been naturalized into narrative fiction by George Pettie's *A petite pallace of ... pleasure* (1576) and Lyly's bestselling *Euphues* (1578). In these fictional contexts, the old techniques "could be used to characterize, to comment on the action, even to advance the plot."[26] *I Henry VI* incorporates just such a cameo controversy. The play's three women are surrounded by allusions to legendary females which problematize their evaluation.

The Countess of Auvergne compares herself to Tomyris, a bloody warrior queen, and is connected by verbal echo with the Queen of Sheba—two entirely opposite figures.[27] Margaret of Anjou is cast in her lover's description of his situation as Helen of Troy (5.5.103ff.), a woman claimed by both attackers and defenders in the controversy. Joan appears amidst a tangle of contradictory allusions: she is among other identifications a Sibyl, an Amazon, Deborah, Helen the mother of Constantine, and Astraea's daughter to the French, but Hecate and Circe to the English. Of the women alluded to in *1 Henry VI*, eleven appear as *exempla* in the formal controversy. The genre itself was tolerant of, not to say dependent upon, divergent evaluations of the same phenomenon: a number of its *exempla*, like Helen of Troy, appeared regularly on both sides, and some writers handily produced treatises both pro and con. It would come as no surprise to readers of the controversy that one man's Sibyl is another man's Hecate.

1 Henry VI should be classed with what Woodbridge calls the "second flurry of plays centering on prominent *exempla* of the formal controversy," which "appeared in the late 1580s and 1590s."[28] Its deployment of these stock figures is as germane to its ideology as its structural alignment of the female characters, but whereas the play's structure points in the direction of synthesis, of the synchronic or temporally transcendent reading, the *exempla* point towards differentiation, the temporally disjunctive reading.

Joan is evaluated by the French choice of *exempla* at the beginning and by the English choice at the end. At all times before Act 5, however, because of the armor she is described as wearing and the military leadership she exercises, she is an example of what the Elizabethans called a virago, a woman strong beyond the conventional expectations for her sex and thus said to be of masculine spirit.[29] The increasing fascination of such women is evident in the proliferation of Amazons, female warriors, and cross-dressing ladies in the English fiction and drama of the late sixteenth century.

The Amazon and the warrior woman were already established as two of the most valued positive *exempla* of the controversy over women. Joan is identified with both immediately on her entry into the play's action: "thou art an Amazon," exclaims the Dauphin, "And fightest with the sword of Deborah" (1.2.104–05). The power of this combination reaches beyond the arena of the formal debate. Spenser had just used it in *The Faerie Queene,* published 1590, in praise of "the brave atchievements" of women (3.4.1.3): those "warlike feates . . . Of bold Penthesilee," the Amazon who aided the Trojans, or the blow with which "Stout Debora strake / Proud Sisera" (3.4.2.4–5, 7–8).[30] For him these two fighters define Britomart, his female knight in armor, who in turn defines Queen Elizabeth, "whose lignage from this lady I derive along" (3.4.3.9). Both Amazons and woman warriors already had some degree of British resonance because the Trojans who received Penthesilea's help were the supposed ancestors of the British, while a proud chapter in legendary English history recounted Queen Boadicea's defense of her country against Roman invasion. The evocation of heroines related to England is continued by Joan's association with Saint Helen, the mother of Constantine; though not a warrior, this finder of the remains of the true cross was by popular tradition British.[31] The Dauphin's welcome to Joan is thus calculated to arouse the most unsuitably positive and even possessive associations in an Elizabethan audience.

Elizabethan literature of course contained many other Amazons besides Penthesilea; the race had a long and honorable history, derived from such respected authorities as Plutarch, Ovid, and Apollonius of Rhodes.[32] In the sixteenth century Amazons became a topic of current relevance when exploration of the Americas and Africa began bringing reports of Amazonian tribes sighted or credibly heard of.[33] Within a brief period after *I Henry VI,* both Ralegh (1596) and Hakluyt (1599) would specify the Amazons' exact location. Perhaps because of their increased timeliness, Amazons were also about to become a vogue onstage; they would appear in at least fourteen dramatic productions from 1592 to 1640.[34]

Elizabethan stage Amazons are all either neutral or positive, an evaluative convention generally in line with their ever more frequent mention in Elizabethan non-dramatic literature. On the other hand, *The Faerie Queene* contains an evil Amazon alongside its positive allusions. For the Amazon figure was inherently double: although "models of female magnanimity and courage" who appeared regularly in lists of the nine female worthies and were venerated both individually and as a race, Amazons were also acknowledged to be at times cruel tormentors of men.[35] From the very beginning, then, Joan's ideological function is complicated to the point of self-contradiction: she seems both French and English, both a type of Penthesilea who helps her countrymen in battle and an unspecified Amazon who may embody threats to men—in fact, a representative of the full complexity of late Elizabethan perception of the strong woman.

These contradictions continue for as long as Joan appears in the role of woman warrior. Although she triumphs over the English and so must be negative, she carries with her a long positive tradition reaching back to Plato's assertions that women could and should be trained for martial exercise and to the figure of the armed goddess Minerva. These classical references as well as invocations of the Old Testament Deborah and Judith figured repeatedly in the formal defenses of women. Female military heroism under special circumstances carried the prestigious sanction of Elyot, More, and Hoby, and Joan's actions conform to the pattern they approved as well as to the current literary conventions defining a praiseworthy female warrior. She fights in defense of her country, "particularly under siege," and converts the Duke of Burgundy to her cause with a simile that likens France to a dying child (3.3.47–49)—defense of her children being a recognized motivation of the virtuous woman fighter.[36] Like Spenser's Britomart and countless others, she deflates male boasts and engages in a validating duel with a would-be lover.

As Spenser's connection of Britomart with Queen Elizabeth suggests, the tradition of the woman warrior acquired particular contemporaneous relevance from her existence. The maiden warrior-goddess Minerva provided an irresistible parallel with the virginal defender of Protestantism, who even before the year of the Armada was called "for power in armes,/And vertues of the minde Minervaes mate" by Peele in *The Arraignment of Paris* (1584).[37] Deborah, a magistrate as well as her country's savior in war, was also adopted immediately into the growing iconology of Elizabeth: the coronation pageant contained a Deborah, and the name was frequently used thereafter for the queen.[38] Not unexpectedly, Spenser identifies the Trojan-oriented Penthesilea as an analogue of his Belphoebe, the avowed representation of Queen Elizabeth.[39]

In light of these accumulated associations, a Minerva-like French leader who is a Deborah and Amazon, and is also called "Astraea's daughter" (1.6.4) at a time when Astraea, goddess of justice, was another *alter ego* of Elizabeth, must be reckoned one of the more peculiar phenomena of the Elizabethan stage.[40] But it is likely that Joan was more than peculiar: she was probably sensational. For the odd fact is that despite all the outpouring of Elizabethan literature both cultivated and popular on the subject of Amazons and warrior women, there seems to be only one rather obscure woodcut of real—as opposed to allegorical—armed women to be found in the English printed books, pamphlets, broadsides, and pictorial narrative strips of the entire era, nor had any such personage (as far as I have yet discovered) ever appeared on the stage.[41] Two Amazons that illustrate Mandeville's *Travels* are clad with impeccable feminine respectability. The coronation Deborah (1559), despite the pageant verses' reference to "the dint of sworde," was equipped with Parliament robes, not with a deadly weapon as in Spenser's fantasy.[42] Holinshed's Boadicea (1577) had a wide skirt and long hair. What is more, there seem to be no pictures of women in men's clothing of any kind. It looks as though there was an unspoken taboo on such representations, a taboo just beginning to be breached occasionally in the 1570s, when Holinshed included in his *History of Scotland* an illustration of Woada's daughters. In this same decade come the first mentions of real Elizabethan women wearing articles of real male apparel, though not armor or weapons, a fashion that was soon to grow into a fad. It is not until the 1580s that a very few cross-dressing ladies appear on stage, and not until after *I Henry VI* that Amazons, women warriors, and girls in male disguise become a triple dramatic vogue. In 1591/92, dressing Joan in armor was a stunning *coup de théâtre*.

It had, however, been anticipated. Outside the world of the stage lived a connoisseur of theatrical effect as daring as Shakespeare. In 1588, on the eve of the expected Spanish invasion, Queen Elizabeth visited her soldiers in the camp at Tilbury "habited like an Amazonian Queene, Buskind and plumed, having a golden Truncheon, Gantlet, and Gorget," according to Heywood's later description.[43] Leonel Sharp, afterwards James I's chaplain and in 1588 "waiting upon the Earl of *Leicester* at *Tilbury* Camp," reported as eyewitness that "the Queen rode through all the Squadrons of her armie, as Armed *Pallas*"[44]—a figure whose iconographic conventions of plumed helmet, spear, and shield coincided with descriptions of Amazon queens.[45] This was the occasion of her famous speech: "I know I have the bodie, but of a weak and feeble woman, but I have the heart and Stomach of a King, . . . and think foul scorn that . . . any Prince of Europe should dare to invade the borders of my Realm. . . . I my self will take up arms, I my self will be your General."[46] This grand gesture of virago-ship, which combined visual uniqueness with enactment of time-honored conventions identifying the woman warrior, is surely the shadowy double behind the sudden appearance in the French camp of Joan, the puzzlingly Astraea-connected Amazonian, to lead her army against the invaders of her country.[47]

This probability does not make life any easier for the critic of *I Henry VI*. One could simplify the situation by seeing Joan as a sarcastic version of such a figure, an anti-Elizabeth, a parodic non-virgin whose soldiership (finally) fails. Perhaps that was the point, or one of the points. But such close mirroring is hard to control. It is difficult to keep doubles separate. An obviously parodic presentation of a figure so suggestive might slide over into parody (dare one breathe it?) of the queen herself.[48] At the same time, the strong honorific associations of the Amazon-Deborah-Elizabeth combination exert their own pull in the opposite direction from parody. If Joan, parodied, functions as inferior foil for English chivalry, Joan honored also functions as its superior. It seems likely, then, that Joan in armor is as fair and foul as the traditional double-potentialed Amazon, and that what she says or does is as likely to undercut "the glorious deeds of the English in France" as to set off their splendor. She is a powerful warrior and a powerful enemy, but also an inverted image of both. Lest this interpretation seem an implausibly modern critical recourse to ambiguity, we should take notice of one elaborate European visual representation in the Elizabethan period of women in armor, Bruegel's *Dulle Griet* or Mad Meg. As described by Natalie Davis in her account of the sociological phenomenon she calls "women on top," the painting sends a similar double message. It "makes a huge, armed, unseeing woman, Mad Meg, the emblem of fiery destruction . . . and disorder. Bruegel's painting cuts in more than one way, however. . . . Nearby other armed women are beating grotesque animals from Hell."[49] This visual oxymoron sorts well with the double-valenced Amazon figure which is the period's prototype of the powerful and active woman.

Amazon, goddess, or queen, the numinous representative of a strength that in its very transcendence of social convention becomes salvific is from another perspective a potential subverter of established order and belief, an overturner of values. Nowhere is this clearer than in the disparity between Elizabethan or Jacobean fictions of cross-dressing women and accounts of real ones from the same period. Both attest to the fascination of the time with gender subversion, as does the cross-dressing phenomenon itself. Fiction could delight in Mary Ambree (1584), who avenged her lover's death in battle by putting on armor to lead the English troops, or in Long Meg of Westminster, said to have lived in Henry VIII's reign: she came from the country to work in a London tavern, dressed in men's clothes, fought and defeated obstreperous males, and went with the soldiers to Boulogne, where she achieved victory over the champion of the French and was honored by the king.[50] Long Meg's story was told in two ballads, a play, and several reprintings of her pamphlet life, all between 1590 and about 1650. And no wonder; for when Long Meg had overcome the (Spanish) aggressor Sir James and humiliated him in the tavern by revealing her womanhood, she "sat in state like her Majesty."[51] Once again the warrior woman is assimilated to that modern numinous exemplar, Queen Elizabeth. But during the same period, women who really do participate in the

growing fashion for wearing men's clothes, including ultimately weapons, are complained against with mounting sarcasm and hysteria. It is one thing to embody, in the
encapsulated realm of fiction or of royalty, transcendence of social constraint—
quite another to undermine on the street the customs around which society is
organized.[52]

If Joan's initial presentation plays with the numinous aura and royal superiority
of the virago, her portrayal in the play's middle section brings to the fore a special
form of the virago's potential for subversion.[53] Uncommitted to convention, Joan
is also uncommitted to the ethical stereotypes that structure the consciousness of
other characters. This is her most threatening and most appealing function. It can
be clearly seen in her comment after her eloquent speech has persuaded Burgundy
to return to the French: "Done like a Frenchman! [Aside.]—turn and turn again"
(3.3.85). Although this is a topical throwaway for the audience, its effect is very like
that of early asides by Richard III, or of Falstaff playing first Henry IV and then Hal.
It is characteristic of her persistent demystification of cherished idealisms, an ideological iconoclasm that does not spare her own achievements once she has finished
with her original claim to divine aid.

Joan's speech constantly invites skepticism at the very moments when values
are in need of affirmation, as when Rouen is captured, when Burgundy is about to
desert, when Talbot falls. We should recall her sardonic response to Talbot's
chivalric challenge—modeled, it is worth remembering, on Essex's conception of
chivalry. Her conversion of Burgundy uses a different mode but achieves a similar
shift of perspective, suddenly presenting an audience that enjoys "the gallant deeds
of the English in France" with a point of view that sees "the cities and the towns
defac'd / By wasting ruin of the cruel foe" (3.3.45–46) and forces them to look at
the enemy "As looks the mother on her lowly babe / When death doth close his
tender dying eyes" (3.3.47–48). This clash of perspectives becomes extreme, and
reaches beyond momentary effect, when the issue is the meaning of death itself.
After the messenger who is searching for Talbot has recited the hero's titles of
honor, performing unawares the eulogistic function of a traditional funeral oration,
Joan observes: "Here is a silly-stately style indeed! / . . . / Him that thou magnifiest
with all these titles, / Stinking and fly-blown lies here at our feet" (4.7.72–76). Like
the cross-dressing woman she is, Joan perceives as futile convention what representatives of the status quo perceive as a visible sign of inner nature, be it formulaic
titles or formulaic clothing. If her view is allowed, honor's a mere scutcheon, as her
fellow subversive Falstaff later agrees. Like Falstaff, Joan must be neutralized on
behalf of stable values, but like his, her point of view is too compelling to be
forgotten even when her circle in the water disperses in the humiliations of the fifth
act. Although Talbot is the play's ostensible hero and nobility's decay its subject, it
is Joan who expresses most forcefully both the vanity of all ideologies and an
unorthodox consolatio. Like the cross-dressing festival ladies of misrule,[54] Joan
offers relief from idealistic codes of behavior—and thus from the need to mourn
their demise.

The need to neutralize the virago, however, even the admired virago, is as pervasive in the period's writing as the evident fascination with her—indeed, it is probably a tribute to the force that fascination exerted. This hypothesis helps in understanding some oddities in the presentation of the period's literary Amazons and warrior women.

Two sets of stage Amazons have no lines at all, nor any action relevant to the plot. Three more are actually men in disguise.[55] But by far the most popular strategy for neutralizing the manly woman was to feminize her. Hippolyta in both Shakespeare and Beaumont and Fletcher is a bride, while in an Elizabethan translation from the French, she is said to have become so eager to serve Theseus that she licked his wounded shoulder with her tongue.[56] Less crude and more congenial was the ancient story that when Penthesilea had been slain by Achilles, her helmet fell off and revealed her beauty, causing Achilles to fall in love with her—sadly, luckily, too late. Amplified by the addition of a flood of golden hair loosed from the fallen helmet, the incident enriched Spanish and Italian romance and made its way to Elizabethan England, where at least six Amazonians, including Britomart, met with a version of this accident—all of them deliciously powerless to hide from admiring male gaze their quintessential femininity.[57] Holinshed's Boadicea with her long tresses and Mandeville's two gowned Amazons present the same feminized picture. Britomart, who sleeps "Al in her snow-white smocke, which locks unbownd" (3.1.63.7), having overcome her opposite number, the wicked Amazon, immediately changes all the rules of Amazon-land and "The liberty of women did repeale, / Which they had long usurpt; ... them restoring / To mens subjection" (5.7.42.5–7). Even robust Long Meg, who looses her hair voluntarily to embarrass her vanquished opponent, returns from her French conquest to recant; having married a soldier who "had heard of her manhood" and "was determined to try her" in a combat with staves, she silently accepts "three or four blows" and then, "in submission, fell down on her knees, desiring him to pardon her, 'For,' said she, ... it behoves me to be obedient to you; and it shall never be said, ... Long Meg is her husband's master; and, therefore, use me as you please.' "[58] The strength of her subversive attraction can be measured by the violence with which she is reintegrated into conservative ideology. She is too powerful to be wedded in another key.

We may anticipate, then, what those in Shakespeare's audience familiar with the conventions defining the woman warrior must also have anticipated: that the more free play Joan's attractive force is permitted, the more completely she will have to be feminized at the end of the play. Her scenes in Act 5 should be read in light of this expectation, in full acceptance of their radical difference from her earlier behavior. Her conjuring, once established, assigns her to an overwhelmingly female class of malefactors: informed estimates place the proportion of women executed as witches at about 93%.[59] Her rejection of her father reduces to female vanity the serious social claim implicit in her male clothing, for, as a number of recent writers point out, cross-dressing attacks the concept of natural hierarchy on which, for the Elizabethans, social class is built.[60] Her terrified snatching at subterfuges in the face of death would count as peculiarly female behavior; and when, finally, she claims to be pregnant, naming everyone and anyone as a lover, her feminization becomes irreversible. She has lost her helmet forever. Her captors' harsh reactions to her pleas are the equivalent of Long Meg's beating: Warwick's sadistically merciful directions, "And hark ye, sirs; because she is a maid, / Spare for no faggots, let there be enow" (5.4.55–56) are followed by York's unequivocal "Strumpet, . . . / Use no entreaty, for it is in vain" (84–85).

The witch is Joan's last topical role. Executions for witchcraft in England reached peaks in the 1580s and 1590s, high points on a long curve that Belsey considers "coterminous with the crisis of the definition of women and the meaning of the family"; she notes that in the last two decades of the sixteenth century "the divorce debate was also reaching a climax."[61] These events coincide with the beginnings of the vogue for Amazons and women warriors on stage and with the early phases of the fad for cross-dressing. But of all that twenty-year span, 1591 was the year of the witch in England. It brought to London the pamphlet *Newes from Scotland,* a full account of the spectacular treason-cum-sorcery trials King James had supervised there in the winter of 1590–91, in which large numbers of his subjects were accused of having made a mass pact with the devil in order to raise storms against the ship bringing the King and his bride from Denmark.[62] The pamphlet had political overtones, as did the trials. King James, described to the English by the tract as "the greatest enemie the Devil hath on earth," was after all an aspirant to their throne. The trials provided him an opportunity to dissociate himself from the memory of his mother's crimes as well as gain a sort of posthumous revenge on his father's probable murderer by urging savage reprisals against a female suspect known to have been Bothwell's friend.[63]

It is not at all clear, however, that James' "forwardness," as the English ambassador called it in a letter to Burghley,[64] elicited the kind of acclaim that could help us read Joan's treatment by York and Warwick as pro-Jamesian political doctrine. There are indications that his self-interested zeal may have worked the other way. The woman he particularly wanted disemboweled was acquitted. Moreover, it appears that popular opinion in Scotland did not support the political aspects of the prosecution.[65] Perhaps still more serious, "the picture of himself as the principal target for witches" might easily look foolish, to say no worse, in a more sophisticated country that had never been as harsh or consistent in its punishment of witches as the continent, where James had first acquired his demonological ideas. As Larner says, "there was a possibility that his new-found interest in witchcraft . . . could . . . damage his image, especially in England."[66] Although England executed witches, it did not burn or torture them, and one wonders what an English audience made of James' vindictiveness or of Warwick's call for plenty of faggots and extra barrels of pitch for Joan's stake (5.4.56–57).[67] Furthermore, it was absolutely standard practice in both England and Scotland to put off a witch's execution if she was pregnant, as was the woman whose grisly punishment James unsuccessfully urged. Although Joan is only pretending, her captors are at best playing cat and mouse with her as they condemn her supposed child to death anew each time she assigns it a different father. Joan is the butt of the brutal joke here, but it is unlikely that York and Warwick come off unscathed by the negative associations of their total violation of English custom: "we will have no bastards live. . . . It dies and if it had a thousand lives. . . . Strumpet, thy words condemn thy brat and thee" (5.4.70, 75, 84).

It is altogether difficult to be sure how an Elizabethan audience might have reacted to Joan's punishment. Opinion on witches in 1591 was by no means monolithic. Skepticism about witch-trials was gathering force; on the continent Montaigne had commented as recently as 1588, "After all, it is putting a very high price on one's conjectures to have a man roasted alive because of them,"[68] and at home Reginald Scot had even earlier published his 600-page attack (1584) on "those same monsterous lies, which have abused all Christendome" and been the undoing of "these poore women."[69] Scot's book was clearly labeled as subversive when it was (appropriately) burnt by the hangman. Later, James attacked Scot by name in his own tract *Daemonologie.* This makes it all the more interesting that the portrayal of Joan divides into a subversively Scot-like main section and a Jamesian demonological coda. In the long middle section of the play already discussed, her triumphs are based simply on boldness, common sense, and resourcefulness. Comically, this supposed witch is the most down-to-earth pragmatist in the play: "had your watch been good / This sudden mischief never could have fallen" (2.1.58–59). In consequence, Talbot's repeated insistence that she is a witch sounds not dissimilar from the deluded allegations recounted by Reginald Scot. Joan herself, unlike Talbot and the French leaders, never falls back on metaphysical notions about her opponent. Whereas her companions suggest that Talbot is "a fiend of hell" or a favorite of the heavens (2.1.46–47), Joan simply expresses realistic respect for his prowess and invents several plans to evade it. Her successes are well served by Scot's commentary: "it is more strange, that we will imagine that to be possible to be doone by a witch, which to nature and sense is impossible; . . . [for in other legal cases] the judge dooth not attend or regard what the accused man saith; or yet would doo: but what is prooved to have beene committed, and naturallie falleth in mans power and will to doo."[70] Yet in Act 5, Joan appears as a witch engaged in a diabolical compact, a demonological feature never very important in English witch trials but topically responsive to James' recent proceedings.

The presentation of Joan as witch is almost as diverse in its implications as her Amazonian image, of which it is a kind of transformation. The common folk belief in witches with beards, like the tradition of the Amazon's armor, renders visible the concept of a woman who "exceeds her sex" (1.2.90).[71] Hall calls her "This wytch or manly woman,"[72] as if the two were so close that he could hardly decide between them. A comment by Belsey illuminates this aspect of Joan's witchhood: "The demonization of women who subvert the meaning of femininity is contradictory in its implications. It places them beyond meaning, beyond the limits of what is intelligible. At the same time it endows them with a (supernatural) power which it is precisely the project of patriarchy to deny. On the stage such figures are seen as simultaneously dazzling and dangerous."[73] Joan's dazzle is of course neutralized by her fifth-act humiliations, but her danger persists in her final curse on England.

Quickly, she is taken off to be neutralized more thoroughly at the stake. Her helplessness vis-à-vis her male captors may serve to remind us that despite folk belief, there were no Elizabethan pictures of witches with beards or any other kind of power-laden sexual ambiguity.[74] Joan's fate enacts that annihilation fantasized for the cross-dressing woman by the anonymous author of a Jacobean pamphlet: "Let ... the powerful Statute of apparell [the sumptuary law] but lift up his Battle-Axe, so as every one may bee knowne by the true badge of their bloud, ... and then these *Chymera's* of deformitie will bee sent backe to hell and there burne to Cynders in the flames of their owne malice."[75] Yet in a final twist of meaning, as we may have seen, the terms of Joan's reintegration into conservative ideology recognizably damage her captors' own ideological sanction.

In my reading of *I Henry VI*, the disjunctive presentation of Joan that shows her first as numinous, then as practically and subversively powerful, and finally as feminized and demonized is determined by Shakespeare's progressive exploitation of the varied ideological potential inherent in the topically relevant figure of the virago. Each of her phases reflects differently upon the chivalric, patriarchal males in the play, especially Talbot, who also have topical referents outside the drama. At no stage is the allocation of value clearcut.

Neither is the definition of dominant ideology clearcut in the play's social context. To bring detailed topical considerations into an assessment of the ideology of *I Henry VI* is to come upon some truisms worth restating: that there is probably more than one opinion on any crucial issue at any time in any society, and that it is often hard to sort out the relationship between views and power. If the queen considers a French expedition disadvantageous but her subordinate succeeds in continuing it, is the dominant ideology war or peace? If pamphleteers complain that women are becoming moral monsters by cross-dressing, but a fad for Amazons arises and women cross-dress more than ever, what is the ideological situation? This kind of uncertainty complicates the concept of subversion, which I have invoked from time to time in my analysis.

Given the multiple uncertainties within the play's milieu and the uncertainties the play itself generates, it becomes strikingly evident that *I Henry VI*, like so much of Shakespeare's later work, locates itself in areas of ideological discomfort. It uses culturally powerful images ambiguously, providing material for different members of a diverse audience to receive the drama in very different ways. Although one must agree with the critical judgment that in this play "the individual consciousness never engages in an *agon* with its milieu, and never asks the great questions,"[76] the presence of Joan does provide a form of *agon*, if a less profound one than in the great tragedies. Even the ending with its strategies of neutralization cannot disqualify the questions raised.

Finally, once the ways in which disturbing ideological positions are neutralized by the play have been made clear, it seems well to point out that the theater is an illusionistic medium and that to neutralize on stage is not necessarily to neutralize in reality. In fact, it is possible that maintaining the illusion that an ideological tendency can be reliably neutralized may help to enable toleration of threatening ideas.[77]

NOTES

[1] This essay was first presented at the 1986 World Shakespeare Conference in Berlin and, in another form, at the Northeast Modern Language Association on 3 April 1987. It shares a common concern about Joan's ideological ambiguity with an independent study by Leah Marcus in her forthcoming book *Shakespeare and the Unease of Topicality,* but we arrive at different conclusions. Professor Marcus emphasizes Queen Elizabeth's complex projected image and its reception by her subjects, while the present essay examines late Elizabethan literary embodiments of the strong woman; Professor Marcus' discussion of topical references in *I Henry VI* is much more extensive than mine and will surely be the definitive treatment of that matter.

[2] Citations are from *The First Part of King Henry VI,* ed. Andrew S. Cairncross, *The Arden Shakespeare* (London, 1962).

[3] Geoffrey Bullough, *Narrative and Dramatic Sources of Shakespeare* (New York, 1960), III, 41.

[4] Robert B. Pierce, *Shakespeare's History Plays: The Family and the State* (Columbus, Oh., 1971), pp. 46–47. In the same spirit, Don M. Ricks identifies the tone she sets as "treachery, depravity, and insolence" in *Shakespeare's Emergent Form: A Study of the Structures of the Henry VI Plays* (Logan, Utah, 1968), p. 45. So common is the critical view of Joan as a moral write-off that she is sometimes assigned reprehensible behavior that does not even occur in the text, as when Catherine Belsey remarks that she "puts heart into the enemy by her rhetoric," in *The Subject of Tragedy: Identity and Difference in Renaissance Drama* (New York, 1985), p. 183. At the very least she is presumed to be the butt of continuous irony (e.g., by David Bevington in "The Domineering Female in *I Henry VI,"* *Shakespeare Studies* 2 [1966], 51–58 and John Wilders in *The Lost Garden: A View of Shakespeare's English and Roman History Plays* [Totowa, N.J., 1978], p. 36). A signal exception is H. M. Richmond in *Shakespeare's Political Plays* (New York, 1967), who allows her "heroic power" and even some "magnetism"; he also goes quite against the current of critical commentary by alluding to "her subtlety and finesse" (p. 23), but he agrees on "the harshness of the portrait" (p. 22).

[5] Bullough, pp. 24–25.

[6] Lisa Jardine, *Still Harping on Daughters: Women and Drama in the Age of Shakespeare* (Sussex, 1983), p. 124.

[7] Belsey, p. 184.

[8] Marilyn French, *Shakespeare's Division of Experience* (New York, 1981), p. 47.

[9] See David Riggs, who admirably elucidates the play's structure in *Shakespeare's Heroical Histories: Henry VI and Its Literary Tradition* (Cambridge, Mass., 1971), pp. 100ff. On the play's ideology we disagree.

[10] Riggs, p. 107. Riggs' view has been more recently affirmed by Norman Rabkin, *Shakespeare and the Problem of Meaning* (Chicago, 1981), pp. 88–89 and n. 39. Ricks and David Sundelson also make explicit, in slightly different ways, a criterion of integration to explain the last act: "her final degeneration in Act V is but a spectacular demonstration of the unsaintliness which has been implicit in her words and behavior all along. There is nothing contradictory, therefore, about the two views of Joan as Pucelle and as 'Puzzel' [whore]" (Ricks, p. 46); "Shakespeare himself seems unable to tolerate any uncertainty about the source of Joan's potency. He resolves the matter with a scene in which she conjures . . . , thus confirming Talbot's explanation" (David Sundelson, *Shakespeare's Restorations of the Father* [New Brunswick, N.J., 1983], p. 20).

[11] See, e.g., Rabkin, pp. 86–87.

[12] Detailed proposals of the play's topicality have been made by T. W. Baldwin, *On the Literary Genetics of Shakespeare's Plays 1592–1594* (Urbana, Ill., 1959), pp. 324–40. Less extended suggestions of parallels have come from J. Dover Wilson in the introduction to his edition of *The First Part of King Henry VI* (Cambridge, 1952), pp. xviii–xix; Emrys Jones, *The Origins of Shakespeare* (Oxford, 1977), pp. 119–26; John Munro in *TLS,* October 11, 1947; Hereward T. Price, *Construction in Shakespeare,* University of Michigan Contributions in Modern Philology No. 17 (Ann Arbor, Mich., 1951), pp. 25–26; and Ernest William Talbert, *Elizabethan Drama and Shakespeare's Early Plays: An Essay in Historical Criticism* (Chapel Hill, N.C., 1963). Leah Marcus offers a most thorough treatment of many of the play's topical allusions that takes full account of their complexity in "Elizabeth," a section of her forthcoming *Shakespeare and the Unease of Topicality.* See note 1 above.

[13] John Munro first interpreted the lines about the phoenix as a reference to Essex. J. Dover Wilson follows suit in his introduction to the play, where he also suggests that "Talbot was intended to stand as in some sort the forerunner of Essex" (p. xix). T. W. Baldwin, in his study of the play's "literary genetics," is dubious about Munro's identification but agrees that the allusion is to "the English armies in France 1589 and following" (p. 334). E. W. Talbert similarly cites Munro and also accepts the play's connection with the Essex expedition (pp. 163–64 and p. 163 n. 6).

[14] J. E. Neale, *Queen Elizabeth I* (Garden City, N.Y., 1957), p. 337.

[15] Dover Wilson sees the parallel between Talbot's and Essex's challenges, but interprets it simply as a reminiscence of Essex's gallantry (p. xix). He considers the play "an outlet for the growing sense of exasperation, anger, and even despair which was felt in London at the impending failure of an invasion of France" (p. xvi.).

[16] Neale, p. 335.

[17] Neale, p. 336. Elizabeth called the campaign "rather a jest than a victory" and ordered Essex home for good in January 1592 (Neale, p. 337).

[18] That a steady stream of ephemera carried bulletins from France to English readers is evident from the entries in the Stationers' Register. The diversity of possible attitudes to the expedition is perhaps suggested by the contrasting titles of two such pieces: an obviously enthusiastic "ballad of the noble departinge of the right honorable the Erle of ESSEX lieutenant generall of her maiesties forces in Ffraunce and all his gallant companie" (23 July 1591) and a possibly more ominous-sounding "letter sent from a gentleman of accoumpte concerning the true estate of the Englishe forces now in Ffraunce under the conduct of the right honorable the Erle of ESSEX" (6 September 1591).

[19] The well-known compliment to Essex in *Henry V*, 5, Cho. 30–34, is also ambiguous in light of the sentence that follows it (ll. 34–35). That this passage refers to Essex has been generally accepted, but the identification has been challenged by W. D. Smith. See G. Blakemore Evans, "Chronology and Sources," *The Riverside Shakespeare*, ed. G. Blakemore Evans (Boston, 1974), p. 53.

[20] E.g. Marilyn French (n. 8 above), following L. C. Knights and Northrop Frye, calls the play a search for legitimacy (p. 43). She believes that legitimacy is presented as a strictly masculine principle—"Shakespeare's women can never attain legitimacy"—although, somewhat confusingly, she also claims that it can contain "the inlaw feminine principle" (p. 49).

[21] Bevington (n. 4 above), pp. 51–58.

[22] Riggs (n. 9 above).

[23] French (n. 8 above), p. 51.

[24] Coppélia Kahn, *Man's Estate: Masculine Identity in Shakespeare* (Berkeley, Cal., 1981), p. 55 and p. 55 n. 11.

[25] Linda Woodbridge, *Women and the English Renaissance: Literature and the Nature of Womankind 1540–1620* (Urbana, Ill., 1984), p. 61. Shakespeare's interest in this controversy is evident not only in his frequent allusions to its *exempla* (Woodbridge cites references, pp. 126–28, and there are many more) but in his use of at least ten of them as characters in his works, four as protagonists. His is an impressive roster even in a period when plays about the controversy's *exempla* were a growth industry (Woodbridge, pp. 126ff.). The four protagonists are Venus, Lucrece, Cressida, and Cleopatra; the other characters, Volumnia in *Coriolanus*, Portia in *Julius Caesar* and Portia in *The Merchant of Venice* (carefully identified, as Woodbridge notes on p. 127, with "Cato's daughter, Brutus' Portia"), Octavia, Helen of Troy, and Hippolyta (Thisbe should also be mentioned). The maligned and repudiated Mariana in *Measure for Measure*, too, may be a relative of Mariamne, Herod's defamed second wife, another favorite of the controversialists.

[26] Woodbridge, pp. 61–62, 66.

[27] Cairncross, 2.3.7–10n., and Bevington.

[28] Woodbridge, p. 126. Woodbridge's account of the controversy is invaluable. I cannot agree with her, however, that the plays written in and after the later 1580s were probably not influenced by it; her own evidence (and there is more she does not cite) seems to point overwhelmingly the other way. She observes that "the drama had many other potential sources," which is true but does not account for the upsurge in plays devoted specifically to *exempla* from the controversy, and she points out that dramatists often treated these *exempla* differently from controversialists—but this objection assumes that to influence is to produce a copy.

[29] The term was almost entirely positive and denoted either physical or spiritual prowess. For the virago's "manly soul," see Simon Shepherd, *Amazons and Warrior Women: Varieties of Feminism in Seventeenth-Century Drama* (Sussex, 1981), pp. 34–35. Various contemporary allusions to the Queen invoked the pun *virgo/virago*, and her "masculine" spirit was frequently remarked upon with admiration. See Winfried Schleiner, *"Divina Virago: Queen Elizabeth as an Amazon," Studies in Philology* 75, 2 (1978), 163–80. I am grateful to Louis Montrose for calling this extremely useful article to my attention.

[30] All citations from *The Faerie Queene* will be identified by book, canto, stanza, and line numbers in my text; these refer to Edmund Spenser, *The Faerie Queene*, ed. R. E. Neil Dodge (Cambridge, Mass., 1936).

[31] I am indebted to F. J. Levy for calling my attention to this fact.

[32] Ironically—or as a calculated symbolic counterstatement to the Maid?—Henry VI's Paris coronation

pageant included "la sage Hippolyte" and her sister Menalippe, as well as Penthesilea and Lempeto, as female worthies. See Robert Withington, *English Pageantry: An Historical Outline*, Vol. I (Cambridge, Mass., 1918), pp. 138–39 n. 4. Celeste Turner Wright calls attention to Henry's coronation pageant in "The Amazons in Elizabethan Literature," *Studies in Philology* 37 (July 1940), 437 n. 41 (n.b.: because of a numbering error in this volume, Wright's article begins on the *second* occurrence of p. 437).

[33] See Abby Wettan Kleinbaum, "The Confrontation," in *The War against the Amazons* (New York, 1983). I appreciate being directed to this book by Daniel Traister, Curator of Rare Books at the University of Pennsylvania.

[34] Schleiner (see n. 29 above) also identifies as "Amazons" the female characters in a mock tournament of 1579, presented for the Queen and the Duke of Alençon's representative (p. 179), although her quotation from her source refers only to "ladies" (pp. 163–64 n. 3). *Tamburlaine* mentions Amazon armies, but they do not appear. Greene's *Alphonsus*, an obvious offspring of *Tamburlaine*, may have preceded *I Henry VI* in presenting visible Amazons as well as a warrior maiden, but this play has never been satisfactorily dated. Rabkin believes it was "probably written 1587," but does not give his reasons (introduction to Robert Greene, "Friar Bacon and Friar Bungay," *Drama of the English Renaissance. I: The Tudor Period*, ed. Russell A. Fraser and Norman Rabkin [New York, 1976] p. 357). The play's general derivative quality suggests, however, that Iphigina is more likely to be a daughter of Joan than the reverse. The other productions I know of containing Amazons are "A Masque of the Amazons . . . played March 3, 1592" (Henslowe's diary, quoted in William Painter, *The Palace of Pleasure*, ed. Joseph Jacobs, 3 vols. [London, 1890], I, lxxxi); "field pastimes with martiall and heroicall exploits" staged for Prince Henry's christening in 1594 (John Nichols, *Progresses, Public Processions, &c. of Queen Elizabeth*, 3 vols. [London, 1823], III, 355); *Midsummer Night's Dream*, 1595; Marston's *Antonio and Mellida*, 1602; *Timon of Athens*, ?1605–1609; Jonson's *Masque of Queens*, 1609; Beaumont and Fletcher's *Two Noble Kinsmen*, ?1613, *The Sea Voyage*, 1622, and *Double Marriage*, 1647; the anonymous *Swetnam, the Woman-Hater*, 1620; Heywood's *Iron Age*, 1632; Shirley's dramatization of the *Arcadia*, 1640; and Davenant's *Salmacida Spolia*, 1640. There is a discussion of Fletcher's *Sea Voyage* and some Amazon dramas 1635–1685 in chapter 11 of Jean Elisabeth Gagen, *The New Woman: Her Emergence in English Drama, 1600–1730* (New York, 1954).

For many of these titles and the beginnings of all my information about Amazons, I have relied on the encyclopedic Wright (n. 32 above). Her non-chronological organization assumes, however, that the degree of interest in Amazons and writers' attitudes towards them remained stable throughout the period from which she takes her examples (some undated). Her evidence suggests otherwise.

[35] Wright, pp. 442–43, 449–54. Wright's data are difficult to get around in chronologically, but it looks as though doubts about the Amazons—including skepticism about their existence—may have increased in England after 1600, although the Amazonian vogue lasted right up to the Civil War.

Although there are Elizabethan accounts of the Amazons' ruthless origins and habits, I do not agree with Shepherd (n. 29 above) that the period's overriding feeling was "Elizabethan distress about Amazons" (p. 14), in support of which view he instances Radigund and the egregious misogynist Knox. Shepherd wants to extrapolate Spenser's opposition between Radigund and Britomart into a pervasive Elizabethan distinction between Amazons and warrior women: "Against the warrior ideal there is the Amazon" (p. 13). This schema will not hold up in the face of a mass of evidence for Elizabethan Amazon-enthusiasm. Shepherd's own evidence for the Elizabethan period is slender and largely extrapolated from Stuart texts. Although he does say that the negative meaning of Amazon "coexists with the virtuous usage" (p. 14), this concession, in itself inadequate, is forgotten in his subsequent loosely supported account.

Nor can I agree with Louis Adrian Montrose's implication in his otherwise insightful and imaginative "'Shaping Fantasies': Figurations of Gender and Power in Elizabethan Culture," *Representations*, 1, 2 (Spring 1983), 61–94, that English Renaissance texts about Amazons generally express "a mixture of fascination and horror" (p. 66). The passages he quotes detail the Amazons' origins and/or customs; others of this type are often flat in tone and delivered without comment, like Mandeville's (1499, rpt. 1568), while some mention no horrors at all. Even the Amazon-shy Spenser compliments the supposed South American tribe: "Joy on those warlike women, which so long/ Can from all men so rich a kingdome hold!" (*F.Q.* 4.11 .22.1–2). Although Montrose calls attention to the association sometimes made between Amazons and the destruction of male children, and in some travel books between Amazons and cannibalism, in an equal number of accounts they produce male children for neighboring tribes and are thought of as desirable breeding stock. By far the greatest number of Amazon allusions, moreover, refer to specific Amazons and appear in a positive context. Penthesilea, the hands-down favorite, is always treated with admiration and respect, as is Hippolyta.

My observations are based on the following Tudor texts: Agrippa, tr. Clapham, *The Nobilitie of Woman Kynde,* 1542 (STC 203), p. 360v; Anghiera (Peter Martyr), tr. Eden, *Decades of the Newe World,* 1555, ed. Arber, *The First Three English Books on America,* 1885, pp. 69, 177, 189; Richard Barckley, *The Felicitie of Man,* 1598 (STC 1381), III, 266–68; Boccaccio, *De Claris Mulieribus,* 1534–47, ed. Wright, EETS (London,1943), pp. 39–42, 66–67, 103–05 and *Tragedies,* tr. Lydgate, 1554 (STC 3178), I, 12; Quintus Curtius, tr. Brende, *History of . . . Alexander,* 1553 (STC 6142), pp. Pii–Piii; Anthony Gibson, tr., *A Womans Woorth,* 1599 (STC 11831), pp. 5, 37v; Richard Madox, *An Elizabethan in 1582: The Diary of Richard Madox . . . ,* ed. Elizabeth Story Donno, Hakluyt Society second series No. 47 (London, 1977), p. 183; Sir John Mandeville, *The Voyage and Travel . . . ,* 1568 (STC 17250), pp. Gviii verso; Ortuñez de Calahorra, tr. T[yler], *The Mirrour of . . . Knighthood,* 1578 (STC 18859), 26.91v, 55.219; Hieronimus Osorius, tr. Blandie, *The Five Books of Civill and Christian Nobilitie,* 1576 (STC 18886), II, 25v; Ovid, tr. Turberville, *Heroycall Epistles,* 1567 (STC 18940.5), p. 23; William Painter, *The Palace of Pleasure,* 1575, ed. Joseph Jacobs, 3 vols. (London, 1890), II, 159–61; Sir Walter Ralegh, *The Discoverie of . . . Guiana,* 1596 (STC 20636), pp. 23–24 and *History of the World,* 1614 (STC 20637), I.4.195–96; William Shakespeare, *King John,* 1594–96, ed. Herschel Baker, in Evans; Sir Philip Sidney, *The Countess of Pembrokes Arcadia,* 1590, ed. Robertson (Oxford, 1973), pp. 21, 36; Edmund Spenser, *The Faerie Queene,* I–III, 1590, IV–VI, 1596 (see n. 30); Andre Thevet, *The New Found World,* tr. 1568 (STC 23950), pp. 101–74 (*recte* 103); William Warner, *Albion's England,* 1586 (STC 15759), pp. 25–26; and two accounts of Spanish voyages known in England, those of Francesco Orellana and Gonzalo Pizarro, *Expeditions into the Valley of the Amazons,* tr. and ed. Clements R. Markham, Hakluyt Society (New York, n.d.), pp. 13, 26, 34, 36). I have also found useful Kleinbaum's chapters "The Net of Fantasy" and "The Confrontation."

[36] Woodbridge, p. 21.

[37] Cited by both Wright and Shepherd.

[38] Wright, p. 455.

[39] He makes this identification in 1590, just a year and a half after the Armada crisis (see discussion below, in text). Penthesilea was frequently used as a comparison for Elizabeth, especially around this time (see Schleiner [n. 29 above], pp. 170–73). The Amazon analogy was still current in 1633, when Phineas Fletcher likened his "warlike Maid, / Parthenia," a recognizable variant of Elizabeth, to Hippolyta in *The Purple Island* 10 .27–40 (STC 11082), pp. 141–44.

[40] In "Elizabeth," Leah Marcus also connects Joan with the queen and comments on the contradiction between Joan's "idealized symbolic identities" and her status as an enemy (p. 51).

[41] For information on woodcuts I am most grateful to Ruth Luborsky, who is currently completing a catalogue of all woodcut-illustrated printed English documents in the period, keyed to the STC. For pictorial narratives, I have consulted David Kunzle, *The Early Comic Strip: Narrative Strips and Picture Stories in the European Broadsheet from 1450–1895* (Berkeley, Cal., 1983). I have examined the engraved representations in Arthur M. Hind, *Engraving in England in the Sixteenth and Seventeenth Centuries,* 3 vols. (Vol. III ed. Margery Corbett and Michael Norton) (Cambridge, 1952–64); in Ronald B. McKerrow, *Printers' and Publishers' Devices 1485–1640 in England and Scotland* (London, 1913); in Ronald B. McKerrow and F. S. Ferguson, *Title-Page Borders Used in England & Scotland 1485–1640* (London,1932 [for 1931] [sic]); and in Margery Corbett and Ronald Lightbown, *The Comely Frontispiece: The Emblematic Title-Page in England, 1550–1660* (London, 1979).

[42] Nichols (n. 34 above), II, 53–54.

[43] Quoted from Thomas Heywood's *Exemplary Lives,* 1640, by Shepherd (n. 29 above), p. 22.

[44] Leonel Sharp, Letter to George Villiers, Duke of Buckingham, n.d. [1623–25], *Cabala, Mysteries of State, in Letters of the Great Ministers of K.* James and K. Charles (1654), p. 259.

[45] Stow in his *Annals* (1615) calls the Queen at Tilbury "Bellona-like" (quoted by Miller Christy, "Queen Elizabeth's Visit to Tilbury in 1588," *English Historical Review 34* [1919], 58), and an anonymous poem of 1600 appeals to her as "Thou that . . . bearest harnesse, speare, and shielde" (Schleiner [n. 29 above], p. 174). Schleiner, who does not know the Sharp letter, calls Heywood's 1640 description "probably on theatrical imagination" (p. 176). There seems little doubt, however, that Elizabeth did wear armor, and that Heywood was only recreating the spectacle staged by a superior dramatist when in 1633 he brought his two-part stage biography of the Queen to its climax with a final Tilbury scene: "Enter . . . Queen ELIZABETH, completely armed." See Thomas Heywood, *The Second Part of If You Know Not Me, You Know No Bodie* (1633), in *Thomas Heywood's Dramatic Works,* ed. J. Payne Collier (London, 1853), II, 156; for the date see editorial note [xxiii]. (The 1606 version of the play does not contain this stage direction, but may of course have used the same costume.)

I do not know where Paul Johnson gets his circumstantial description of a white velvet dress, etc.

In *Elizabeth I: A Study in Power and Intellect* (London, 1974), p. 320, which Montrose (n. 35 above) follows, p. 77. The description is not in any of the sources Johnson cites in his footnote.

[46] Sharp, p. 260. J. E. Neale, "Sayings of Queen Elizabeth," *History* n.s. 10 (October 1925), pp. 212–33, considers this speech substantially authentic (pp. 226–27). Sharp, who recounted it soon after 1623, must have received a copy of it in 1588, for at Tilbury he had been "commanded to re-deliver" the oration to "all the Armie together, to keep a Publique Fast" (Sharp, p. 259) after Elizabeth's departure.

For evidence that Elizabeth's rhetorical self-presentations often implied androgyny, see Leah S. Marcus, "Shakespeare's Comic Heroines, Elizabeth I, and the Political Uses of Androgyny," *Women in the Middle Ages and the Renaissance*, ed. Mary Beth Rose (Syracuse, N.Y., 1986).

[47] In "Elizabeth," Leah Marcus notes numerous similarities between Joan and the queen, including the proposed celebration of a saint's day commemorating each woman (p. 68) and the identity in name between two of Joan's supposed lovers and two of Elizabeth's suitors (p. 69).

[48] Leah Marcus, in "Elizabeth," does interpret Joan as a figure of parody that "brings into the open a set of suppressed cultural anxieties" about Elizabeth (p. 51).

[49] Natalie Zemon Davis, "Women on Top," *Society and Culture in Early Modern France* (Stanford, Cal., 1975), p. 129.

[50] "The Life of Long Meg of Westminster," *The Old Book Collector's Miscellany*, ed. Charles Hindley, Vol. II (London, 1872). See also Shepherd (n. 29 above), pp. 70–71. The outlines of Long Meg's story exhibit striking similarities with the outlines of Joan's; according to Hall, Joan too came from the country and "was a greate space a chamberleyn in a commen hostrey" (Bullough, p. 56) before going off to lead the army against the English champion and being honored by the Dauphin.

[51] Hindley, p. xii, quoted by Shepherd, p. 73. The ballad of Mary Ambree is given in Thomas Percy, *Reliques*, Vol. III (1823), pp. 46–51 (series 2, Bk. 2, no. 19). She was a well-known figure, mentioned by Fletcher and Ben Jonson (Percy, p. 46). Long Meg was even more familiar; she is referred to by Lyly, Nashe, Harvey, Deloney, Taylor, Dekker, Jonson, Beaumont and Fletcher, Middleton, and William Gamage's collection of epigrams (see Hindley and Shepherd).

All modern critics who discuss Long Meg give a wrong date of 1582 for the first pamphlet account of her life. This edition's title page and colophon are forged from an unrelated book published 1582; the rest of the text is ca. 1650. See William A. Jackson, ed., *Records of the Court of the Stationers' Company 1602–1640* (London, 1957), pp. 112–13 and n. 6 (this information is incorporated in the STC's revised Vol. II, ed. Katharine Pantzer). The earliest mention I know of Meg's story is the 18 August 1590 entry in the *Stationers' Register* for her life, followed in 27 August the same year by an entry for a ballad about her. On 14 March 1594/95, another ballad is entered. The first extant life would thus become one printed in 1620 (STC 17782.5), followed by further editions in 1635 and 1636 (STC 17783, 17783.3). After these would come the "1582" (*recte* ca. 1650). Hindley, who reprints the 1635 edition, includes in his introduction another reprint, which he believes to be an abridged version (n.d.) of the supposed 1582 text. It does seem to be Elizabethan, for it contains the casual reference to "Her Majesty"; later, this phrase was economically altered by the printer to "she sat in her Majesty" (1635; I have not seen the 1620 edition). Thus the life in Hindley's introduction may be the version registered 1590; if so, it is our earliest text.

[52] Lawrence Stone believes that female cross-dressing was a reflection of the Jacobean court's homosexuality and that "The playwrights noticed what was happening and gave it further circulation"; see *The Crisis of the Aristocracy 1558–1641* (Oxford, 1966), pp. 666–67. Given the early beginnings of both real and fictional cross-dressing, however, behavior at the Jacobean court comes much too late to be an explanation.

[53] There is contemporaneous evidence for the possibility of regarding Joan as a heroine. Gabriel Harvey in his commonplace book set her between Alexander and her shepherd-analogue David (Shepherd, p. 35). By the 1620s, she was publicly entered among warlike and valorous women in Thomas Heywood's *Gynaikeion* (Jardine [n. 6 above], p. 137 n. 66) and admitted to membership in the long-running formal controversy in Christopher Newstead's *An Apology for Women*, a positive *exemplum* after all (Woodbridge [n. 25 above], p. 80).

[54] Davis (n. 50 above), pp. 138–39.

[55] The Amazon army in Greene's *Alphonsus* stands by silently while its non-Amazon leader fights; the Amazons in the masque of Shakespeare's *Timon* sing and dance. Since these are early manifestations of the Amazon vogue in drama, their extraneousness probably reflects their initial use as spectacle rather than integrated content. Marston's *Antonio and Mellida*, the anonymous *Swetnam the Woman-Hater*, and Shirley's dramatization of the *Arcadia*, which fall into the later part of the period, contain men disguised as Amazons.

[56] Anthony Gibson, tr., *A Womans Woorth* (1599), cited by Wright (n. 32 above), p. 437.

[57] Ortuñez's Claridiana (tr. 1585), Spenser's Britomart and Radigund (although the latter's loss of helmet releases no golden hair), Ariosto's Bradamante (tr. 1591), Tasso's Clorinda (tr. 1600), and Phineas Fletcher's Hippolyta (*The Purple Island*, 1633). See Wright, p. 441, and Shepherd, pp. 9–10. Mary Ambree (1584) removes her helmet to astonish the besieging forces; Shepherd says she "was forced to reveal her true gender to avoid being killed" (p. 222 n. 2), but the tone of the ballad is triumphant. Nevertheless, Ambree does share in the woman warrior's climactic feminization.

[58] Hindley (n. 51 above), p. xx; quoted in a slightly different form by Shepherd, pp. 71–72.

[59] Belsey (n. 4 above), p. 185. Christina Larner gives the proportion of females among those put on trial for witchcraft in England at close to 95–100% in *Witchcraft and Religion: The Politics of Popular Belief,* ed. Alan Macfarlane (New York, 1984), p. 85. Belsey's figure is taken from earlier work by Larner.

[60] Cf. Mary Beth Rose's comment that cross-dressing women are "obscuring ... the badge of their social status as well, and thereby endangering critically the predictable orderliness of social relations" ("Women in Men's Clothing: Apparel and Social Stability in *The Roaming Girl,*" *English Literary Renaissance* 14 [1984], 374).

[61] Belsey, p. 185. Overall, Belsey is concerned with an extended period of "crisis" lasting from 1542 to 1736, when the last statute against witchcraft was repealed.

[62] This tract, with its new emphasis on the spectacular pact with the Devil, which had not previously been a factor in Scottish witch trials and was never very important in English ones (Larner, pp. 4, 8, 80–81, 88), seems to have evoked a little spate of conjuring dramas in the early 1590s, including *Dr. Faustus* and possibly *Friar Bacon and Friar Bungay* (written between 1589 and 1592).

[63] Larner, pp. 69, 9–10, 12.

[64] Larner, p. 12.

[65] Larner, pp. 12–13.

[66] Larner, pp. 14, 4, 10–11, 15.

[67] Warwick does say "That so her torture may be shortened" (5.4.58), but it seems at best a mixed recommendation. As for the usual English treatment of witchcraft, although it sounds sufficiently grim to us, it was "fairly far down the scale" of intensity compared with that of other countries, sufficiently different to be often called "unique" by recent investigators, although Larner is not willing to go that far (pp. 70–71).

[68] Michel de Montaigne, "Ignorance and Witchcraft," *Witchcraft in Europe 1100–1700: A Documentary History,* ed. Alan C. Kors and Edward Peters (Philadelphia,1972), p. 337.

[69] Reginald Scot, "Credulity and Witchcraft," Kors, pp. 327, 326.

[70] Scot, in Kors, pp. 318–19.

[71] This phrase and its variants (sometimes in Latin) were regularly applied to Queen Elizabeth. James' eulogistic inscription on her monument identifies her, typically, as *"super sexum"* (see Schleiner [n. 29 above], pp. 172–73).

On witches' beards, Belsey (p. 186) cites Keith Thomas' *Religion and the Decline of Magic*, p. 678. Thomas Alfred Spalding, *Elizabethan Demonology* (London, 1880), p. 99, instances *The Honest Man's Fortune, The Honest Whore,* and *The Merry Wives of Windsor*—besides, of course, *Macbeth,* to which both Belsey and Spalding refer.

[72] Bullough, p. 61.

[73] Belsey, p. 185.

[74] For information on pictures of witches, I am again indebted to Ruth Luborsky. Many illustrations are also reproduced in Kors, including some of witches with animal heads and limbs, but none with transsexual characteristics.

[75] *Hic Mulier*, C1v, cited by Rose (n. 61 above), p. 375.

[76] Ronald S. Berman, "Shakespeare's Conscious Histories," *Dalhousie Review* 41, 4 (Winter 1961–62), 486.

[77] The research for this essay has relied greatly on the knowledgeable and generous help of Georgiana Zeigler, curator of the Furness Collection at the University of Pennsylvania, to whom I owe much gratitude.

John A. Bertolini

SAINT JOAN:
THE SELF AS IMAGINATION

In his notice of the first production of Shaw's *Saint Joan,* Pirandello asserted that the play was "a work of poetry from beginning to end."[1] What Pirandello may have meant by that encompassing statement is not clear, but that he thought of the play as something other than either an impudent historical pamphlet masquerading as drama or a flippant treatment of a sacred subject *is* clear. My purpose now is to explore what Pirandello asserted about the play: its deeply poetic nature—a quality of the play that has as often been denied as asserted.[2] The play's poetic nature lives as much in its subject, which I take to be the workings of the imagination more than Joan's particular sainthood, as it does in its artistry. To make my point, I shall begin with the Epilogue, where I see the clearest evidence of Shaw's preoccupation with the nature of imagination.[3]

The famous Epilogue to *Saint Joan* (or notorious Epilogue, if one reads any fair sampling of the reviews and criticism of the play from 1925 on) begins with a description of Charles' reading in bed, or rather, as Shaw puts it, *"looking at the pictures in Fouquet's Boccaccio."* At first, that stage direction looks like a characteristic good-humored joke at the expense of the foolish Charles, whom Shaw continually portrays as a childishly self-centered individual, shrewd in certain matters, but of nevertheless singularly limited intellectual capacity. The joke is that Charles interests himself only in the dirty pictures found in the book. Neither Fouquet's coloring nor Boccaccio's prose style holds Charles' attention; the dirty pictures do, however. And Charles' insensitivity to art here is meant to tell us how he will respond to Joan's proposal that she return to life. Indeed, it reminds us of how he misunderstood Joan while she was alive. Charles' insensitivity to art and to Joan amount to the same thing.

Fouquet's Boccaccio is only one of the means by which Shaw insinuates into the play notions about art and how people respond to products of the imagination. It is part of a pattern of symbols and metaphors through which Shaw dramatizes his

From *The Playwrighting Self of Bernard Shaw* (Carbondale: Southern Illinois University Press, 1991), pp. 125–31, 137–44.

sense of what art can and should be. To continue with the opening stage directions of the Epilogue is to see Shaw's preoccupation with art emerge more and more clearly. From Fouquet's illustrations, Shaw directs our attention to a *"picture of the Virgin, lighted by candles of painted wax."* He then describes the walls of the room as *"hung from ceiling to floor with painted curtains which stir at times in the draughts."* And lastly, he tells us that Charles' watchman's rattle is *"handsomely designed and gaily painted."* In short, Shaw takes some pains to point out that Charles is surrounded by painting of one kind or another—a painted manuscript, painted candles, painted curtains, and a painted toy—but painting used to satisfy the human need for a decorous living space, adornment to please the eye.

Against this decorative use of art, Shaw sets Joan as symbol and metaphor. Joan enters when *"A rush of wind through the open doors sets the walls swaying agitatedly. The candles go out. He [Charles] calls in the darkness."* Whatever visual pleasure we took in Charles' colorful surroundings ends as, *"A flash of summer lightning shews up the lancet window"* and *"A figure is seen in silhouette against it."* The movement of light that Shaw depicts here, from darkness to a figure seen in silhouette, to Joan dimly seen, culminates in the last moments of the Epilogue when *"The last remaining rays of light gather into a white radiance descending on Joan."* At that moment, Joan stands literally and figuratively illuminated, for Shaw intends the Epilogue to make us see Joan more clearly as a metaphor that has meaning for the world, not merely as a decorative figure in memory and imagination.

Shaw has Joan herself articulate this significance: "I hope men will be the better for remembering me; and they would not remember me so well if you [Peter Cauchon] had not burned me." The rays of white light are also a transfiguration of the light from the fire that burned her, a connection Shaw suggests to us through Cauchon's words, "even as she burned, the flames whitened into the radiance of the Church Triumphant," as well as through the description of the curtains in Charles' bedroom: *"At first glance the prevailing yellow and red in these hanging pictures is somewhat flamelike when the folds breathe in the wind."* Since the Epilogue follows shortly after Joan is dragged away to be burned, Shaw's stage directions cannot fail to remind us of those flames.

It could be charged that the final vision of the illuminated and solitary Saint Joan is a conventional tableau that has no more meaning than other such melodramatic stage-lighting effects, that it is visual rhetoric merely, a counterpart to her final rhetorical question: "O God that madest this beautiful earth, when will it be ready to receive Thy saints? How long, O Lord, how long?" No doubt the emotion of those last moments derives partly from the rhetorical strategy, but the emotion is also genuinely and complexly poetic. The final "radiance" fulfills the imagistic movement from darkness to light that the figure of Joan follows before our eyes. Poetic, too, is the ritualistic structuring of the immediately preceding episode. With a Te Deum-like sequence of lauds to Joan, each character in the Epilogue kneels in turn to hymn her praises, only to be asked by Joan if she should then return to earth. With their sadly comic volte-faces, each one rises to reject her proposal and leave her on stage alone. This ritual-like stage action points to Joan's isolation as a symbolic figure as well as to her personal isolation. She remains a scapegoat rejected by her comrades and community, and therefore a tragic figure. The kneeling to praise, the rising to reject, and the successive desertions of Joan in the Epilogue reenact the whole drama, which consists of her rise to influence and power in Scenes I to III and her fall in Scenes IV and V.[4]

Shaw liked this patterned action of successive desertions so well he used versions of it for the conclusions of *The Apple Cart* (1928) and *Too True to Be Good* (1931), but he did not invent it for *Saint Joan;* he invented it for the conclusion of *Back to Methuselah,* where Lilith corresponds to Joan figuratively and where Adam, Eve, Cain, and the Serpent correspond to Charles, Dunois, and the rest. Shaw there uses a similar ritual-like stage action and plays similarly with light and darkness: *"It is now quite dark. A vague radiance appears near the temple and shapes itself into the ghost of Adam."* As each ghost appears, it announces itself, hears the voice of the next to appear, and asks whose the voice is. Then the voice introduces itself, and the person appears.

This progress repeats itself for Adam, Eve, Cain, the Serpent, and lastly Lilith, who then starts a new pattern, whereby each ghost defines its contribution to life, notes the condition of the world, and asks the next ghost what he or she makes of it. The new pattern ends with the Serpent, who defines her contribution thus: "I chose wisdom and the knowledge of good and evil; and now there is no evil; and wisdom and good are one. It is enough." With her muted expression of philosophical content, the new ritual enters its final phase as, first the Serpent vanishes, and then Cain, Eve, and Adam express resignation, confidence, and dismay, respectively, and each vanishes in turn, leaving Lilith alone on stage to give her peroration to the whole play cycle that makes up *Back to Methuselah.* The order of the ghosts' exit lines reverses the order of their entrance lines, just as in *Saint Joan,* the order of the Te Deum speakers is reversed for their exit speeches. (The order of exits in *Saint Joan* is not so schematic as in *Back to Methuselah;* but it is close enough so that the audience has the sense of reverse order.)

Shaw's use of similarly structured endings for both plays suggests that Shaw's imagination connects Lilith's ritualistic isolation with Joan's. Both are icons in the scripture of Creative Evolution; both look to the future for fulfillment of their meaning. Here is how Lilith does so (with a strange consciousness of her metaphoric dimension):

> I brought life into the whirlpool of force, and compelled my enemy, Matter, to obey a living soul. . . . and now I shall see . . . the whirlpool become all life and no matter. And because these infants that call themselves ancients are reaching out towards that, I will have patience with them still; though I know well that when they attain it they shall become one with me and supersede me, and Lilith will be only a legend and a lay that has lost its meaning. Of Life only is there no end; and though of its million starry mansions many are empty and many still unbuilt, and though its vast domain is as yet unbearably desert, my seed shall one day fill it and master its matter to its uttermost confines.

And for what may be beyond, the eyesight of Lilith is too short. It is enough that there is a beyond. [*She vanishes*].

Lilith looks forward to the time when she will have been so successfully incorporated into the imagination of humankind ("they shall become one with me") that she will become a dead metaphor ("a lay that has lost its meaning"). But in that incorporation and that becoming Lilith is reborn ("my seed shall one day fill it"), for she lives on in her acceptance by the imagination. Joan looks forward to a similar death and rebirth in the imagination of her audience (with, however, less visionary confidence), when her meaning will be so fully understood and accepted that her image is no longer necessary in humankind's memory. Joan's illuminated isolation at the end of the Epilogue is an attempt by Shaw the poet to help us imagine Saint Joan, which means above all to see her clearly.

But seeing Joan clearly requires imagination from the audience and reader. That is why the basic metaphors for lack of imagination in this play are poor eyesight and darkness, images that are associated chiefly with John de Stogumber and Charles. When de Stogumber realizes (in the Epilogue) that he may again be in Joan's presence, he reacts immediately by denying that she is Joan: "My sight is bad: I cannot distinguish your features: but you are not she." Just before he says this, de Stogumber explains how he was saved: "I had not seen it [cruelty] you know. That is the great thing: you must see it. And then you are redeemed and saved." Cauchon asks him if the sufferings of Christ were not enough for him, and de Stogumber replies: "I had seen them in pictures, and read of them in books, and been greatly moved by them, as I thought. But it was no use: it was not our Lord that redeemed me, but a young woman whom I saw actually burned to death. It was dreadful: oh, most dreadful. But it saved me." Cauchon then asks what I take to be a central question of the play, "Must then a Christ perish in torment in every age to save those that have no imagination?" In the play's terms, then, imagination is how the human mind bridges the gap between life and art, between reality and fantasy, distinguishes the real toad in the imaginary garden. For that gap to be bridged the word must be made flesh in our minds. It is not so much a question of action in the real world (though that may be partly its consequence), but rather of what takes place in the human mind: understanding.

To understand Shaw's art and thought here it will be helpful to turn to two other plays that contain both imagistic connections with *Saint Joan* and explicit illustrations of Shaw's idea of the imagination: *Back to Methuselah* (again) and *On the Rocks*. As part of the Preface to *On the Rocks*, Shaw presents a short imaginary dialogue between Jesus and Pontius Pilate in which the following exchange takes place:

PILATE: A Salutary severity—
JESUS: Oh please!... I am so made by God that official phrases make me violently sick.... I have spoken to you as one man to another in living words. Do not be so ungrateful as to answer me in dead ones.... a thought is the substance of a word. I am no mere chance pile of flesh and

bone: If I were only that, I should fall into corruption and dust before your eyes. I am the embodiment of a thought of God: I am the Word made flesh: that is what holds me together before you in the image of God.... The Word is God. And God is within you....

PILATE: There are many sorts of words; and they are all made flesh sooner or later.... Your truth, as you call it, can be nothing but the thoughts for which you have found words which will take effect in deeds if I set you loose to scatter your words broadcast among the people.

What is most striking at first in this dialogue is Shaw's evident concern with language, that words matter, that they are efficacious in the real world. But words are not reality (and here Shaw shows his intellectual inheritance from Coleridge); their substance is thought. When Shaw has Jesus declare Himself to be "the embodiment of a thought of God . . . the Word made flesh," and then has Him explain "that is what holds me together . . . in the image of God," Shaw means that God created humankind by first imagining it. Things can become real after they have been imagined. Shaw as a dramatist habitually converts words into flesh on stage before an audience, but that conversation is only complete when the audience accepts the imaginative reality of Joan, in short, when the audience also imagines Joan. ⟨. . .⟩

The central drama of *Saint Joan* lies in her conquest of the fear of death in the trial scene. Plainly, the locus of powerful emotion in the play is Joan's recantation when she tears up her confession. Learning that she will not go free, but suffer life imprisonment instead, makes her assert the value of freedom over life itself. However, the freedom she desires is not merely freedom of movement (though that is important to her), but also the freedom of the imagination: "if only I could still hear the wind in the trees, the larks in the sunshine, the young lambs crying through the healthy frost, and the blessed blessed church bells that send my angel voices floating to me on the wind. But without these I cannot live." The imaginative freedom Joan asserts here is exclusively aural.[5] In Shaw's mind Joan's voices replicate the voices Adam and Eve hear in the garden in "In the Beginning." Real death for Joan means being cut off from the voice of imagination: her dread of the imprisoning of her imagination crushes her fear of the fire.

Shaw makes Joan not only imaginative herself, but a stimulus to imagination in others (that is one of the reasons why she, like Falstaff, can be seen as an emblem of the imagination). The first Shaw does, humorously, through a pair of stage directions. At her first entrance, Shaw describes Joan as having *"eyes very wide apart and bulging as they often do in very imaginative people."* In contrast, when Shaw introduces the Dauphin, he describes him as having *"little narrow eyes, near together."* Shaw does not need to indicate any more explicitly the Dauphin's lack of imagination. We remember his description of Joan and draw our own conclusion: the Dauphin has no imagination (rather like Herodias in Wilde's *Salome*, for whom "the moon is like the moon, that is all"). The Dauphin's later assertion to Joan, "I have my eyes open," adds ironic counterpoint to Shaw's humorous hinting at

Charles' lack of imagination: his eyes may be open, but only to see what lies in front of him; he has no vision of what France should be as Joan does.

Shaw also makes Joan stimulate imagination in others (again humorously). For example, after de Baudricourt is finally convinced to send her to the Dauphin, Joan says, "Oh, squire! Your head is circled with light, like a saint's," and he looks *"up for his halo rather apprehensively."* Joan can make people see more than what is in front of their eyes. In short, Joan enables people to see the metaphoric dimension of reality. That poetic power in her is brought into high relief through the discussion of miracles between the Archbishop and La Trémouille, where the Archbishop explains that the church nourishes the people's "faith by poetry."

> THE ARCHBISHOP: Parables are not lies because they describe events that never happened. . . . if they [the people] feel the thrill of the supernatural, and forget their sinful clay in a sudden sense of the glory of God, it will be a miracle.

Shortly thereafter, Shaw underlines his point through a deft bit of characterization, when he has the Archbishop identify Pythagoras as "A sage who held that the earth is round and that it moves around the sun," at which La Trémouille exclaims, "What an utter fool! Couldnt he use his eyes?" La Trémouille, like Charles and like de Stogumber, has limited vision because he cannot see the metaphoric dimension of reality, the poetry in life, its miracles.

More important, however, than these two aspects of Joan is her identity as an emblem of imagination itself, especially in its essence of freedom. Nowhere does Shaw bring this identification out more clearly than in the short scene before Orléans between Dunois and his Page. That scene opens with Dunois invoking the west wind in an attempt at poetic incantation (echoing Shelley's "Ode to the West Wind," of which more later). As Dunois finishes his prayer-poem, the Page bounds to his feet:

> THE PAGE: See! There! There she goes!
> DUNOIS: Where? Who? The Maid?
> THE PAGE: No: the kingfisher. Like blue lightning.

A bit later, they watch another kingfisher fly by the reeds and *"They follow the flight till the bird takes cover."* That they are waiting for Joan, and that Dunois thinks the Page means Joan when he first cries out, suffices to enforce our identifying Joan with the kingfisher. But if we think of the bird's name and back to how Joan, at the court of the Dauphin in the preceding scene, searches *"along the row of courtiers, and presently makes a dive, and drags out Charles by the arm,"* we can see that Shaw's mind symbolically identifies Joan with the kingfisher bird. (Summer lightning presages Joan's appearance in the Epilogue—a reminder of the "blue lightning" to which the Page compares the kingfisher.) That identification, however, goes beyond the merely picturesque or the punning senses in the bird's name and in Charles' label, Dauphin (Dolphin), for in the next exchange between the Page and

Dunois, we see the kingfisher image expand into a multivalent metaphor for Joan that reaches to the core of the play's meaning:

THE PAGE: Arnt they lovely? I wish I could catch them.
DUNOIS: Let me catch you trying to trap them, and I will put you in the iron cage for a month to teach you what a cage feels like.

Dunois' words proleptically point to the trial scene where Joan's imprisonment is in question, and where Shaw maintains Joan's association with the image of flying: "JOAN: And why must I be chained by the feet to a log of wood? Are you afraid I will fly away? . . . COURCELLES: If you cannot fly like a witch, how is it that you are still alive?"[6] The instinctive reaction of unimaginative people to the "lovely" things in life, the free things, like the kingfisher, is to capture and cage them. So too it is with Joan: her lovely, free imagination provokes them to want to destroy her, or failing that, at least to cage her for life. In their desire to imprison Joan, Shaw shows that they want to deny metaphor. For Joan embodies imagination, the freedom to soar beyond things, to metaphorize the world by seeing more. After Dunois utters a second prayer-poem, this time to the kingfisher bird, asking it to send a west wind, Joan immediately enters, and at the end of the scene the west wind comes, as if there were a silent consonance between them. Indeed, there is, but the consonance alludes loudly to Shelley's "Ode to the West Wind":

> Be thou, Spirit fierce,
> My spirit! Be thou me, impetuous one!
>
> Drive my dead thought over the universe
> Like withered leaves to quicken a new birth!
> And, by the incantation of this verse,
>
> Scatter, as from an unextinguished hearth
> Ashes and sparks, my words among mankind!
> Be through my lips to unawakened earth
>
> The trumpet of a prophecy! O wind,
> If Winter comes, can Spring be far behind?[7]

Joan imagines into existence a new France out of the blood and death of Orleans. That is why Shaw sounds overtones of sexual attraction between Joan and Dunois as they discuss tactics for laying siege to Orleans. Their conversation veers off midway onto the topic of love and marriage. With her enthusiasm and familiarity Joan could be said to seduce Dunois into believing in her, not through feminine wiles or any means so overt, but through her innocent self-assurance and intimacy of address, even as she seduces de Baudricourt and Charles. In Joan's meeting with Dunois, feminine sexuality combines with maternal caring (as is typical in Shaw). Dunois' decorative masculinity asserts itself playfully even before Joan arrives: he *"has had his lance stuck up with a pennon"* and *"has his commander's baton in his hand."* And when the wind changes, the seduction ends in union: the surrender of

Dunois (he kneels and hands her his baton), and Joan's seizing of him (she flings *"her arms around Dunois, kissing him on both cheeks"*). But Joan's conquest of Dunois is not only a lover's conquest, for she simultaneously mothers him: "I will deliver you from fear." (In Scene V she says to him, "You are the pick of the basket here, Jack.")

The crowning of Charles as king of a new France out of the victory at Orleans adumbrates Shelley's imagery only in a general way, with Joan as a rejuvenating, fertility figure, but what Joan as a martyred saint can do for the rejuvenation of the world echoes Shelley more specifically: "You will all be glad to see me burnt; but if I go through the fire I shall go through it to their hearts [of the common people] for ever and ever." Shelley's prayer that the west wind "Scatter, as from an unextinguished hearth/Ashes and sparks, my words among mankind!"[8] turns into "the trumpet of a prophecy," like Joan's prediction, and modulates finally into a temperate, yet half-fearful, faith in time's transforming power—"If Winter comes, can Spring be far behind?"—tonally not unlike the ending of *Saint Joan*, "How long, O Lord, how long?" (though there is also anguish in Joan's question).

Shelley's theme of time brings me to my final point about the central drama in *Saint Joan*: the possibility of overcoming the fear of death through imagination. For Joan's final question, "O God that madest this beautiful earth, when will it be ready to receive thy saints? How long, O Lord, how long?," is a real question, not just a rhetorical flourish to conclude the play.

Shaw calls *Saint Joan* a *chronicle* play, and he means it in three senses. *Saint Joan* is a historical play that represents actual persons and events of the past. It is a play that rivals Shakespeare's history plays (based as they were on sixteenth-century chronicles), particularly *Henry VI, Part One*, which had so maligned the historical Joan that Shaw could appear to be rewriting Shakespeare for the sake of justice. But it is also a play about time. Much of what characters spend their time doing in *Saint Joan* is waiting: in the first scene, waiting for the hens to lay; in Scene II, the court waits for the Dauphin ("LA TRÉMOUILLE: What the devil does the Dauphin mean by keeping us waiting like this?"); in Scene III, Dunois waits for the west wind and for Joan; in Scene IV, Warwick waits for Cauchon to arrive; in Scene V, after the coronation, the people wait to see Joan; in Scene VI, the English wait for the outcome of the trial ("WARWICK: Is this trial never going to end?"); and in the Epilogue, Joan remains waiting for the earth to be ready to receive God's saints. The recurring sense of expectancy, of waiting upon time, works as a structural force in the play and gives Joan's last line its peculiar power to move. We have been waiting all through the play for historical time to unfold, and at the end of the play we wait for imaginative time to unfold; that is, we ask ourselves what our imaginations can create in time.

Shaw places the Epilogue in historical time: *"night in June 1456."* But more than that, he tells us the exact time for the beginning, the middle, and the end of the scene, midnight. Before the dialogue begins, he tells us, *"A distant clock strikes the half-hour softly,"* which we know means 11:30 P.M. Approximately halfway through the scene, just before the Soldier enters, *"The clock strikes the third quarter."* In other words, the time Shaw indicates as passing during the action of the Epilogue equals half an hour. Although Shaw locates the action chronologically and represents it as transpiring in real time, yet the action is not realistic, for characters who are dead appear in it (Joan herself, Cauchon, et al.), as well as characters who are alive but who could not actually be present in Charles' chamber.

Moreover, Shaw creates unrealistic entrances for his characters. For example, Dunois enters *"through the tapestry on Joan's left, the candles relighting themselves at the same moment, and illuminating his armor and surcoat cheerfully,"* and Shaw thereby metaphorically underlines his sense of the Epilogue as a pure product of art and the imagination, while at the same time rehearsing the larger illumination provided by the end of the play. Thus, Shaw collapses time and space in the Epilogue[9]—a normal procedure for a dramatist who wishes to represent the action of a dream on stage. It is clear, however, that Shaw does not intend the Epilogue to be Charles' dream merely, and certainly not his wish fulfillment.[10] Indeed, it cannot be the dream of any character on stage, for toward the end of the scene, *"a clerical-looking gentleman,"* dressed *"in the the fashion of the year 1920, suddenly appears."* It can only be the audience's dream projected on stage as a fantastical, Lucianic adventure: a "what if Joan were free to talk with her friends and foes after her death and learn of her canonization?" proposition.

The author helps the audience to imagine the situation, to ask itself when it will be ready to receive God's saints. And the moment when it contemplates this question is midnight, in stage time and in real time (Shaw surely must have planned that the last half-hour of the play from 11:30 to midnight would also correspond to the time the audience would be hearing the play—assuming an evening performance beginning at 8:00), so that imagination and reality come together artfully on the borderline between the death of the midnight bell's last chime and the day's rebirth into the white radiance descending on Joan. In the ritualized ending to the play, the pallid green light of the false images and dim sight yields to the visionary white light around the lonely figure of Joan, praying her quietly urgent question, "How long, O Lord, how long?" Shaw wrote *Saint Joan* to help us imagine Saint Joan, that is to help us sense what imagination is.

But Shaw knows he can only go so far in the direction of representing imagination. In doing so he appeals to three kinds of imagination in the audience: the hallucinatory imagination through the dream setting; the auditory through the chimes; and the visual through the white radiance. Yet there remains something ineffable about the imagination that the dramatist can only hint at—JOAN: "I cannot tell you the whole truth: God does not allow the whole truth to be told." Shaw has Joan express this idea during the cathedral scene (V), midway through the play, where he creates a moment that rehearses the use of the chimes in the Epilogue. In speaking to Dunois after Charles' coronation, Joan tries to explain her sense of imagination resonating within her:

> It is in the bells I hear my voices. Not today, when they all rang: that was nothing but jangling. But here in this corner, where the bells come down from heaven, and the echoes linger, or in the fields, where they come from a

distance through the quiet of the countryside, my voices are in them. [*The cathedral clock chimes the quarter*] Hark! [*She becomes rapt*] Do you hear? "Dear-child-of-God": just what you said. At the half-hour they will say "Be-brave-go-on." At the three-quarters they will say "I-am-thy-Help." But it is at the hour, when the great bell goes after "God-will-save-France": it is then that St Margaret and St Catherine and sometimes even the blessed Michael will say things that I cannot tell beforehand. Then, oh then—

Dunois interrupts her at this point, for to him, when Joan talks this way, she seems "a bit cracked," but surely his interruption is timely. The filling in of that dash that halts her speech is the Epilogue, especially its final moments when we hear those chimes Joan only describes here, and we see the white radiance descending on her head. The poetry of the play concentrates itself in the theatrical gestures of light, sound, and language combining together to make us feel what we might otherwise be incapable of feeling. Shaw's use of theatrical metaphor creates a heightened and therefore new sense of reality in his audience, as well as in those of his readers who have imagination themselves.

The delicacy and feeling with which Shaw accomplishes his meaning elude demonstration somewhat, in part because aural and visual stage rhythm account for much of the proper effect. The ritual isolation of Joan proceeds regularly as each character in turn demurs from her proposal that she return to life, and then rises and exits. When we reach the last two characters, Charles and the Soldier, Shaw applies a *ritardando* to the rhythm of the exit speeches: first, as Charles "[*mumbling in his pillows*] Goo ni," falls asleep, finally weary of Joan and irredeemably uncon-scious of her sadness, while Joan bids him "Goodnight, Charlie," showing her affection for him in her use of his nickname, notwithstanding his indifference to her; and second, as the Soldier with an instinctive, if not fully conscious, sense of the pain caused by the others' rejection of her, counsels her not to pay any heed to such lofty personages as kings and archbishops. He even starts to explain why she "has as good a right to [her] notions as they have to theirs," but before he can get on with his "lecture," the chimes of midnight begin to sound and Joan never hears his lecture: "Excuse me: a pressing appointment—[*He goes on tiptoe*]." All during his half-attempted consolation of her, his friendly chattiness focuses the audience's attention, not on himself, but on the chimes and on Joan's silence as she attends to them.[11]

"A work of poetry from beginning to end," wrote Pirandello. What Joan hears in those chimes—the Word made flesh, poetic imagination overcoming the fear of death—Shaw makes her embody as a character and a symbol, thus helping us to imagine imagination herself, Saint Joan.

NOTES

[1] "Bernard Shaw's *Saint Joan*" in *Bernard Shaw's Plays*, ed. Warren S. Smith (New York: W. W. Norton, 1970), 450.

[2] Denied in *The Harvest of Tragedy* (New York: Barnes and Noble, 1966), 194–95, by T. R. Henn, for example (whose objections to Joan's diction seem to me way off the mark insofar as they do not take

into account Joan's mystical bent); asserted by J. I. M. Stewart, *Eight Modern Writers,* Vol. 12 of the Oxford *History of English Literature* (Oxford: Oxford Univ. Press, 1963), 179: "... certainly Shaw's outstanding play, conceivably the finest and most moving English drama since *The Winter's Tale* or *The Tempest."*

[3] A shorter version of this chapter was published in 1983 in *Shaw: The Annual of Bernard Shaw Studies,* Vol. 3, *Shaw's Plays in Performance,* ed. Daniel Leary (University Park: The Pennsylvania State Univ. Press, 1983), as "Imagining *Saint Joan";* almost at the same time Bryan Tyson published his fine book, *The Story of Saint Joan* (Kingston and Montreal: McGill-Queen's Univ. Press, 1982). It is a pleasure to note here that Tyson and I had reached independently similar readings of how Shaw used the theme of imagination in *Saint Joan.* I refer the reader to Tyson's book for insights parallel and additional to those I try to articulate here regarding the role of imagination in the play.

[4] I should like to note here that I believe Robert Bolt borrowed this structure (whether consciously or unconsciously) for the screenplay of *Lawrence of Arabia,* where the "miraculous" taking of Aqaba corresponds to Joan's victory at Orleans, and where Lawrence's becoming persona non grata to the British and the Arabs corresponds to Joan's becoming a thorn to both church and state. There are many further parallels.

[5] That is partly because her speech derives from Milton's invocation to Light at the beginning of Bk. III of *Paradise Lost:* "Thus with the year/Seasons return, but not to me returns/Day, or the sweet approach of ev'n or morn,/Or sight of vernal bloom, or summer's rose,/Or flocks, or herds, or human face divine" (40–44). Both set pieces express the feeling of loss, but Shaw disguises his inspiration by shifting the terms of loss from the visual in Milton to the aural in Joan. Moreover, Shaw characteristically shifts the emphasis away from the experience of the loss to the affirmation of Joan's feeling for nature.

[6] When Shaw prepared a screenplay of *Saint Joan,* he added a scene set in the marketplace of Rouen in which the Executioner is seen preparing the stake for Joan's burning; Shaw suggests that "If a bird or two could be induced to light on the stake, the effect would be deadly" (see *Saint Joan: A Screenplay by Bernard Shaw,* ed. Bernard F. Dukore [Seattle: Univ. of Washington Press, 1968], 158)—a Hitch-cockian touch, that, and simultaneously additional and ironic enforcement of the connection between Joan and flight.

[7] Cf. Milton: "Meanwhile/The world shall burn, and from her ashes spring/New heav'n and earth, wherein the just shall dwell/And after all their tribulation long/See golden days, fruitful of golden deeds,/ With joy and love triumphing and fair truth." *Paradise Lost,* Bk. III, 333–38.

[8] Cf. Pilate's speech from *On the Rocks,* particularly, "... if I set you loose to scatter your words broadcast among the people."

[9] In the Preface, Shaw hints at his self-conscious treatment of time in the play: "... as it [the play] is for stage use I have had to condense into three and a half hours a series of events which in their historical happening were spread over four times as many months; for the theatre imposes unities of time and place from which Nature in her boundless wastefulness is free. Therefore the reader must not suppose that Joan really put Robert de Baudricourt in her pocket in fifteen minutes, nor that her excommuni-cation, recantation, relapse, and death at the stake were a matter of half an hour or so." The point, as I see it, of Shaw's playful patronizing of his reader here, his exhortation to a willing suspension of disbelief (as if some readers might be unfamiliar with the conventions of stage time), is to make the reader aware in an indirect way that Shaw is playing with time in the play for a reason.

[10] "The Epilogue is obviously not a representation of an actual scene, or even of a recorded dream; but it is none the less historical," says Shaw in his "Note by the Author" in *Collected Plays,* Vol. 6, 213. Shaw *does* use the technique of dramatic action as wish-fulfillment dream in *Too True to Be Good,* where, as Northrop Frye points out, for the anonymous heroine, "the action ... is really her own wish-fulfillment dream." See *The Secular Scripture: A Study of Romance* (Cambridge: Harvard Univ. Press, 1976), 79.

[11] The interplay between Joan and the Soldier repeats that between Major Barbara and Peter Shirley, when the latter tries to console Barbara for her loss of purpose in life at the end of Act II: "Ah, if you would only read Tom Paine in the proper spirit, miss!" Peter's limited awareness (like the Soldier's) intensifies our sense of Barbara's (and Joan's) pain.

CHRONOLOGY

c. 1590–92   William Shakespeare, *1 Henry VI*

1730   François Marie Arouet (Voltaire) begins work on *La Pucelle* (first authorized publication 1762)

1796   Robert Southey, *Joan of Arc*

1801   Friedrich Schiller, *Die Jungfrau von Orleans*

1895–96   Serialization of Mark Twain's *Personal Recollections of Joan of Arc* (first book publication 1896)

1897   Charles Péguy's *Jeanne d'Arc* trilogy

1908   Anatole France, *La Vie de Jeanne d'Arc*

1910   Charles Péguy, *La Mystère de la charité de Jeanne d'Arc*

1923   Georg Kaiser, *Gilles und Jeanne*

1923   First performance of George Bernard Shaw's *Saint Joan* (first book publication 1924)

1932   Bertolt Brecht, *Der heilige Johanna der Schlachthöfe*

1946   First performance of Maxwell Anderson's *Joan of Lorraine* (first book publication 1947)

1953   Jean Anouilh, *L'Alouette*

1974   Thomas Keneally, *Blood Red, Sister Rose*

CONTRIBUTORS

HAROLD BLOOM is Sterling Professor of the Humanities at Yale University and Henry W. and Albert A. Berg Professor of English at the New York University Graduate School. He is a 1985 MacArthur Foundation recipient, served as the Charles Eliot Norton Professor of Poetry at Harvard University (1987–88), and is the author of nineteen books, the most recent being *The Book of J* (1990). Currently he is editing the Chelsea House series Modern Critical Views and The Critical Cosmos, and other Chelsea House series in literary criticism.

JOHAN HUIZINGA (1872–1945) was one of the most distinguished historians of his time. Educated in the Netherlands, he spent most of his career at the University of Groningen and the University of Leiden. Among his books translated into English are *The Waning of the Middle Ages* (1924), *Erasmus* (1924), *Homo Ludens: A Study of the Play-Element in Culture* (1949), and *America: A Dutch Historian's Vision, from Afar and Near* (1972).

ROGER B. SALOMON is Director of Graduate Studies and Professor of English at Case Western Reserve University in Cleveland. He is the author of *Twain and the Image of History* (1961) and *Desperate Story-Telling: Post-Romantic Elaborations of the Mock-Heroic Mode* (1987).

FRANK M. FOWLER, Professor of German Language and Literature at Queen Mary and Westfield College in London, is the co-editor of the 1983 and 1984 volumes of the *Publications of the English Goethe Society.*

HANS MAYER has taught at the University of Leipzig and the Technical University at Hanover. Among his many books are *Deutsche Literatur und Weltliteratur: Reden und Aufsätze* (1957), *Doktor Faust und Don Juan* (1979), *Thomas Mann* (1980), and *Versuche über Schiller* (1987). Several of his works have been translated into English, including *Steppenwolf and Everyman* (1971), *Portrait of Wagner* (1972), and *Richard Wagner in Bayreuth 1876–1976* (1976).

PAUL HERNADI is the author of *Beyond Genre: New Directions in Literary Classification* (1972) and *Interpreting Events: Tragicomedies of History on the Modern Stage* (1985) and the editor of *What Is Literature?* (1978), *What Is Criticism?* (1981), and *The Horizon of Literature* (1982). He is Professor of English at the University of California–Santa Barbara.

GABRIELE BERNHARD JACKSON is Professor of English at Temple University and has written *Vision and Judgment in Ben Jonson's Drama* (1968) and has edited Jonson's *Every Man in His Humor* (1969).

JOHN A. BERTOLINI is Professor of English at Middlebury College (Middlebury, VT). He is the author of *The Playwrighting Self of Bernard Shaw* (1991).

BIBLIOGRAPHY

Abbott, Anthony S. *"Saint Joan."* In *Shaw and Christianity*. New York: Seabury Press, 1965, pp. 157–73.

Allison, D. E. "The Spiritual Element in Schiller's *Jungfrau* and Goethe's *Iphigenie."* *German Quarterly* 32 (1959): 316–29.

Amar, Yvonne A. "Mark Twain's Joan of Arc: An 'Asbestos' Character Rising from the Ashes." *Mark Twain Journal* 19, No. 3 (Winter 1978–79): 13–19.

Austin, Don. "Comedy through Tragedy: Dramatic Structure in *Saint Joan."* *Shaw Review* 5 (1965): 52–62.

Bailey, Mabel Driscoll. "Jesus and Joan, and Final Affirmation." In *Maxwell Anderson: The Playwright as Prophet*. London: Abelard-Schuman, 1957, pp. 153–70.

Bell, Neil. "Mark Twain's Joan of Arc." *Mark Twain Journal* 11, No. 3 (Fall 1961): 4–6.

Bermel, Albert. "The Virgin as Heretic: *Saint Joan* by Bernard Shaw (1923)." In *Contradictory Characters: An Interpretation of the Modern Theatre*. New York: Dutton, 1973, pp. 185–206.

Berry, Edward I. *"1 Henry VI:* Chivalry and Ceremony." In *Patterns of Decay: Shakespeare's Early Histories*. Charlottesville: University Press of Virginia, 1975, pp. 1–28.

Bhalla, Alok. "An Obstinate Margin in Tragedy (Shaw's *Saint Joan*)." *Quest* No. 54 (July–September 1967): 45–51.

Blankenagel, John C. "Shaw's *Saint Joan* and Schiller's *Jungfrau von Orleans."* *Journal of English and Germanic Philology* 25 (1926): 379–92.

Bloom, Harold, ed. *George Bernard Shaw's* Saint Joan. New York: Chelsea House, 1987.

Boas, Frederick S. "Joan of Arc in Shakespeare, Schiller, and Shaw." *Shakespeare Quarterly* 2 (1951): 35–45.

Bostock, J. Knight. "The Maid of Orleans in German Literature." *Modern Language Review* 22 (1927): 298–309.

Brooking, Jack. "Jeanne d'Arc, the Trial Notes, and Anouilh." *Theatre Annual* 16 (1959): 20–29.

Brown, John Mason. "The Prophet and the Maid." In *As They Appear*. New York: McGraw-Hill, 1952, pp. 71–76.

Calin, William. "Love and War: Comic Themes in Voltaire's *Pucelle."* *French Forum* 2 (1977): 34–46.

Canby, Henry Seidel. "Saint George and Joan." *Saturday Review of Literature*, August 2, 1924, p. 4.

Chenais, Margaret. "New Light on the Publication of the *Pucelle."* *Studies on Voltaire and the Eighteenth Century* 12 (1960): 9–20.

Chiari, Joseph. "Jean Anouilh." In *The Contemporary French Theatre: The Flight from Naturalism*. London: Rockliff, 1958, pp. 170–204.

Clemens, Cyril. "Mark Twain's Joan of Arc." *Commonweal*, July 26, 1935, pp. 323–24.

Collins, Joseph. "Interpreting Joan of Arc." *Bookman* (New York) 63 (1926): 19–22.

Crompton, Louis. *"Saint Joan."* In *Shaw the Dramatist*. Lincoln: University of Nebraska Press, 1969, pp. 192–210.

Crosby, Donald H. "Freedom through Disobedience: *Die Jungfrau von Orleans*, Heinrich von Kleist, and Richard Wagner." In *Friedrich Schiller and the Drama of Human Experience*, edited by Alexej Ugrinsky. Westport, CT: Greenwood Press, 1988, pp. 37–42.

Curry, Kenneth. *Southey*. London: Routledge & Kegan Paul, 1975.

Cutts, John P. *"I Henry VI."* In *The Shattered Glass: A Dramatic Pattern in Shakespeare's Early Plays.* Detroit: Wayne State University Press, 1968, pp. 109–13.

De Quincey, Thomas. "Joan of Arc" [1847]. In *Collected Writings.* Edited by David Masson. Edinburgh: Adam & Charles Black, 1890, Volume 5, pp. 384–416.

DiSalvo, Jacqueline. "Milton and Shaw Once More: *Samson Agonistes* and *Saint Joan." Milton Quarterly* 22 (1988): 115–20.

Dolis, John J., Jr. "Bernard Shaw's *Saint Joan:* Language Is Not Enough." *Massachusetts Studies in English* 4, No. 4 (1975): 17–25.

Dukore, Bernard F. *Bernard Shaw, Playwright.* Columbia: University of Missouri Press, 1973.
——. "Brecht's Shavian Saint." *Quarterly Journal of Speech* 40 (1964): 136–39.

Emerson, Everett. *The Authentic Mark Twain: A Literary Biography of Samuel L. Clemens.* Philadelphia: University of Pennsylvania Press, 1984.

Evans, G. Blakemore. *"Die Jungfrau von Orleans:* A Drama of Philosophical Idealism." *Monatshefte für Deutschen Unterricht* 35 (1943): 188–94.

Ewen, Frederic. "Pity Is Not Enough: *Saint Joan of the Stockyards."* In *Bertolt Brecht: His Life, His Art, and His Times.* New York: Citadel Press, 1967, pp. 257–69.

Falb, Lewis W. *"L'Alouette* and the *Pièces Costumées."* In *Jean Anouilh.* New York: Ungar, 1977, pp. 100–113.

Fenn, Bernard. *Characterisation of Women in the Plays of Bertolt Brecht.* Frankfurt am Main: Peter Lang, 1982.

Fetscher, Iring. "Bertolt Brecht and America." In *The Legacy of the German Refugee Intellectuals,* edited by Robert Boyers. New York: Schocken Books, 1972, pp. 246–72.

Fielden, John. "Shaw's *Saint Joan* as Tragedy." *Twentieth Century Literature* 3 (1957–58): 59–67.

Fowler, Frank M. "Storm and Thunder in Gluck's and Goethe's *Iphigenie auf Tauris* and in Schiller's *Die Jungfrau von Orleans." Publications of the English Goethe Society* 43 (1972–73): 28–56.

French, A. L. "Joan of Arc and *Henry VI." English Studies* 49 (1968): 425–29.

Garland, H. B. *"Die Jungfrau von Orleans."* In *Schiller the Dramatic Writer.* Oxford: Clarendon Press, 1969, pp. 210–32.

Gerber, John C. *Mark Twain.* Boston: Twayne, 1988.

Grab, Frederic. "Introduction" to *Saint Joan of the Stockyards* by Bertolt Brecht, translated by Frank Jones. Bloomington: Indiana University Press, 1969, pp. 7–17.

Graham, Ilse. *"Die Jungfrau von Orleans:* A Saint out of Season." In *Schiller's Drama: Talent and Integrity.* New York: Barnes & Noble, 1974, pp. 171–91.

Gribben, John L. "Shaw's *Saint Joan:* A Tragic Heroine." *Thought* 40 (1965): 549–66.

Harben, Niloufer. "George Bernard Shaw: *Saint Joan."* In *Twentieth-Century English History Plays.* Totowa, NJ: Barnes & Noble, 1988, pp. 22–62.

Harrell, Don. "Mark Twain's *Joan of Arc:* Fact or Fiction?" *Markham Review* 4 (1975): 95–97.

Harris, Susan K. "Narrative Structure in Mark Twain's *Joan of Arc." Journal of Narrative Technique* 12 (1982): 48–56.

Harvey, John. *Anouilh: A Study in Theatrics.* New Haven: Yale University Press, 1964.

Hayman, Ronald. *Bertolt Brecht: The Plays.* London: Heinemann Educational Books, 1984.

Hill, Claude. *Bertrolt Brecht.* Boston: Twayne, 1975.

Hill, Holly, ed. *Playing Joan: Actresses on the Challenge of Shaw's* Saint Joan. New York: Theatre Communications Group, 1987.

Hoffpauir, Richard. "The Thematic Structure of Southey's Epic Poetry." *Wordsworth Circle* 6 (1975): 240–48.

Hulse, James W. "Shaw: Beyond Socialism." In *Revolutionists in London: A Study of Five Unorthodox Socialists.* Oxford: Clarendon Press, 1970, pp. 192–228.

John, S. Beynon. *Anouilh:* L'Alouette *and* Pauvre Bitos. London: Grant & Cutler, 1984.

Jones, Emrys. "*I Henry VI:* Hereafter Ages." In *The Origins of Shakespeare.* Oxford: Clarendon Press, 1977, pp. 142–60.

Kasimov, Harold. "The Conflict between the Mystic and the Church as Reflected in Bernard Shaw's *Saint Joan* and Jean Anouilh's *The Lark.*" *Mystics Quarterly* 14 (1988): 94–100.

Kaul, A. N. "George Bernard Shaw: From Anti-Romance to Pure Fantasy." In· *The Action of English Comedy.* New Haven: Yale University Press, 1970, pp. 284–327.

Kronenberger, Louis. "Shaw." In *The Thread of Laughter: Chapters on English Stage Comedy from Jonson to Maugham.* New York: Knopf, 1952, pp. 227–78.

Krumpelmann, John T. "Schiller and Saint Joan of Arc." *Monatshefte für Deutschen Unterricht* 34 (1942): 159–68.

Langner, Lawrence. "*Saint Joan*—1923." In *G.B.S. and the Lunatic.* New York: Atheneum, 1963, pp. 56–81.

Laverty, Moya. "*Jeanne d'Arc au bûcher* and Its Place in the Work of Claudel." In *Claudel: A Reappraisal,* edited by Richard Griffiths. Oxford: Rapp & Whiting, 1968, pp. 63–78.

Ley, Ralph. *Brecht as Thinker: Studies in Literary Marxism and Existentialism.* Normal, IL: Applied Literature Press, 1979.

Lightbody, Charles Wayland. *The Judgements of Joan: Joan of Arc, a Study in Cultural History.* Cambridge, MA: Harvard University Press, 1961.

MacCarthy, Desmond. *"St. Joan."* In *Shaw's Plays in Review.* New York: Thames & Hudson, 1951, pp. 162–75.

Macksoud, S. John, and Ross Altman. "Voices in Opposition: A Burkeian Rhetoric of *Saint Joan.*" *Quarterly Journal of Speech* 57 (1971): 140–46.

Marcus, Leah S. "Elizabeth." In *Puzzling Shakespeare: Local Reading and Its Discontents.* Berkeley: University of California Press, 1988, pp. 51–105.

Meisel, Martin. *Shaw and the Nineteenth-Century Theater.* Princeton: Princeton University Press, 1963.

Milfull, John. *From Baal to Keuner: The "Second Optimism" of Bertolt Brecht.* Bern: Herbert Lang, 1974.

Miller, R. D. *"Die Jungfrau von Orleans."* In *Interpreting Schiller: A Study of Four Plays.* Harrogate: Duchy Press, 1986, pp. 38–59.

Mott, Bertram, Jr. "Twain's Joan: A Divine Anomaly." *Etudes Anglaises* 23 (1970): 245–55.

Nathan, George Jean. *"Joan of Lorraine"* [by Maxwell Anderson]. In *The Theatre Book of the Year 1946–1947.* New York: Knopf, 1947, pp. 189–96.

Newman, C. M. "Joan of Arc in English Literature." *Sewanee Review* 34 (1926): 431–39.

Parmalee, Patty Lee. *Brecht's America.* Columbus: Miami University/Ohio State University Press, 1981.

Passage, Charles E. *Friedrich Schiller.* New York: Ungar, 1975.

Pierce, Robert B. "The Henry VI Plays." In *Shakespeare's History Plays: The Family and the State.* Columbus: Ohio State University Press, 1971, pp. 35–88.

Pronko, Leonard Cabell. *The World of Jean Anouilh.* Berkeley: University of California Press, 1961.

Rackin, Phyllis. *Stages of History: Shakespeare's English Chronicles.* Ithaca: Cornell University Press, 1990.

Richmond, H. M. *Shakespeare's Political Plays.* New York: Random House, 1967.

Ricks, Don M. *Shakespeare's Emergent Form: A Study of the Structures of the* Henry VI *Plays.* Logan: Utah State University Press, 1968.

Robertson, J. M. *Mr. Shaw and "the Maid."* London: Richard Cobden-Sanderson, 1926.

Russo, Gloria M. "Sexual Roles and Religious Images in Voltaire's *La Pucelle.*" *Studies on Voltaire and the Eighteenth Century* 171 (1977): 31–53.

Salls, Helen Harriet. "Joan of Arc in English and American Literature." *South Atlantic Quarterly* 35 (1936): 167–84.

Salomon, Roger B. "The Cosmic Woman: *Joan of Arc.*" In *Twain and the Image of History.* New Haven: Yale University Press, 1961, pp. 167–90.

Schmitt, Hans A. *Charles Péguy: The Decline of an Idealist.* Baton Rouge: Louisiana State University Press, 1967.

Searle, William. "Shaw's Saint Joan as 'Protestant.'" *Shaw Review* 15 (1972): 110–16.

Sellner, Timothy F. "The Lionel-Scene in Schiller's *Jungfrau von Orleans:* A Psychological Interpretation." *German Quarterly* 50 (1977): 264–82.

Servais, Yvonne. *Charles Péguy: The Pursuit of Salvation.* Westminster, MD: Newman Press, 1953.

Severin, Nelly H. "Voltaire's Saint Joan: A Burlesque on Saints and Chastity." *South Central Bulletin* 36 (1976): 150–52.

Sharpe, Lesley. *"Die Jungfrau von Orleans."* In *Schiller and the Historical Character.* Oxford: Oxford University Press, 1982, pp. 127–41.

Shivers, Alfred S. *Maxwell Anderson.* Boston: Twayne, 1976.

Simons, John D. *Friedrich Schiller.* Boston: Twayne, 1981.

Smith, Warren Sylvester. "The Web of Ambiguity." In *Bishop of Everywhere: Bernard Shaw and the Life Force.* University Park: Pennsylvania State University Press, 1982, pp. 125–37.

Spengemann, William C. "The Saint: *Joan of Arc.*" In *Mark Twain and the Backwoods Angel.* Kent, OH: Kent State University Press, 1966, pp. 105–19.

Stahl, E. L. "Guilt and Redemption." In *Friedrich Schiller's Drama: Theory and Practice.* Oxford: Clarendon Press, 1954, pp. 106–25.

Stone, Albert E., Jr. "Mark Twain's *Joan of Arc:* The Child as Goddess." *American Literature* 31 (1959): 1–20.

Stone, Susan S. "Shaw's Heroic Model in Flux: From Caesar to Charles." *English Studies in Canada* 2 (1976): 306–13.

Suvin, Darko. "*Saint Joan of the Slaughterhouses:* Structures of a Slaughterhouse World." In *Essays on Brecht: Theater and Politics,* edited by Siegfried Mews and Herbert Knust. Chapel Hill: University of North Carolina Press, 1974, pp. 11–40.

Tadie, Andrew. "Introduction" to *Personal Recollections of Joan of Arc* by Mark Twain. San Francisco: Ignatius Press, 1989, pp. 9–17.

Tillyard, E. M. W. *Shakespeare's History Plays.* London: Macmillan, 1944.

Topazio, Virgil W. "Voltaire's *Pucelle:* A Study in Burlesque." *Studies on Voltaire and the Eighteenth Century* 2 (1956): 207–23.

Tyson, Brian. *The Story of Shaw's* Saint Joan. Kingston: McGill-Queen's University Press, 1982.

Wagner, Paul. "Frank Harris and the Maid of Orleans." *Princeton University Library Chronicle* 30 (1968–69): 25–38.

Watson, Donald G. *Shakespeare's Early History Plays: Politics at Play on the Elizabethan Stage.* Athens: University of Georgia Press, 1990.

Weintraub, Stanley. "Bernard Shaw's Other Saint Joan." *Shavian* 2, No. 10 (October 1964): 7–13.

————. "The Genesis of *Joan.*" In *The Unexpected Shaw: Biographical Approaches to G.B.S. and His Work.* New York: Ungar, 1982, pp. 181–93.

West, Alick. *"A Good Man Fallen among Fabians."* London: Lawrence & Wishart, 1950.

Wilson, Edmund. "Bernard Shaw since the War." *New Republic,* August 27, 1924, pp. 380–81.

Wisenthal, J. L. *"Saint Joan."* In *The Marriage of Contraries: Bernard Shaw's Middle Plays.* Cambridge, MA: Harvard University Press, 1974, pp. 172–92.

Witte, William. *Schiller.* Oxford: Basil Blackwell, 1949.

Wood, Ruth Kedzie. "The Literary Annals of Jeanne d'Arc." *Bookman* (New York) 39 (1914): 287–98.

Woodbridge, Homer E. *"Saint Joan."* In *George Bernard Shaw: Creative Artist.* Carbondale: Southern Illinois University Press, 1963, pp. 116–26.

ACKNOWLEDGMENTS

"Preface" to *Saint Joan* by George Bernard Shaw from *Collected Plays with Their Prefaces,* Volume 4, by George Bernard Shaw, © 1924, 1930 by George Bernard Shaw, © 1951, 1957 by The Public Trustee as Executor of the Estate of George Bernard Shaw, © 1973 by The Trustees of the British Museum, The Governors and Guardians of The National Gallery of Ireland and Royal Academy of Dramatic Art. Reprinted by permission of The Society of Authors on behalf of the Estate of Bernard Shaw.

"Pirandello Distills Shaw" by Luigi Pirandello from *New York Times Magazine,* January 13, 1924, © 1924 by The New York Times Company. Reprinted by permission of The New York Times Company.

"The Saint as Tragic Hero: *Saint Joan* and *Murder in the Cathedral"* by Louis L. Martz from *Tragic Themes in Western Literature,* edited by Cleanth Brooks, © 1955 by Yale University. Reprinted by permission of the author.

"The Domineering Female in *I Henry VI"* by David M. Bevington from *Shakespeare Studies* 2 (1966), © 1967 by The Center for Shakespeare Studies. Reprinted by permission of *Shakespeare Studies.*

"The Visions of a New Man: The Expressionist Plays" by Ernst Schürer from *Georg Kaiser* by Ernst Schürer, © 1971 by Twayne Publishers, Inc. Reprinted by permission of Twayne Publishers, a division of G. K. Hall & Co.

"The Woman as Stranger: or 'None but woman left ...'" by Leslie A. Fiedler from *The Stranger in Shakespeare* by Leslie A. Fiedler, © 1972 by Leslie A. Fiedler. Reprinted by permission of the author.

Review of *Blood Red, Sister Rose* by A. G. Mojtabai from *New York Times Book Review,* February 9, 1975, © 1975 by The New York Times Company. Reprinted by permission of The Darhansoff & Verrill Literary Agency.

"La Pucelle, 1755" by Theodore Besterman from *Voltaire* by Theodore Besterman, © 1969, 1976 by Theodore Besterman. Reprinted by permission of Basil Blackwell.

"Joan's Last Trial" by William Searle from *The Saint and the Skeptics: Joan of Arc in the Work of Mark Twain, Anatole France, and Bernard Shaw* by William Searle, © 1976 by Wayne State University Press. Reprinted by permission of Wayne State University Press.

"The Dark Comedy of the Henry VI Plays" by Donald G. Watson from *Thalia* 1, No. 2 (Autumn 1978), © 1978 by R. G. Collins and Jacqueline Tavernier-Courbin. Reprinted by permission.

"Heroes and Antiheroes" by H. G. McIntyre from *The Theatre of Jean Anouilh* by H. G. McIntyre, © 1981 by George G. Harrap & Co. Reprinted by permission of Harrap Publishing Group Ltd.

"Mark Twain's Capers: A Chameleon in King Carnival's Court" by Rolande Ballorain from *American Novelists Revisited: Essays in Feminist Criticism,* edited by Fritz Fleischmann, © 1982 by Fritz Fleischmann. Reprinted by permission of the author.

"Shakespeare's *Henry VI* Trilogy and Elizabethan 'Romance' Histories: The Origins of a Genre" by Paul Dean from *Shakespeare Quarterly* 18, No. 1 (Spring 1982), © 1982 by The Folger Shakespeare Library. Reprinted by permission of *Shakespeare Quarterly*.

"Shaw's *Saint Joan* and the Modern History Play" by Stephen Watt from *Comparative Drama* 19, No. 1 (Spring 1985), © 1985 by *Comparative Drama*. Reprinted by permission of *Comparative Drama*.

"Anti-Historians: Women's Roles in Shakespeare's Histories" by Phyllis Rackin from *Theatre Journal* 37, No. 3 (October 1985), © 1985 by The Johns Hopkins University Press. Reprinted by permission of the author and The Johns Hopkins University Press.

"The Middle Ages, the Renaissance, and After" by J. L. Wisenthal from *Shaw's Sense of History* by J. L. Wisenthal, © 1988 by Jonathan Wisenthal. Reprinted by permission of Oxford University Press.

"Bernard Shaw's Saint" by Johan Huizinga from *Men and Ideas: History, the Middle Ages, the Renaissance* by Johan Huizinga, translated by James S. Holmes and Hans van Marle, © 1959 by The Free Press, A Corporation, translation © 1959 by Meridian Books, Inc. Reprinted by permission of the Estate of Johan Huizinga.

"Escape from History: Mark Twain's *Joan of Arc*" by Roger B. Salomon from *Philological Quarterly* 40, No. 1 (January 1961), © 1961 by the State University of Iowa, Iowa City. Reprinted by permission of *Philological Quarterly*.

"Sight and Insight in Schiller's *Die Jungfrau von Orleans*" by Frank M. Fowler from *Modern Language Review* 68, No. 2 (April 1973), © 1973 by Modern Humanities Research Association. Reprinted by permission of the author and the Modern Humanities Research Association.

"The Scandal of Joan of Arc" by Hans Mayer from *Outsiders: A Study in Life and Letters* by Hans Mayer, translated by Denis M. Sweet, © 1975 by Suhrkamp Verlag, Frankfurt am Main, translation © 1982 by Massachusetts Institute of Technology. Reprinted by permission of The MIT Press.

"Re-presenting the Past: *Saint Joan* and *L'Alouette*" by Paul Hernadi from *Interpreting Events: Tragicomedies of History on the Modern Stage* by Paul Hernadi, © 1985 by Cornell University. Reprinted by permission of Cornell University Press.

"Witches, Amazons, and Shakespeare's Joan of Arc" (originally titled "Topical Ideology: Witches, Amazons, and Shakespeare's Joan of Arc") by Gabriele Bernhard Jackson from *English Literary Renaissance* 18, No. 1 (Winter 1988), © 1988 by *English Literary Renaissance*. Reprinted by permission of *English Literary Renaissance*.

"*Saint Joan*: The Self as Imagination" by John A. Bertolini from *The Playwriting Self of Bernard Shaw* by John A. Bertolini, © 1991 by the Board of Trustees, Southern Illinois University. Reprinted by permission.

INDEX